Praise for *Eloquent Ruby*

"Reading *Eloquent Ruby* is like programming in Ruby itself: fun, surprisingly deep, and you'll find yourself wishing it was always done this way. Wherever you are in your Ruby experience from novice to Rails developer, this book is a must read."

—Ethan Roberts
Owner, Monkey Mind LLC

"*Eloquent Ruby* lives up to its name. It's a smooth introduction to Ruby that's both well organized and enjoyable to read, as it covers all the essential topics in the right order. This is the book I wish I'd learned Ruby from."

—James Kebinger
Senior Software Engineer, PatientsLikeMe
www.monkeyatlarge.com

"Ruby's syntactic and logical aesthetics represent the pinnacle for elegance and beauty in the ALGOL family of programming languages. *Eloquent Ruby* is the perfect book to highlight this masterful language and Russ's blend of wit and wisdom is certain to entertain and inform."

—Michael Fogus
Contributor to the Clojure programming
language and author of *The Joy of Clojure*

ELOQUENT RUBY

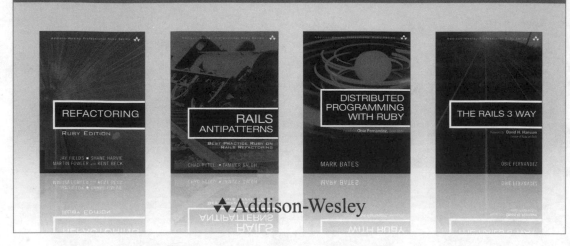

ELOQUENT RUBY

Russ Olsen

✦✦Addison-Wesley

Upper Saddle River, NJ • Boston • Indianapolis • San Francisco
New York • Toronto • Montreal • London • Munich • Paris • Madrid
Capetown • Sydney • Tokyo • Singapore • Mexico City

Many of the designations used by manufacturers and sellers to distinguish their products are claimed as trademarks. Where those designations appear in this book, and the publisher was aware of a trademark claim, the designations have been printed with initial capital letters or in all capitals.

The author and publisher have taken care in the preparation of this book, but make no expressed or implied warranty of any kind and assume no responsibility for errors or omissions. No liability is assumed for incidental or consequential damages in connection with or arising out of the use of the information or programs contained herein.

The publisher offers excellent discounts on this book when ordered in quantity for bulk purchases or special sales, which may include electronic versions and/or custom covers and content particular to your business, training goals, marketing focus, and branding interests. For more information, please contact:

U.S. Corporate and Government Sales
(800) 382-3419
corpsales@pearsontechgroup.com

For sales outside the United States please contact:

International Sales
international@pearson.com

Visit us on the Web: www.informit.com/aw

Library of Congress Cataloging-in-Publication Data

Olsen, Russ.
  Eloquent Ruby / Russ Olsen.
        p.   cm.
  Includes index.
  ISBN-13: 978-0-321-58410-6 (pbk. : alk. paper)
  ISBN-10: 0-321-58410-4 (pbk. : alk. paper)
  1. Ruby (Computer program language) I. Title.
  QA76.73.R83O47 2011
  005.13'3—dc22
                        2010048388

ISBN-13: 978-0-321-58410-6
ISBN-10:   0-321-58410-4

Text printed in the United States on recycled paper at RR Donnelley in Crawfordsville, Indiana.
Sixth Printing March 2015

To My Dad
Charles J. Olsen
Who never had a chance to write a book of his own,
which is a shame because it would have been
hilarious

Contents

Foreword *xix*

Preface *xxi*

Acknowledgments *xxv*

About the Author *xxvii*

PART I: The Basics   **1**

Chapter 1: Write Code That Looks Like Ruby   **3**

The Very Basic Basics   4

Go Easy on the Comments   6

Camels for Classes, Snakes Everywhere Else   8

Parentheses Are Optional but Are Occasionally Forbidden   9

Folding Up Those Lines   10

Folding Up Those Code Blocks   11

Staying Out of Trouble   12

In the Wild   13

Wrapping Up   15

Chapter 2: Choose the Right Control Structure   **17**

If, Unless, While, and Until   17

Use the Modifier Forms Where Appropriate   19

Use each, Not for   20

A Case of Programming Logic   21

Staying Out of Trouble   23
In the Wild   25
Wrapping Up   27

Chapter 3: Take Advantage of Ruby's Smart Collections   29

Literal Shortcuts   29
Instant Arrays and Hashes from Method Calls   30
Running Through Your Collection   33
Beware the Bang!   36
Rely on the Order of Your Hashes   38
In the Wild   38
Staying Out of Trouble   40
Wrapping Up   42

Chapter 4: Take Advantage of Ruby's Smart Strings   43

Coming Up with a String   44
Another API to Master   47
The String: A Place for Your Lines, Characters, and Bytes   49
In the Wild   50
Staying Out of Trouble   51
Wrapping Up   52

Chapter 5: Find the Right String with Regular Expressions   53

Matching One Character at a Time   54
Sets, Ranges, and Alternatives   55
The Regular Expression Star   57
Regular Expressions in Ruby   58
Beginnings and Endings   60
In the Wild   62
Staying Out of Trouble   63
Wrapping Up   64

Chapter 6: Use Symbols to Stand for Something   65

The Two Faces of Strings   65
Not Quite a String   66
Optimized to Stand for Something   67

In the Wild   69
Staying Out of Trouble   70
Wrapping Up   71

Chapter 7: Treat Everything Like an Object—Because Everything Is   73

A Quick Review of Classes, Instances, and Methods   74
Objects All the Way Down   76
The Importance of Being an Object   77
Public, Private, and Protected   79
In the Wild   81
Staying Out of Trouble   82
Wrapping Up   84

Chapter 8: Embrace Dynamic Typing   85

Shorter Programs, But Not the Way You Think   85
Extreme Decoupling   89
Required Ceremony Versus Programmer-Driven Clarity   92
Staying Out of Trouble   93
In the Wild   94
Wrapping Up   96

Chapter 9: Write Specs!   97

Test::Unit: When Your Documents Just Have to Work   98
A Plethora of Assertions   101
Don't Test It, Spec It!   101
A Tidy Spec Is a Readable Spec   104
Easy Stubs   105
. . . And Easy Mocks   107
In the Wild   108
Staying Out of Trouble   110
Wrapping Up   113

PART II: Classes, Modules, and Blocks   115

Chapter 10: Construct Your Classes from Short, Focused Methods   117

Compressing Specifications   117
Composing Methods for Humans   121

Composing Ruby Methods   122
One Way Out?   123
Staying Out of Trouble   126
In the Wild   127
Wrapping Up   128

Chapter 11: Define Operators Respectfully   129

Defining Operators in Ruby   129
A Sampling of Operators   131
Operating Across Classes   134
Staying Out of Trouble   135
In the Wild   137
Wrapping Up   139

Chapter 12: Create Classes That Understand Equality   141

An Identifier for Your Documents   141
An Embarrassment of Equality   142
Double Equals for Everyday Use   143
Broadening the Appeal of the == Method   145
Well-Behaved Equality   146
Triple Equals for Case Statements   149
Hash Tables and the eql? Method   150
Building a Well-Behaved Hash Key   152
Staying Out of Trouble   153
In the Wild   154
Wrapping Up   156

Chapter 13: Get the Behavior You Need with Singleton and Class Methods   157

A Stubby Puzzle   158
A Hidden, but Real Class   160
Class Methods: Singletons in Plain Sight   162
In the Wild   164
Staying Out of Trouble   165
Wrapping Up   167

Chapter 14: Use Class Instance Variables   169

A Quick Review of Class Variables   169
Wandering Variables   171
Getting Control of the Data in Your Class   174
Class Instance Variables and Subclasses   175
Adding Some Convenience to Your Class Instance Variables   176
In the Wild   177
Staying Out of Trouble   179
Wrapping Up   179

Chapter 15: Use Modules as Name Spaces   181

A Place for Your Stuff, with a Name   181
A Home for Those Utility Methods   184
Building Modules a Little at a Time   185
Treat Modules Like the Objects That They Are   186
Staying Out of Trouble   189
In the Wild   190
Wrapping Up   191

Chapter 16: Use Modules as Mixins   193

Better Books with Modules   193
Mixin Modules to the Rescue   195
Extending a Module   197
Staying Out of Trouble   198
In the Wild   202
Wrapping Up   205

Chapter 17: Use Blocks to Iterate   207

A Quick Review of Code Blocks   207
One Word after Another   209
As Many Iterators as You Like   210
Iterating over the Ethereal   211
Enumerable: Your Iterator on Steroids   213
Staying Out of Trouble   215
In the Wild   217
Wrapping Up   218

Chapter 18: Execute Around with a Block   219

Add a Little Logging   219
When It Absolutely Must Happen   224
Setting Up Objects with an Initialization Block   225
Dragging Your Scope along with the Block   225
Carrying the Answers Back   227
Staying Out of Trouble   228
In the Wild   229
Wrapping Up   231

Chapter 19: Save Blocks to Execute Later   233

Explicit Blocks   233
The Call Back Problem   234
Banking Blocks   236
Saving Code Blocks for Lazy Initialization   237
Instant Block Objects   239
Staying Out of Trouble   240
In the Wild   243
Wrapping Up   244

PART III: Metaprogramming   247

Chapter 20: Use Hooks to Keep Your Program Informed   249

Waking Up to a New Subclass   250
Modules Want To Be Heard Too   253
Knowing When Your Time Is Up   255
. . . And a Cast of Thousands   256
Staying Out of Trouble   257
In the Wild   259
Wrapping Up   261

Chapter 21: Use method_missing for Flexible Error Handling   263

Meeting Those Missing Methods   264
Handling Document Errors   266
Coping with Constants   267
In the Wild   268

Staying Out of Trouble   270
Wrapping Up   271

Chapter 22: Use method_missing for Delegation   273

The Promise and Pain of Delegation   274
The Trouble with Old-Fashioned Delegation   275
The method_missing Method to the Rescue   277
More Discriminating Delegation   278
Staying Out of Trouble   279
In the Wild   281
Wrapping Up   283

Chapter 23: Use method_missing to Build Flexible APIs   285

Building Form Letters One Word at a Time   286
Magic Methods from method_missing   287
It's the Users That Count—All of Them   289
Staying Out of Trouble   289
In the Wild   290
Wrapping Up   292

Chapter 24: Update Existing Classes with Monkey Patching   293

Wide-Open Classes   294
Fixing a Broken Class   295
Improving Existing Classes   296
Renaming Methods with alias_method   297
Do Anything to Any Class, Anytime   299
In the Wild   299
Staying Out of Trouble   303
Wrapping Up   303

Chapter 25: Create Self-Modifying Classes   305

Open Classes, Again   305
Put Programming Logic in Your Classes   308
Class Methods That Change Their Class   309
In the Wild   310

Staying Out of Trouble   314
Wrapping Up   315

Chapter 26: Create Classes That Modify Their Subclasses   317

A Document of Paragraphs   317
Subclassing Is (Sometimes) Hard to Do   319
Class Methods That Build Instance Methods   321
Better Method Creation with define_method   324
The Modification Sky Is the Limit   324
In the Wild   327
Staying Out of Trouble   330
Wrapping Up   332

PART IV: Pulling It All Together   333

Chapter 27: Invent Internal DSLs   335

Little Languages for Big Problems   335
Dealing with XML   336
Stepping Over the DSL Line   341
Pulling Out All the Stops   344
In the Wild   345
Staying Out of Trouble   347
Wrapping Up   349

Chapter 28: Build External DSLs for Flexible Syntax   351

The Trouble with the Ripper   352
Internal Is Not the Only DSL   353
Regular Expressions for Heavier Parsing   356
Treetop for Really Big Jobs   358
Staying Out of Trouble   360
In the Wild   362
Wrapping Up   364

Chapter 29: Package Your Programs as Gems   367

Consuming Gems   367
Gem Versions   368

The Nuts and Bolts of Gems   369
Building a Gem   370
Uploading Your Gem to a Repository   374
Automating Gem Creation   375
In the Wild   376
Staying Out of Trouble   377
Wrapping Up   380

Chapter 30: Know Your Ruby Implementation   381
A Fistful of Rubies   381
MRI: An Enlightening Experience for the C Programmer   382
YARV: MRI with a Byte Code Turbocharger   385
JRuby: Bending the "J" in the JVM   387
Rubinius   388
In the Wild   389
Staying Out of Trouble   389
Wrapping Up   390

Chapter 31: Keep an Open Mind to Go with Those Open Classes   391

Appendix: Going Further   393

Index   397

Foreword

Do you know why experienced Ruby programmers tend to reach for basic collections and hashes while programmers from other languages go for more specialized classes? Do you know the difference between strip, chop, and chomp, and why there are three such similar methods when apparently one might suffice? (Not to mention lstrip and rstrip!) Do you know the downsides of dynamic typing? Do you know why the differences between strings and symbols get so blurry, even to experienced Ruby developers? How about metaprogramming? What the heck is an eigenclass? How about protected methods? Do you know what they're really about? Really? Are you sure?

Russ knows all that stuff and more. And if books are like babies, then Russ is that experienced mom who pops out her second child after a couple of hours of labor and is back at work a week later in her pre-pregnancy clothes as if nothing out of the ordinary happened. You know: the one all the other moms talk about in hushed tones of disbelief and reverence. That's the way my series authors discuss Russ.

Not that there's anything small or insignificant about Russ' bouncing new baby . . . eh, I mean book. On the contrary, weighing in at just over 400 pages, this tome is slightly larger than its older sibling *Design Patterns in Ruby*. The family resemblance is crystal clear: Russ is first and foremost your friend. His approachable writing style makes even the driest Ruby language topics engaging and funny. Like the way that symbols remind Russ "of the eyes peering out from the tilted head of a confused but friendly dog."

Truth is, we need this kind of book now more than ever. Ruby has hit the mainstream with the force of a Hulk Smash, and the masses are paddling along well-known routes without full (heck, sometimes any) understanding of what makes their favorite

frameworks and library APIs so vibrant and navigable. So for those not content with
the basics, those who want to go beyond shallow understanding, this book goes deep.
It helps readers achieve true mastery of Ruby, a programming language with some of
the deepest, darkest pools of nuance and texture of all the major languages of modern
times.

I know you're going to enjoy this book, just like I did. And if you do, please join
me in encouraging Russ to get knocked up again soon.

—Obie Fernandez, Professional Ruby Series Editor

Preface

I've taught a fair number of Ruby classes over the years, but one particular class stands out in my mind. Class was over, and as I was going out the door one of my students, an experienced Java programmer, stopped me and voiced a complaint that I have heard many times since. He said that the hardest part of learning Ruby wasn't the syntax or the dynamic typing. Oh, he could write perfectly correct Ruby, sans semicolons and variable declarations. The problem was that something was missing. He constantly found himself falling back into his same old Java habits. Somehow his Ruby code always ended up looking much like what he would have written in Java. My answer to him was not to worry, you haven't missed anything—you just aren't done learning Ruby.

What does it mean to learn a new programming language? Clearly, like my frustrated student, you need to understand the basic rules of the grammar. To learn Ruby you need to be aware that a new line usually starts a new statement, that a class definition starts with the word `class`, and that variable names start with a lowercase letter—unless they start with an @. But you can't really stop there. Again, like my erstwhile student you will also need to know what all of that code does. You'll need to know that those statements are really expressions (since they all return a value) and that all of those classes starting with the `class` keyword can change over time. And you'll need to know why those `@variables` are different from the plain vanilla variables.

But the punch line is that even after you master all of this, you are still not quite there. It turns out that computer languages share something fundamental with our everyday order-a-pizza human tongues: Both kinds of languages are embedded in a culture, a way of thinking about the world, an approach to solving problems. A formal understanding of the mechanics of Ruby isn't the same as really looking at the programming world through Ruby-colored glasses. You need to absorb the cultural part of Ruby, to see how real Rubyists use the language to solve problems.

This is a book about making that final leap, about absorbing the Ruby programming culture, about becoming truly fluent in Ruby. The good news is that for most people the final step is the best part of learning Ruby—a series of "Ah ha!" moments— as it suddenly becomes clear why those funny symbol things exist, why classes are never final, and how this wonderful language works so hard to just stay out of your way.

Who Is This Book For?

This book is for you if you have a basic understanding of Ruby but feel that you haven't quite gotten your arms around the language. If you find yourself wondering what anyone could possibly do with all those odd language features that seem so important to Ruby, keep reading.

This book is also for you if you are a programmer with experience in other object oriented languages, perhaps Java or C# or Python, and you want to see what this Ruby thing is all about. While I'm not going to explain the basic details of Ruby in this book, the basics of Ruby are really very basic indeed. So, if your learning style involves simply jumping into the deep end, welcome to the pool.

How Is This Book Organized?

Mostly, this book works from small to large. We will start with the most tactical questions and work our way up to the grand strategy behind pulling whole Ruby projects together. Thus the first few chapters will concentrate on one-statement, one-method, one-test, and one-bug–sized issues:

- How do you write code that actually looks like Ruby?

- Why does Ruby have such an outsized collection of control structures?

- Why do Ruby programmers use so many hashes and arrays in their code?

- How do I get the most out of Ruby's very powerful strings and regular expressions?

- What are those symbol things, and what do you do with them?

- Is everything in Ruby really an object?

- How do I take advantage of dynamic typing?

- How can I make sure that my code actually works?

From there we will move on to the bigger questions of building methods and classes:

- Why are Ruby classes so full of tiny little methods?

- Why would you overload an operator? And, more importantly, why would you not?

- Do I really need to care about object equality?

- What good is a module?

- Can I really assign a method to an individual object? And what does that have to do with class methods?

- How do I hang some data on a class?

- How do you use blocks to good effect?

- Why would you ever call a method that doesn't actually exist?

- Can I really get notified when a class gets created? Why would I do that?

- Can I really modify classes on the fly? Why would I do that?

- Can I really write code that writes code? Why would I do that?

Finally, we will look at some of the techniques you can use to pull your programming project together into a unified whole:

- Would you really build a whole language simply to solve an ordinary programming problem?

- How do I make it easy for others to use my work?

- How does my Ruby implementation work?

- Where do I go from here?

About the Code Examples

The trouble with writing books about programming is that all the interesting stuff is in a constant state of flux. This is, after all, what makes it interesting. Certainly Ruby is something of a moving target these days: Although the great bulk of the Ruby code base was written for Ruby 1.8.X, version 1.9 has been out for some time and is clearly the future. In the pages that follow I have tried to split the coding difference by writing all of the examples in the 1.9 dialect,[1] taking care to note where Ruby 1.8 would be different. The good news is that there aren't all that many differences.

I have also consistently used the traditional pp command to print out more complex objects. However, to keep from driving everyone[2] crazy, I'm not going to endlessly repeat the require 'pp' call needed to make pp work. Just assume it is there at the top of each example.

---

1. Specifically, the examples all use Ruby-1.9.1-p430.

2. Especially me!

Acknowledgments

Sometimes I love to write and other times it's like squeezing out that last bit of toothpaste—from the point of view of the tube. At those times the constant support of my friends and family made the difference between a finished book and a smashed computer. In return I would like to say thanks, starting with my lovely wife Karen and my noble son Jackson for their constant support, and for putting up with me when that last sentence would just not settle down. Thanks especially to Karen for sneaking into my office in the middle of the night to remove the extraneous of's and the's from the manuscript.

Thanks to my good friend Bob Kiel for his constant encouragement. Couldn't have done it without you, Bob.

Thanks, too, to Eileen Cross for simply being there for me for all these years.

Thanks to the fine folks at FGM, especially Scott Gessay, Mike Fortier, Mike Morehouse, and Kirk Maskalenko. It really is a great place to work. Also thanks to George Croghan for continuing to speak to me even after I had used the parental voice of death on him.

Thanks to Chris Bailey for keeping me from taking a match to the whole project.

I also owe some serious gratitude to Gene, Laura, and Derek Stokes for their company and cheer as well as occasionally providing me with a quiet place to think and write: I've spent many a happy hour toiling away at the kitchen table of their beach house. I'd especially like to thank Gene for his rocket fuel martinis. I have only myself to blame if Gene's concoctions occasionally enhanced the happiness of the hour at the expense of the toiling. And thanks to Laura for injecting just the right level of zaniness into my life.

Special thanks to Scott Downie (the brightest intern who ever fetched coffee) for introducing me to the TV series *Firefly* and thereby getting me through the dark days of Chapters 15 and 16.[1]

Thanks to everyone behind the Northern Virginia Ruby Users' Group, RubyNation, and the National Capital Area Clojure User Group for their encouragement. Through their efforts hundreds of gallons of beer have found a decent home.

Thanks to everyone who reviewed the early versions of this book, including Rob Sanheim, James Kebinger, and Ethan Roberts.

Special thanks for Beth Gutierrez for providing her unique perspective on the manuscript.

Thanks to Carl Fyffe for helping me find a way out of the dark days of Chapters 15 and 16.

Thanks to Mike Abner and the aforementioned Carl for helping me to settle on a title.

Thanks also to Steve Ingram for starting the e-mail discussion that eventually gave birth to Chapter 6.

Thanks to my friend Diana Greenberg for her constant support, and for not buying a copy of this book before I can give her one.

Special thanks to Diane Freed. If you can imagine trying to correct a manuscript full of technical terms, tortured syntax, and typos (I can't), you have an idea of the job of a copy editor, a job that Diane performed with real finesse.

Thanks also to Rob and Denise Cross for putting up with me over a long Thanksgiving weekend as I went through my end of the copyediting of this book.

Thanks to Raina Chrobak of Addison-Wesley for her help and patience.

Finally special thanks to my editor Chris Guzikowski for putting up with the delays caused by the dark days of Chapters 15 and 16.

P.S. Thanks to Peter Cooper, Sonia Hamilton, John G. Norman, and Bodo Tasche for suggesting corrections to the first printing.

---

1. Well, originally they were Chapters 11, 12, and 13, and then they became Chapter 10 before settling down as 15 and 16. Now you know why those days were so dark.

About the Author

Russ Olsen's career spans three decades, during which he has written everything from graphics device drivers to document management applications. These days, Russ diligently codes away at GIS systems, network security, and process automation solutions. Otherwise, Russ spends a lot of his free time writing and talking about programming, especially Ruby and Clojure.

Russ' first book is the highly regarded *Design Patterns in Ruby* (Addison-Wesley, 2008). Russ is also the lurking presence behind the Technology As If People Mattered blog (www.russolsen.com). Russ' technical pontifications have been translated into six languages, and Russ is a frequent speaker at technical conferences.

Russ lives in the Washington, D.C., area with his lovely wife, Karen, and noble son, Jackson, both of whom are smarter than he is.

PART I
The Basics

CHAPTER 1

Write Code That Looks Like Ruby

Some years ago I did a long stint working on a huge document management system. The interesting thing about this job was that it was a joint development project: Part of the system was developed by my group here in the United States and part was built by a team of engineers in Tokyo. I started out doing straight programming, but slowly my job changed—I found myself doing less and less programming and more and more translating. Whenever a Japanese–American meeting collided with the language barrier my phone would ring, and I would spend the rest of the afternoon explaining to Mr. Smith just exactly what Hosokawa-San was trying to say, and vice versa. What is remarkable is that my command of Japanese is practically nil and my Japanese colleagues actually spoke English fairly well. My special ability[1] was that I could understand the very correct, but very unidiomatic classroom English spoken by our Japanese friends as well as the slangy, no-holds-barred Americanisms of my U.S. coworkers.

You see the same kind of thing in programming languages. The parser for any given programming language will accept any valid program—that's what makes it a valid program—but every programming community quickly converges on a style, an accepted set of idioms. Knowing those idioms is as much a part of learning the language as knowing what the parser will accept. After all, programming is as much about communicating with your coworkers as writing code that will run.

---

1. I had developed this talent over numerous lunches, happy hours, and late-night bull sessions. Oh, how I do devote myself to the cause.

In this chapter we'll kick off our adventures in writing good Ruby with the very smallest idioms of the language. How do you format Ruby code? What are the rules that the Ruby community (not the parser) have adopted for the names of variables and methods and classes? As we tour the little things that make a Ruby program stylistically correct, we will glimpse at the thinking behind the Ruby programming style, thinking that goes to the heart of what makes Ruby such a lovely, eloquent programming language. Let's get started.

The Very Basic Basics

At its core, the Ruby style of programming is built on a couple of very simple ideas: The first is that code should be crystal clear—good code tells the reader exactly what it is trying to do. Great code shouts its intent. The second idea is related to the first: Since there is a limit to how much information you can keep in your head at any given moment, good code is not just clear, it is also concise. It's much easier to understand what a method or a class is doing if you can take it all in at a glance.

To see this in practice, take a look at this code:

```ruby
class Document
  attr_accessor :title, :author, :content

  def initialize(title, author, content)
    @title = title
    @author = author
    @content = content
  end

  def words
    @content.split
  end

  def word_count
    words.size
  end
end
```

The Document class is nothing special technically—just a field for an author, one for a title, and one for the document content along with a few simple methods.[2] The thing to note about the code above is that it follows the Ruby indentation convention: In Ruby you indent your code with two spaces per level. This means that the first level of indentation gets two spaces, followed by four, then six, and then eight. The two space rule may sound a little arbitrary, but it is actually rooted in very mundane practicality: A couple of spaces is about the smallest amount of indentation that you can easily see, so using two spaces leaves you with the maximum amount of space to the right of the indentation for important stuff like actual code.

Note that the rule is to use two *spaces* per indent: The Ruby convention is to never use tabs to indent. Ever. Like the two space rule, the ban on tabs also has a very prosaic motivation: The trouble with tabs is that the exchange rate between tabs and spaces is about as stable as the price of pork belly futures. Depending on who and when you ask, a tab is worth either eight spaces, four spaces, two spaces, or, in the case of one of my more eccentric former colleagues, three. Mixing tabs and spaces without any agreement on the exchange rate between the two can result in code that is less than readable:

```ruby
class Document
  attr_accessor :title, :author, :content

    def initialize(title, author, content)
      @title = title
      @author = author
      @content = content
  end

  def words
      @content.split
    end

    def word_count
    words.size
        end
  end
```

2. But do take a good long look at the Document class because it's going to be with us for much of the book.

Life, not to mention the schedule, is too short to deal with problems like this,[3] so idiomatic Ruby should be serenely tab free.

Go Easy on the Comments

The mechanics of Ruby comments are simple enough: Anything following a # in the code is a comment.[4] The real questions regarding comments are when and how much? When is it a good idea to insert a comment into your code? And how much commenting is enough?

Good Ruby code should speak for itself, and most of the time you should let it do its own talking. If it's obvious how someone would use your method—if the class or program needs no explanation—then don't explain it. Above all, avoid boilerplate comments: Never put in a comment simply because you always put a comment there.

There are good reasons for adding comments to your code, the best being to explain how to use your software masterpiece. These kinds of "how to" comments should focus on exactly that: how to use the thing. Don't explain why you wrote it, the algorithm that it uses, or how you got it to run faster than fast. Just tell me how to use the thing and remember that examples are always welcome:

```
# Class that models a plain text document, complete with title
# and author:
#
# doc = Document.new( 'Hamlet', 'Shakespeare', 'To be or...' )
# puts doc.title
# puts doc.author
# puts doc.content
#
# Document instances know how to parse their content into words:
#
# puts doc.words
# puts doc.word_count
#
```

---

3. The "problem like this" in the example is that it was written with randomly mixed tabs and spaces, with each tab worth two spaces. Now expand the tabs to four spaces each and you have the formatting chaos that we see.

4. Ruby also supports multiline comments delimited by =begin and =end, but Ruby programmers tend to stick with the # style of comments most of the time.

```
class Document
  # class omitted...
end
```

This is not to say that you shouldn't have comments that explain some of the background of the code. Just keep the background separate from the instructions:

```
# Author: Russ Olsen
# Copyright 2010 Russ Olsen
#
# Document: An example Ruby class
```

Sometimes it's also wise to include a "how it works" explanation of particularly complicated bits of code. Again, keep this kind of explanation separate from the "how to":

```
# Using ngram analysis, compute the probability
# that this document and the one passed in were
# written by the same person. This algorithm is
# known to be valid for American English and will
# probably work for British and Canadian English.
#
def same_author_probability( other_document )
  # Implementation left as an exercise for the reader...
end
```

The occasional in-line comment can also help:

```
return 0 if divisor == 0    # Avoid division by zero
```

Whatever you do, don't fall into the trap of sprinkling those "pesky younger sibling" comments throughout your code, comments that follow on the heels of each line, repeating everything it says:

```
count += 1  # Add one to count
```

The danger in comments that explain how the code works is that they can easily slide off into the worst reason for adding comments: to make a badly written program somewhat comprehensible. That voice you hear in your head, the one whispering that you need to add some comments, may just be your program crying out to be rewritten. Can you improve the class, method, and variable names so that the code itself tells you what it is doing? Can you rearrange things, perhaps by breaking up a long method or collapsing two classes together? Can you rethink the algorithm? Is there anything you can do to let the code speak for itself instead of needing subtitles?

Remember, as the old bit of programming wisdom says, good code is like a good joke: It needs no explanation.

Camels for Classes, Snakes Everywhere Else

Once we get past the relatively easy issues of indentation and comments, we come face to face with the question of names. Although this isn't the place to talk about the exact words you would use to describe your variables, classes and methods, this is the place to talk about how those words go together. It's really very simple: With a few notable exceptions, you should use `lowercase_words_separated_by_underscores`.[5] Almost everything in this context means methods, arguments, and variables, including instance variables:

```ruby
def count_words_in( the_string )
  the_words = the_string.split
  the_words.size
end
```

Class names are an exception to the rule: Class names are camel case, so `Document` and `LegalDocument` are good but `Movie_script` is not. If all of this seems a bit doctrinaire for you, there is a place where you can exercise some creativity: constants. Ruby programmers seem divided about whether constants should be rendered in camel case like classes:

```ruby
FurlongsPerFortnight = 0.0001663
```

Or all uppercase, punctuated by underscores:

```ruby
ANTLERS_PER_MALE_MOOSE = 2
```

---

5. Because of its low, streamlined look, this naming style is known as "snake case."

My own preference—and the one you will see throughout this book—is the ALL_UPPERCASE flavor of constant.

Parentheses Are Optional but Are Occasionally Forbidden

Ruby tries hard not to require any syntax it can do without and a great example of this is its treatment of parentheses. When you define or call a method, you are free to add or omit the parentheses around the arguments. So if we were going to write a method to find a document, we might write it with the parentheses:

```ruby
def find_document( title, author )
  # Body omitted...
end

# ...

find_document( 'Frankenstein', 'Shelley' )
```

Or leave them out:

```ruby
def find_document title, author
  # Body omitted...
end

# ...

find_document 'Frankenstein', 'Shelley'
```

So, do you put them in or leave them out? With some notable exceptions, Ruby programmers generally vote *for* the parentheses: Although this isn't a hard and fast rule, most Ruby programmers surround the things that get passed into a method with parentheses, both in method definitions and calls. Somehow, having those parentheses there makes the code seem just a bit clearer.

As I say, this is not a rigid law, so Ruby programmers do tend to dispense with the parentheses when calling a method that is familiar, stands alone on its own line, and whose arguments are few in number. Our old friend `puts` fits this description to a tee, and so we tend to leave the parentheses off of calls to `puts`:

```
puts 'Look Ma, no parentheses!'
```

The other main exception to the "vote yes for parentheses" rule is that we don't do empty argument lists. If you are defining—or calling—a method with no parameters, leave the parentheses off, so that it is:

```
def words
  @content.split
end
```

And not:

```
def words()
  @content.split()
end
```

Finally, keep in mind that the conditions in control statements don't require parentheses—and we generally leave them off. So don't say this:

```
if ( words.size < 100 )
  puts 'The document is not very long.'
end
```

When you can say this:

```
if words.size < 100
  puts 'The document is not very long.'
end
```

Folding Up Those Lines

Although most Ruby code sticks to the "one statement per line" format, it is possible to cram several Ruby statements onto a single line: All you need to do is to insert a semicolon between the statements:

```
puts doc.title; puts doc.author
```

As I say, mostly we don't. There are a few exceptions to this rule. For example, if you are defining an empty, or perhaps a very, very simple class, you might fold the definition onto a single line:

```
class DocumentException < Exception; end
```

You might also do the same thing with a trivial method:

```
def method_to_be_overriden; end
```

Keep in mind that a little bit of this kind of thing goes a long way. The goal is code that is clear as well as concise. Nothing ruins readability like simply jamming a bunch of statements together because you can.

Folding Up Those Code Blocks

Ruby programs are full of code blocks, chunks of code delimited by either a pair of braces, like this:

```
10.times { |n| puts "The number is #{n}" }
```

Or, by the do and end keywords:

```
10.times do |n|
  puts "The number is #{n}"
  puts "Twice the number is #{n*2}"
end
```

The two forms of code block are essentially identical: Ruby doesn't really care which you use. Ruby programmers have, however, a simple rule for formatting of code blocks: If your block consists of a single statement, fold the whole statement into a single line and delimit the block with braces. Alternatively, if you have a multi-statement block, spread the block out over a number of lines, and use the do/end form.

Staying Out of Trouble

More than anything else, code that looks like Ruby looks *readable*. This means that although Ruby programmers generally follow the coding conventions that we have covered in this chapter, sometimes circumstances—and readability—call for the unconventional. Take the rule about folding up a one line code block, so that instead of this:

```
doc.words.each do |word|
   puts word
end
```

You would write this:

```
doc.words.each { |word| puts word }
```

The time to break this convention is when it would make your single line of code too long:

```
doc.words.each { |word| some_really_really_long_expression( ... with
lots of args ... ) }
```

Although coders differ about how long is too long,[6] at some point you're going to confront a block that might live on a single line, but shouldn't.

This kind of thinking should also go into the question of parentheses. There are times when, according to the "rules," you might omit the parentheses, but readability says that you should leave them in. For example, we have seen that `puts` generally goes sans parentheses:

```
puts doc.author
```

Another method that is frequently without parentheses is `instance_of?`, which tells you whether an object is an instance of some class:

```
doc.instance_of? Document
```

---

6. In fact, given the formatting limitations of this book, a good number of the blocks you'll see in this book will be multiline rather than single line, simply because the longer line will not fit on the page.

If, however, you assemble these two methods into a more complex expression, like this:

```
puts doc.instance_of? self.class.superclass.class
```

Then perhaps it is time for some parentheses:

```
puts doc.instance_of?( self.class.superclass.class )
```

Thus, the final code formatting rule is to always mix in a pinch of pragmatism.

In the Wild

Absolutely the best way to learn to *write* idiomatic Ruby code is to *read* idiomatic Ruby code. The Ruby standard library, the lump of Ruby code that came with your Ruby interpreter, is a great place to start. Just pick a class that interests you; perhaps you have always been fascinated by the Set class.[7] Find set.rb in your Ruby install and settle in for some interesting reading.

If you do go looking at set.rb, you will find, along with two-space indentation and well-formed variable names, that the file starts with some comments[8] explaining the background of the class:

```
# Copyright (c) 2002-2008 Akinori MUSHA <knu@iDaemons.org>
#
# Documentation by Akinori MUSHA and Gavin Sinclair.
#
# All rights reserved. You can redistribute and/or modify it
# under the same terms as Ruby.
```

This is followed by a quick explanation of what the class does:

```
# This library provides the Set class, which deals with a
# collection of unordered values with no duplicates.  It
# is a hybrid of Array's intuitive inter-operation facilities
```

---

7. Perhaps you should get out more often.

8. If you do look you will discover that I reformatted the comments a bit to make them fit on the page.

```
# and Hash's fast lookup.  If you need to keep values ordered,
# use the SortedSet class.
```

And then a few examples:

```
#    require 'set'
#    s1 = Set.new [1, 2]              # -> #<Set: {1, 2}>
#    s2 = [1, 2].to_set              # -> #<Set: {1, 2}>
#    s1 == s2                         # -> true
```

If you want to add useful comments to your own code, you could do worse than follow the model of set.rb.

If you look closely at the Set class you will see a couple of additional method name conventions at work. The first is that Ruby programmers will usually end the name of a method that answers a yes/no or true/false question with a question mark. So if you do peek into Set you will find the include? method as well as superset? and empty?. Don't be fooled by that exotic-looking question mark: It's just an ordinary part of the method name, not some special Ruby syntax. The same thing is true of exclamation points at the end of a method name: The Ruby rules say that ! is a fine character with which to end a method name. In practice, Ruby programmers reserve ! to adorn the names of methods that do something unexpected, or perhaps a bit dangerous. So the Set class has flatten! and map!, both of which change the class in place instead of returning a modified copy.

Although set.rb is a model of Ruby decorum, there are also notable spots where the code that comes built into Ruby breaks some of the Ruby conventions. Exhibit one: the Float method. Shock! Imagine a method name that begins with an uppercase letter. [Cue ominous music.]

Actually, there is some excuse for this momentous breach of manners: The Float method turns its argument—usually a string—into a floating point number.[9] Thus you can use Float as a kind of stand-in for the class name:

```
pi = Float('3.14159')
```

---

9. Note that the Float('3.14159') is not quite the same as '3.14159'.to_f. The Float method will throw an exception if you pass it bad input, while to_f will quietly return 0.

Float vs .to_f

The best part of having rules is that they inevitably create rule breakers—and it's even better when the rule breakers are the authorities.

Wrapping Up

So there we have the very basics of the Ruby programming style. Shallow, space-based indentation. A definite set of rules for formatting names. Optional parentheses, mostly supplied. Comments that tell you how to use it, or how it works, or who wrote it, but in stingy moderation. Above all else, pragmatism: You cannot make readable code by blindly following some rules.

This is, however, just the beginning: In a very real sense, this whole book is devoted to Ruby conventions of one kind or other. In particular, in Chapters 10 and 18 we will return to the subject of method names, while the last chapter is all about breaking the rules.

For the moment, however, we're going to stick to the basics, so in the next chapter we'll look at the Ruby control structures and how they contribute to clear and concise code.

CHAPTER 2

Choose the Right Control Structure

If indentation, comments, and the form of your variable names are the things that give your program its look, then it's the control structures—the ifs and elses and whiles—that bring it to life: It's no accident that the generic name for a program is "logic." Ruby includes a fairly familiar set of control structures, not much different than those available in more traditional languages. Look at any Ruby program and you will see the ifs, elses, and whiles of your programming youth. But if you look a little closer, you will also come across some odd-looking logical constructs, things with much less familiar names like unless and until.

In this chapter we will look at creating Ruby programs full of idiomatic control structures, at why sometimes you want to say *if this then do that* and at other times *do this unless that*. Along the way we will also explore Ruby's take on what is true and what is false, and learn how you can avoid having your program logic take a wrong turn.

If, Unless, While, and Until

Good news always bears repeating, so let me say it again: Ruby's most basic control structure, the if statement, contains no surprises. For example, if we wanted to add the idea of unmodifiable read-only documents to our Document class, we might end up with this very boring example of an if statement:

```
class Document
  attr_accessor :writable
  attr_reader :title, :author, :content

  # Much of the class omitted...

  def title=( new_title )
    if @writable
      @title = new_title
    end
  end

  # Similar author= and content= methods omitted...

end
```

Now the `if` statement in the `title=` method above is completely generic: Plus or minus some parentheses around the condition, it could have come out of a program written in any one of a dozen programming languages. Consider, however, what would happen if we turned the logic around: What if, instead of an `@writable` attribute, we had coded `@read_only` instead? The natural tendency would be to simply throw in a `!` or a `not`:

```
def title=( new_title )
  if not @read_only
    @title = new_title
  end
end
```

The trouble with this `if` statement is that it is just slightly more verbose than it needs to be. A more concise—and idiomatic—way to say the same thing is:

```
def title=( new_title )
  unless @read_only
    @title = new_title
  end
end
```

With `unless`, the body of the statement is executed only if the condition is false. The unless-based version of `title=` has two advantages: First, it is exactly one token (the not) shorter than the `if` not rendition. Second—and much more important—is that once you get used to it, the `unless`-based decision takes less mental energy to read and understand. The difference between `if` not and `unless` may seem trivial, but it is the difference between saying that "It is not true that Ruby is like Java" and saying "Ruby is different than Java": It's just a little clearer. Of course, the operative phrase is "once you get used to it." If you aren't familiar with `unless`, using it can feel a bit like wearing your shoes on the wrong feet. But do be persistent: For most programmers, the `unless` statement very rapidly loses its weirdness and becomes the way you do a backward `if` statement. And yes, getting rid of that one token is worth it.

In exactly the same way that `if` has `unless`, `while` has a negative doppelganger in `until`: An `until` loop keeps going until its conditional part becomes true. In the same way that Ruby coders avoid negated conditions in `ifs`, we also shy away from negated conditions in `while` loops. Thus, it's not:

```
while ! document.is_printed?
  document.print_next_page
end
```

It's:

```
until document.printed?
  document.print_next_page
end
```

Writing clear code is a battle of inches, and you need to contest every extraneous character, every bit of reversed logic.

Use the Modifier Forms Where Appropriate

Actually, our code is still not as clutter free as it might be. Take a look at the last version of our "can we modify this document?" logic:

```
unless @read_only
  @title = new_title
end
```

Since the body of this `unless` is only one statement long, we can—and probably should—collapse the whole thing into a single line with the `unless` at the end:

```
@title = new_title unless @read_only
```

You can also pull the same trick with an `if`:

```
@title = new_title if @writable
```

You can also do similar things with both `while`:

```
document.print_next_page while document.pages_available?
```

And `until`:

```
document.print_next_page until document.printed?
```

These last examples show off the two advantages of the modifier form: Not only do they enable you to fit a lot of programming logic into a small package, but they also read very smoothly: *Do this if that.*

Use each, Not for

In contrast to the somewhat strange-looking `unless` and `until`, Ruby sports a very familiar `for` loop. You can, for example, use `for` to run through all the elements of an array:

```
fonts = [ 'courier', 'times roman', 'helvetica' ]

for font in fonts
  puts font
end
```

The unfortunate thing about the `for` loop is that we tend not to use it! In place of the `for` loop, idiomatic Ruby says that you should use the `each` method:

```
fonts = [ 'courier', 'times roman', 'helvetica' ]

fonts.each do |font|
```

```
    puts font
end
```

Since the two versions of the "print my fonts" code are essentially equivalent,[1] why prefer one over the other? Mainly it is a question of eliminating one level of indirection. Ruby actually defines the for loop in terms of the each method: When you say for font in fonts, Ruby will actually conjure up a call to fonts.each. Given that the for statement is really a call to each in disguise, why not just pull the mask off and write what you mean?

A Case of Programming Logic

Along with the garden variety if, Ruby also sports a case statement, a multi-way decision statement similar to the switch statement that you find in many programming languages. Ruby's case statement has a surprising number of variants. Most commonly it is used to select one of a number of bits of code to execute:

```
case title
when 'War And Peace'
  puts 'Tolstoy'
when 'Romeo And Juliet'
  puts 'Shakespeare'
else
  puts "Don't know"
end
```

Alternatively, you can use a case statement for the value it computes:

```
author = case title
         when 'War And Peace'
           'Tolstoy'
         when 'Romeo And Juliet'
           'Shakespeare'
```

---

1. Almost. The code block in the each version actually introduces a new scope. Any variables introduced into a code block are local to that block and go away at the end of the block. The more traditional for version of the loop does not introduce a new scope, so that variables introduced inside a for are also visible outside the loop.

```
      else
        "Don't know"
      end
```

Or the equivalent, and somewhat more compact:

```
author = case title
         when 'War And Peace' then 'Tolstoy'
         when 'Romeo And Juliet' then  'Shakespeare'
         else "Don't know"
         end
```

These last two examples rely on the fact that virtually everything in Ruby returns a value. Logically enough, a `case` statement returns the values of the selected `when` or `else` clause—or `nil` if no `when` clause matches and there is no `else`. Thus the following just might evaluate to `nil`:

```
author = case title
         when 'War And Peace' then 'Tolstoy'
         when 'Romeo And Juliet' then  'Shakespeare'
         end
```

What all this means is that you can use the `case` statement for exactly what it is: a giant, value-returning expression.

A key thing to keep in mind about all of these `case` statements is that they use the ===[2] operator to do the comparisons. We will leave the details of === to Chapter 12, but the practical effect of the `case` statement's use of === is that it can make your life easier. For example, since classes use === to identify instances of themselves, you can use a `case` statement to switch on the class of an object:

```
case doc
when Document
  puts "It's a document!"
when String
  puts "It's a string!"
```

---

2. That's three equals signs!

```
else
  puts "Don't know what it is!"
end
```

In the same spirit, you can use a case statement to detect a regular expression match:

```
case title
when /War And .*/
  puts 'Maybe Tolstoy?'
when /Romeo And .*/
  puts 'Maybe Shakespeare?'
else
  puts 'Absolutely no idea...'
end
```

Finally, there is a sort of degenerate version of the case statement that lets you supply your own conditions:

```
case
when title == 'War And Peace'
  puts 'Tolstoy'
when title == 'Romeo And Juliet'
  puts 'Shakespeare'
else
  puts 'Absolutely no idea...'
end
```

This last example is really not much more than an if/elsif statement dressed up like a case statement, and, in fact, most Ruby programmers seem to prefer the if.

Staying Out of Trouble

One of the best ways to lose control of your programming logic is to forget the fundamentals of Ruby's boolean logic. Remember, when you are making decisions in Ruby, only false and nil are treated as false. Ruby treats everything else—and I do mean everything—as true. Former C programmers should keep in mind that the number 0, being neither false nor nil, is true in Ruby. So, this:

```
puts 'Sorry Dennis Ritchie, but 0 is true!' if 0
```

Will print an apology to the inventor of C. In the same spirit, the string "false" is also not the same as the boolean value false and thus, this:

```
puts 'Sorry but "false" is not false' if 'false'
```

Will also print something.

Ruby's treatment of booleans means that there are two things that are false and an infinite number of things that are true. Thus you should avoid testing for truth by testing for specific values. In Ruby, this:

```
if flag == true
  # do something
end
```

Is not just overly wordy, it is an invitation to disaster. After all, the value of flag may have been the result of a call to defined?. The idea behind defined? is that it will tell you whether some Ruby expression is defined or not:

```
doc = Document.new( 'A Question', 'Shakespeare', 'To be...' )
flag = defined?( doc )
```

The rub is that although defined? does indeed return a boolean, it never, ever returns true or false. Instead, defined? returns either a string that describes the thing passed in—in the example above, defined?(doc) will return "local-variable". On the other hand, if the thing passed to defined? is not defined, then defined? will return nil. So defined?—like many Ruby methods—works in a boolean context, as long as you don't explicitly ask if it returns true or false.

It's also possible to go wrong by taking nil for granted. Imagine you have some method, get_next_object that gives you one object after another, returning nil when there are no more objects:

```
# Broken in a subtle way...
while next_object = get_next_object
  # Do something with the object
end
```

This code is relying on the fact that `nil` is false and almost everything else is true to propel the loop round and round. The trouble with this example can be summed up in a question: What happens if the next object happens to be the object `false`? The answer is that the loop will terminate early. Much better is:

```
until (next_object = get_next_object) == nil
  # Do something with the object
end
```

Or:

```
until (next_object = get_next_object).nil?
  # Do something with the object
end
```

If you are looking for `nil` and there is any possibility of `false` turning up, then look for `nil` explicitly.

In the Wild

As we have seen, you can take advantage of the expression-oriented nature of Ruby to pull values back from a `case` statement. Although relatively rare, you will sometimes come across code that captures the values of a `while` or `if` statement. Here, for instance, is a fragment of code from the RubyGems system, which uses an `if` statement as a big expression to check on the validity of an X509 certificate:

```
ret = if @not_before && @not_before > time
    [false, :expired, "not valid before '#@not_before'"]
  elsif @not_after && @not_after < time
    [false, :expired, "not valid after '#@not_after'"]
  elsif issuer_cert && !verify(issuer_cert.public_key)
    [false, :issuer, "#{issuer_cert.subject} is not issuer"]
  else
    [true, :ok, 'Valid certificate']
  end
```

Another expression-based way to make a decision, one that you will see quite a bit, is the ternary operator or ?: operator. Here's an example, again from RubyGems:

```
file = all ? 'specs' : 'latest_specs'
```

The ?: operator acts like a very compact if statement with the condition part coming right before the question mark. If the condition (in the example, the value of all) is true, then the value of the whole expression is the thing between the question mark and the colon—'specs' in the example. If the condition is false, then the expression evaluates to the last part, the bit after the colon, 'latest_specs' in the example. The ?: operator has been around since at least the C programming language, but many programming communities tend to ignore it. Ruby coders, always looking for a succinct way getting the point across, do use ?: quite a bit.

Another common expression-based idiom helps with a familiar initialization problem: Sometimes you are just not sure if you need to initialize a variable. For example, you might want to ensure that an instance variable is not nil. If the variable has a value you want to leave it alone, but if it is nil you want to set it to some default:

```
@first_name = '' unless @first_name
```

Although this code does work, an experienced Ruby programmer is much more likely to write it this way:

```
@first_name ||= ''
```

This construct may look a little odd, but there is (literally) logic behind it. Recall that:

```
count += 1
```

Is equivalent to:

```
count = count + 1
```

Do the same expansion on the first ||= expression and you get:

```
@first_name = @first_name || ''
```

Translated into English, the expansion says "Set the new value of `@first_name` to the old value of `@first_name`, unless that is `nil`, in which case set it to the empty string." So why do Ruby programmers tend to favor `||=` over the alternatives? It's the same old answer: The `||=` is a little bit less code, and (more importantly) you don't have to repeat the name of the variable you are initializing.

Finally, be aware that this use of `||=` suffers from exactly the kind of `nil`/`false` confusion that I warned you about earlier. If `@first_name` happened to start out as `false`, the code would cheerfully go ahead and reset it to the empty string. Moral of the story: Don't try to use `||=` to initialize things to booleans.

Wrapping Up

In this chapter we looked over the control structures available to the Ruby programmer. We've seen that when it comes to control structures, Ruby has our old friends `if` and `while` along with less familiar choices like `unless` and `until`. Spend the time and you will rapidly discover that having an extensive menu of control structures lets you say what needs to be said with as little fuss—and clutter—as possible.

So much for the control structures. Programs do not, however, live by code alone: There is always that pesky data clamoring to be read, sorted, massaged, displayed, and saved. So in the next chapter we'll see how you can make effective use of the twin Swiss Army knives of Ruby data structures, the array and the hash.

CHAPTER 3

Take Advantage of Ruby's Smart Collections

Here's something to do the next time you have a rainy afternoon to kill: Download two or three significant Ruby programs, maybe utilities that you use every day or applications you have heard of or perhaps projects whose names you just happen to like. Once you have the code, settle in and start reading it; figure out how it works and why it's put together the way it is. One of the things you are likely to find is arrays, lots and lots of arrays. You will probably also come across a good number of hashes mixed in with those arrays.

In the pages that follow we are going to look at the Ruby versions of these two venerable data structures and discover that they have some surprising talents. Along the way we will also see how you can create arrays in a surprising number of ways, how you can run through the elements of an array without a hint of an index, and how orderly the Ruby hash class is. We will also take a tour of some of the rougher parts of the Ruby collection landscape and, finally, we will visit a bit with one of the lesser known of the Ruby collection classes.

Literal Shortcuts

Before you can do anything with a collection you need to have one. A common way to conjure up a collection is with a literal, but the trouble with collection literals is that they have parts—the things in the collection—and spelling out all of those individual elements can make for very inelegant code. Thus a simple literal array of words can turn into a thicket of quotes and commas:

```
poem_words = [ 'twinkle', 'little', 'star', 'how', 'I', 'wonder' ]
```

Fortunately, Ruby gives us some convenient syntactical shortcuts for exactly this situation. If you need to initialize an array of strings, where none of the strings have embedded spaces, you can simply say:

```
poem_words = %w{ twinkle little star how I wonder }
```

Hash literals also present you with a couple of choices. The traditional hash literal has you associating your keys with your values with the so-called **hash rocket**, =>, like this:

```
freq = { "I" => 1, "don't" => 1, "like" => 1, "spam" => 963 }
```

This last form is perfectly general purpose in that it doesn't care about the types of the hash keys. If you happen to be using symbols as your keys—a very common practice—then you can cut this:

```
book_info = { :first_name => 'Russ', :last_name => 'Olsen' }
```

Down to this:

```
book_info = { first_name: 'Russ', last_name: 'Olsen' }
```

Either way you get exactly the same hash.[1]

Instant Arrays and Hashes from Method Calls

Another way to get hold of a collection is to have Ruby manufacture one for you during the method-calling process. Although Ruby methods typically take a fixed number of arguments, it is possible to build methods that take a variable number of

---

1. Well, you get the same hash if you are using Ruby 1.9, which is where this shorter hash literal syntax made its appearance.

arguments. If you have a basic set of arguments and simply want to allow your callers to be able to omit one here or there, you can simply specify defaults. This method, for instance, will take one or two arguments:

```
def load_font( name, size = 12 )
  # Go font hunting...
end
```

Sometimes, however, what you need is a method that will take a completely arbitrary set of arguments. Ruby has a special syntax for this: If, in your method definition, you stick an asterisk before one of your parameter names, that parameter will soak up any extra arguments passed to the method. The value of the starred parameter will be an array containing all the extra arguments. Thus this method:

```
def echo_all( *args )
  args.each { |arg| puts arg }
end
```

Will take any number of arguments and print them out. You can only have one starred parameter, but it can be pretty much anywhere in your parameter list:[2]

```
def echo_at_least_two( first_arg, *middle_args, last_arg )
  puts "The first argument is #{first_arg}"
  middle_args.each { |arg|puts "A middle argument is #{arg}" }
  puts "The last argument is #{last_arg}"
end
```

In practice this means that you can sometimes rely on Ruby to manufacture an array for you. Take the add_authors method for example:

```
class Document

  # Most of the class omitted...
```

---

2. In Ruby 1.9 it can be anywhere. In 1.8 the starred argument needed to be at the end of the argument list.

```
    def add_authors( names )
      @author += " #{names.join(' ')}"
    end
  end
```

The `add_authors` method lets the caller specify a number of different names as the author of a document. As it is written above, you pass the `add_authors` method an array of names:

```
    doc.add_authors( [ 'Strunk', 'White' ] )
```

Once it has the array of author's names, `add_authors` uses the array method `join` to combine the elements into a single space-delimited string, which it then appends onto `@author`.

This initial stab at `add_authors` does work, but it is not as smooth as it might be: By adding a star to the `names` argument you can turn your method into one that takes any number of arguments—all delivered in an array.[3] Adding the star, like so:

```
  class Document

    # Most of the class omitted...

    def add_authors( *names )
      @author += " #{names.join(' ')}"
    end
  end
```

Means that you can relieve your users of the need to wrap the names in an array:

```
    doc.add_authors( 'Strunk', 'White' )
```

The jargon for a star used in this context is **splat**, as in "splat names." Think of an exploding array, with elements flying every which way.

---

3. The star actually works the other way too: If you happen to find yourself holding a three-element array and want to pass that trio of objects to a method that takes three arguments, you can simply say `some_method( *my_array )`. Ah, symmetry.

Hashes also have a bonus method-passing feature. Any method can, of course, take a literal hash as an argument. Thus, we might have a method that will locate a font by name and size, and pass the values in as a hash:

```
def load_font( specification_hash )
  # Load a font according to  specification_hash[:name] etc.
end
```

So that we can load a font like this:

```
load_font( { :name => 'times roman', :size => 12 } )
```

The bonus comes if the hash is at the end[4] of the argument list—as it is in the load_font example. In that case we can leave the braces off when we call the method. Given this, we can shorten our call to load_font down to:

```
load_font( :name => 'times roman', :size => 12 )
```

Written without the braces, this method call has a nice, named parameter feel to it. You can even go one step further and leave the parentheses off, resulting in something that looks more like a command and less like a method call:

```
load_font :name => 'times roman', :size => 12
```

Running Through Your Collection

Once you have a collection, you will probably want to do something with it. Frequently that something will involve iterating through the collection one element at a time. Depending on your programming background, you might be tempted to do the iterating with an index-based loop, perhaps like this:

```
words = %w{ Mary had a little lamb }

for i in 0..words.size
  puts words[i]
end
```

---

4. That is, the end of the argument list not counting any explicit block argument. More about this in Chapter 19.

I said it in the last chapter, but it bears repeating here: Don't do that. The way to run through a Ruby collection is with the each method:

```
words.each { |word| puts word }
```

Hashes also sport an each method, though the Hash version comes with a twist: If the block you supply to the Hash rendition of each takes a single argument, like this:

```
movie = { title: '2001', genre: 'sci fi', rating: 10 }

movie.each { |entry| pp entry }
```

Then each will call the block with a series of two element arrays, where the first element is a key and the second the corresponding value, so that the code above will print:

```
[:title, "2001"]
[:genre, "sci fi"]
[:rating, 10]
```

Alternatively, you can supply a block that takes two arguments, like this:

```
movie.each { |name, value| puts "#{name} => #{value}"}
```

Both hashes and arrays have many talents beyond the each method: Both of these classes come equipped with very extensive APIs. To take a simple example, imagine that we want to add a method to the Document class, a method that will return the index of a particular word. Without thinking we might just grab for each:

```
def index_for( word )
  i = 0
  words.each do |this_word|
    return i if word == this_word
    i += 1
  end
  nil
end
```

A much better way is to look at the `Array` API and come up with the `find_index` method:

```
def index_for( word )
  words.find_index { |this_word| word == this_word }
end
```

Two other collection methods you want to be sure to include in your mental toolkit are `map` and `inject`. Like `each` and `find_index`, `map` takes a block and runs through the collection calling the block for each element. The difference is that instead of making some kind of decision based on the return from the block the way `find_index` does, `map` cooks up a new array containing everything the block returned, in order. The `map` method is incredibly useful for transforming the contents of a collection en mass. For example, if you wanted an array of all the word lengths, you might turn to `map`:

```
pp doc.words.map { |word| word.size }
```

Which would print:

```
[3, 5, 2, 3, 4]
```

Alternatively, you might want an all-lowercase version of the words in your document. That's easy, too:

```
lower_case_words = doc.words.map { |word| word.downcase }
```

The `inject` method is a bit harder to get your arms around but well worth the trouble. To see what `inject` can do for you, imagine that you need to write a method that will compute the average length of the words in a document. To compute the average, we need two things: the total number of words—which we can easily get by calling `word_count`—and the total length of all the words (not counting white space), which is going to take some work. To do that work, we might use `each`, something like this:

```
class Document

  # Most of the class omitted...
```

```
    def average_word_length
      total = 0.0
      words.each { |word| total += word.size }

      total / word_count
    end
  end
```

Can we improve on this? You bet: This is the kind of problem that the `inject` method is tailor-made to solve. Like `each`, `inject` takes a block and calls the block with each element of the collection. Unlike `each`, `inject` passes in two arguments to the block: Along with each element, you get the current result—the current sum if you are adding up all of the word lengths. Each time `inject` calls the block, it replaces the current result with the return value of the previous call to the block. When `inject` runs out of elements, it returns the result as its return value.

Here, for example, is our `average_word_length` method, reworked to use `inject`:

```
    def average_word_length
      total = words.inject(0.0){ |result, word| word.size + result}
      total / word_count
    end
```

The argument passed into `inject`—0.0 in the example—is the initial value of the result. If you don't supply an initial value, `inject` will skip calling the block for the first element of the array and simply use that element as the initial result.

Altogether, array instances carry around an even one hundred public methods while hashes include more than eighty. A key part of knowing how to program in Ruby is getting to know this extensive toolkit.

Beware the Bang!

One thing you really want to know is which methods will actually change your collection and which will leave it be. This is not as obvious as you might expect. For example, arrays come with a `reverse` method, which, unsurprisingly, switches the order of the elements. You would think that reversing any nontrivial array is surely going to change it:

```
a = [ 1, 2, 3]
a.reverse
```

Unfortunately, you would think wrong: The `reverse` method does not change anything. Print out the array from the previous example and you would see its order undisturbed. The `reverse` method actually returns a reversed *copy* of the array, so that this:

```
pp a.reverse
pp a
```

Will print:

```
[3, 2, 1]
[1, 2, 3]
```

If you really want to reverse the array in place, you need `reverse!`, with an exclamation point at the end:

```
a.reverse!
pp a
```

Run this code and you will see:

```
[3, 2, 1]
```

In the same way, the array `sort` method returns a sorted copy, while `sort!` sorts the array in place.

Don't, however, get the idea that only methods with names ending in `!` will change your collection. Remember, the Ruby convention is that an exclamation point at the end of a method name indicates that the method is the dangerous or surprising version of a pair of methods. Since making a modified copy of a collection seems very safe while changing a collection in place can be a bit dicey, we have `sort` and `sort!`. The punch line is that there are many `!`-less methods in Ruby's collection classes, methods that will cheerfully change your collection in place as an intrinsic part of what they do. Thus, `push`, `pop`, `delete`, and `shift` are as capable of changing your array as sort!. Be sure you know what a method is going to do to your collection before you call it.

Rely on the Order of Your Hashes

Ruby arrays and hashes have one thing in common that takes many programmers by surprise: They are both ordered. Order and arrays go together like coders and coffee—it's hard to imagine one without the other. But hashes have, in many programming languages and in earlier versions of Ruby, usually been any unruly bunch. The hashes available in many other languages and in the bad old days of Ruby would mix up the entries in a more or less random order. With the advent of Ruby 1.9, however, hashes have become firmly ordered. Create a new hash, perhaps with a literal:

```
hey_its_ordered = { first: 'mama', second: 'papa', third: 'baby' }
```

And iterate through it:

```
hey_its_ordered.each { |entry| pp entry }
```

And the items will stay firmly ordered:

```
[:first, "mama"]
[:second, "papa"]
[:third, "baby"]
```

If you add items to an existing hash, they get sent to the end of the line. Thus if we add a fourth entry to our hash:

```
hey_its_ordered[:fourth] = 'grandma'
```

Then granny will take up residence at the far end of the hash. Changing the value of an existing entry, however, does not disturb its place in line, so if we set hey_its_ordered[:first] to 'mom', it would stay right there at the front.

In the Wild

One reason that the basic collections are so pervasive in the Ruby code base is that Ruby programmers tend to reach for them at times when programmers from other

language traditions might go for a more specialized class. Thus, if you call `File`
`.readlines('/etc/passwd')` you *don't* get back an instance of some specific line
holding class: What you do get is a simple array full of strings. In the same spirit, ask
an object for its public methods by calling `object.public_methods` or a class for its
forebearers by calling `my_class.ancestors` and in each case you will get back a plain
old array of method names or super classes.[5] And it's not just arrays: Ruby programmers frequently use hashes to specify all sorts of things. Thus Rails applications tend
to have lots of code that looks like this:

```
link_to "Font", :controller =>"fonts", :action =>"show", :id =>@font
```

Perhaps the ultimate expression of this "use the simple collections" philosophy can
be found in the `XmlSimple` gem. This wonderful bit of software allows you to turn any
XML file, like this:

```
<characters>
  <super-hero>
    <name>Spiderman</name>
    <origin>Radioactive Spider</origin>
  </super-hero>
  <super-hero>
    <name>Hulk</name>
    <origin>Gamma Rays</origin>
  </super-hero>
  <super-hero>
    <name>Reed Richards</name>
    <origin>Cosmic Rays</origin>
  </super-hero>
</characters>
```

Into a convenient set of nested hashes and array:

```
{"super-hero"=>
  [{"name"=>["Spiderman"], "origin"=>["Radioactive Spider"]},
   {"name"=>["Hulk"], "origin"=>["Gamma Rays"]},
   {"name"=>["Reed Richards"], "origin"=>["Cosmic Rays"]}]}
```

---

5. Well, superclasses and mixed-in modules.

With just a couple of lines of code:

```
require 'xmlsimple'
data = XmlSimple.xml_in('dc.xml')
```

There are two reasons for this preference for the bare collections over more specialized classes. First, the Ruby collection classes are so powerful that often there is no practical reason to create a custom-tailored collection simply to get some specialized feature. Frequently, a call to each or map is all you really need. And second, all things being equal, Ruby programmers actually prefer to work with generic collections. To the Ruby way of thinking, one less class is one less thing to go wrong. In addition, I know exactly how an array is going to react to a call to each or map, which isn't necessarily true of the SpecializedCollectionOfStuff. When the problem is complexity, the cure might just be simplicity.

Staying Out of Trouble

If you look back over the pages of this chapter you will see that it is just full of calls to methods like each and map, methods that run through some collection, calling a block for each element. There is a lot of coding goodness in these methods, but beware: They will turn on you if you abuse them. The easiest way to screw up one of these iterating methods is to change the collection out from underneath the method. Here, for example, is a seriously misguided attempt to remove all of the negative numbers from an array:

```
array = [ 0, -10, -9, 5, 9 ]
array.each_index {|i| array.delete_at(i) if array[i] < 0}
pp array
```

The trouble with this code is that it will tend to leave some negative numbers behind: Removing the first one (the -10) from the array messes up the internal indexing of the each method, so much that it will miss the second negative number, leaving us with a result of:

```
[0, -9, 5, 9]
```

Although the problem in this example is reasonably easy to spot,[6] this is sadly not always the case: In particular, if your collection is being shared by several different threads, you run the real risk of one thread modifying a collection that the other thread is iterating over.

You will also want to take care when adding new elements well past the existing end of your array. Although there is not much danger of tacking on elements one by one with push or <<, you can also plug new values anywhere you want:

```
array = []
array[24601] = "Jean Valjean"
```

Since arrays are continuous, the second line above instantly created 24,602 new elements of array, most of them set to nil.

Another problem with arrays and hashes is that because they are so tremendously useful we sometimes reach for them when we should really be using something else. Imagine, for instance, that we are interested in knowing whether a specific word appears in a document. We could do this with a hash, using the words for keys and anything—perhaps true—as the values:

```
word_is_there = {}
words.each { |word| word_is_there[ word ] = true }
```

Alternatively, we might create an array that will keep track of each unique word:

```
unique = []
words.each { |word| unique << word unless unique.include?(word) }
```

The trouble with both of these approaches is that they are roundabout: The whole point of a hash is to map keys to values, but in our hash-based implementation we are really just interested in the keys—the words. The array-based version is not much better. Since arrays don't really mind duplicate values, every time we put a new word in

---

6. . . . and fix: A much cleaner way to get rid of those pesky negative numbers—a way that actually works—is to simply say array.delete_if {|x| x < 0}.

the array we need to search the whole thing (via the `include?` method) to see if the word is already there.

What we really need is a collection that doesn't allow duplicates but does feature very fast and easy answers to the "is this object in there?" question. The punch line is that we need a *set*. Fortunately, Ruby comes with a perfectly serviceable, if sometimes forgotten, `Set` class:

```
require 'set'

word_set = Set.new( words )
```

In coding, as in carpentry, you need the right tool for the job.

Wrapping Up

Making effective use of the collection classes is every bit as much a part of writing clear, idiomatic Ruby as getting the indentation and variable names right. The reason for this is very simple: The Ruby collection classes are like giant levers—if you know how to use them you can move a lot of computing weight with very little effort. Part of being a good Ruby programmer is knowing the `Array` and `Hash` classes, knowing what they can do, and knowing when to use them and when to reach for something else.

Of course, once you have your collections you are going to need to put something in them. Frequently that something will be a string.

CHAPTER 4

Take Advantage of Ruby's Smart Strings

Ask a nonprogrammer what we software types do all day and their answer will probably involve numbers. It's true: Programs are often knee deep in numerical values, everything from account balances to the number of milliseconds it takes to store a balance in a database. It ain't called computing for nothing. The thing that non-coders don't realize is just how much text processing goes on alongside all the number-crunching. Real-world programs tend to overflow with text, everything from the name of the account owner, to the name of the table that stores the balance, to the name of the program doing the storing. Because text processing is so central to just about every programming problem, every modern programming language comes equipped with some kind of string facility, typically a container that will not just store your text but also help you to fold, bend, and mutilate it.

The place for text in a Ruby program is in instances of the String class. In this chapter we will take a quick tour of Ruby's strings, starting with the surprising number of ways that you create a string and progressing to a fast look at the String API. We will also explore some of the ways that newcomers to Ruby can come to grief with strings and look at a few of the powerful things that Ruby applications do with just a pinch of string processing.

Coming Up with a String

What strikes many new Ruby coders about the language's strings is not the strings themselves but the number of ways that you can write a string literal. For example, just about every programming language features quoted strings. Some languages use single quotes as delimiters; others rely on double quotes. Ruby uses both kinds: There is the single-quoted string literal that is very literal indeed, doing almost no interpretation on the text between the quotes. In fact, the only fancy things you can do in a single-quoted string are to embed a literal quote in it, escaped by a backslash:

```
a_string_with_a_quote = 'Say it ain\'t so!'
```

And embed a literal backslash, also escaped by a backslash:[1]

```
a_string_with_a_backslash = 'This is a backslash: \\'
```

Double-quoted strings do quite a bit more interpretation: You can put characters like tabs and newlines in a double-quoted string with the appropriate character after a backslash:

```
double_quoted = "I have a tab: \t and a newline: \n"
```

You can also embed arbitrary expressions in a double-quoted string by enclosing the expression between #{ and }, so that this:

```
author = "Ben Bova"
title = "Mars"
puts "#{title} is written by #{author}"
```

Will print:

```
Mars is written by Ben Bova
```

---

1. Do be aware that Ruby will print backslashes embedded in strings in different ways, depending on how you output the string. If you use puts to print out a string with a backslash, Ruby will just print the backslash. If you use pp, however, Ruby will print the same double backslash you would use to embed the backslash character in the string. Either way, it's the same string with the same (single) backslash.

Keep in mind that since a single quote is not special in a doubled-quoted string and vice versa, you can sometimes avoid a lot of quote escaping by surrounding your string with a different quote flavor, so that instead of this:

```
str = "\"Stop\", she said, \"I cannot deal with the backslashes.\""
```

You can simply say:

```
str = '"Stop", she said, "I cannot deal with the backslashes."'
```

Although simple single- and double-quoted strings will suffice for about 98% of your string literal needs, occasionally you do need something a little more exotic. What if, for example, you had a string full of both types of quotation marks:

```
str = '"Stop", she said, "I can\'t live without \'s and "s."'
```

Ruby offers a couple of ways out of this kind of backslash Hell. In this case, the best choice is probably the arbitrary quote mechanism, which looks like this:

```
str = %q{"Stop", she said, "I can't live without 's and "s."}
```

Arbitrarily quoted strings always start with a percent sign (%) followed by the letter q. The character after the q is the actual string delimiter—we used a brace ({) in the example above. If your delimiter has a natural partner, the way } goes with {, then that's the character you use to close the string. In the example above we could have used (and) instead of { and }:

```
str = %q("Stop", she said, "I can't live without 's and "s.")
```

Or < and >:

```
str = %q<"Stop", she said, "I can't live without 's and "s.">
```

The [and] characters also work this way. Alternatively, you can use any of the other special characters as your delimiter, ending the string with the same character. Here we use a dollar sign:

```
str = %q$"Stop", she said, "I can't live without 's and "s."$
```

The case of the letter q that leads off your string also matters: If it is lowercase, as it has been in all of our examples so far, the string gets the limited interpretation, single-quote style treatment. A string with an uppercase Q gets the more liberal doubled-quoted interpretation:

```
str = %Q<The time in now #{Time.now}>
```

One nice feature of all Ruby strings is that they can span lines:

```
a_multiline_string = "a multi-line
string"

another_one = %q{another multi-line
string}
```

Keep in mind that if you don't do anything about it, you will end up with embedded newlines in those multiline strings. You can cancel out the newlines in double-quoted strings (and the equivalent %Q form) with a trailing backslash:

```
yet_another = %Q{another multi-line string with \
no newline}
```

Finally, if you happen to have a very long multiline string, consider using a here document. A here document allows you to create a (usually long) string by sticking it right in your code:

```
heres_one = <<EOF
This is the beginning of my here document.
And this is the end.
EOF
```

Literal strings are frequently necessary and sometimes very messy. You can reduce the messiness by picking the best form for the situation.

Another API to Master

The real utility in strings lies in the things you can do with—and to—them. Like collections, Ruby strings support a very extensive API, an API that every Ruby programmer needs to master. For example, once you have your string you can call the `lstrip` method, which will return a copy of the string with all of the leading whitespace clipped off, so that `' hello'.lstrip` will return `'hello'`.

Similarly, there is `rstrip`, which will peel the white space off of the end of your string as well as plain old `strip`, which will take the white space off of both ends. Similar to the trio of strip methods are `chomp` and `chop`. The `chomp` method is useful for those times when you are reading lines from a text file, something that tends to produce strings with unwanted line-terminating characters at the end. The `chomp` method will return a copy of the string with at most one newline character[2] lopped from the end. Thus,

```
"It was a dark and stormy night\n".chomp
```

Will give you the dark and stormy night without the newline. Note that `chomp` only does one newline at a time, so that `"hello\n\n\n".chomp` will return a string ending with two newlines. Be careful not to confuse `chomp` with the `chop` method. The `chop` method will simply knock off the last character of the string, no matter what it is, so that `"hello".chop` is just `"hell"`.

If the case of your characters concerns you, then you can use the `upcase` method to get a copy of your string with all of the lowercase letters made uppercase or the `downcase` method to go the opposite direction, or you can use `swapcase` to go from `'Hello'` to `'hELLO'`.

If you need to make more extensive changes to your string you might reach for the `sub` method. The name of this method is short for substitute, and the method will enable you to search for some substring and replace it with another. Thus, this:

```
'It is warm outside'.sub( 'warm', 'cold' )
```

---

2. Strictly speaking, `chomp` removes at most one record separator character from your string. Since the record separator is by default your system's newline character, most of the time this is a distinction without a difference.

Will evaluate to `'It is cold outside'`. If you need to be more enthusiastic about your substitutions, you might turn to gsub. While sub does at most one substitution, gsub will replace as many substrings as it possibly can. Thus, this:

```
puts 'yes yes'.sub( 'yes', 'no' )
puts 'yes yes'.gsub( 'yes', 'no' )
```

Will print out:

```
no yes
no no
```

Sometimes it's handy to be able to break your strings into smaller strings, and for that we have split. Call split with no arguments and it will return an array containing all the bits of your string that were separated by white space. Thus:

```
'It was a dark and stormy night'.split
```

Will return the following array:

```
["It", "was", "a", "dark", "and", "stormy", "night"]
```

Pass a string argument to split and it will break things up using that string as a delimiter, so that:

```
'Bill:Shakespeare:Playwright:Globe'.split( ':' )
```

Will evaluate to:

```
["Bill", "Shakespeare", "Playwright", "Globe"]
```

Like the collection classes, many of the string methods have counterparts whose names end with a !, which modify the original string instead of returning a modified copy. Thus, along with sub, we have sub!. So if you run this:

```
title = 'It was a dark and stormy night'
title.sub!( 'dark', 'bright' )
title.sub!( 'stormy', 'clear' )
```

Then `title` will end up as `'It was a bright and clear night'`.

If your interest runs more towards searching for things than changing them, you can locate a string within a bigger string with the `index` method:

```
"It was a dark and stormy night".index( "dark" )  # Returns 9
```

The String: A Place for Your Lines, Characters, and Bytes

Along with being things themselves, strings are also collections of other things. One odd aspect of strings is that they can't quite make up their minds as to the kinds of things they collect. Most commonly we think of strings as being collections of characters—after all, if you say `@author[3]` you are trying to get at the fourth character of the `@author` string. If you do think of your strings as collections of characters, you can use the `each_char` method to iterate. Thus, if `@author` is `'Clarke'`, this:

```
@author.each_char {|c| puts c}
```

Will produce:

```
C
l
a
r
k
e
```

You can also look at a string as a collection of bytes—after all, behind all those pretty characters are some utilitarian bytes. If you want to look at the bytes behind your string, you can loop through them with the aptly named `each_byte` method:

```
@author.each_byte { |b| puts b }
```

This code will print out a series of numbers, one for each byte:[3]

```
67
108
97
114
107
101
```

Strings can also hold more than one line, and if you find yourself with such a string, then you can look at it as a collection of lines:

```
@content.each_line { |line| puts line }
```

Interestingly, since the "collection of what?" question is not one that can really be answered for strings, Ruby's string class omits the plain old each method.[4]

In the Wild

As I said at the beginning of this chapter, most real-world programs spend their lives swimming through a sea of strings. For example, five minutes of poking around in the Ruby standard library uncovered this:

```ruby
def html_escape(s)
  s.to_s.gsub(/&/, "&amp;").gsub(/\"/, "&quot;").
    gsub(/>/, "&gt;").gsub(/</, "&lt;")
end
```

This code,[5] which decontaminates a string so that it is suitable for use in HTML and XML, is from the RSS library. The slashes around the first arguments to gsub mark those arguments as regular expressions, which we will look at in the next chapter.

---

3. The difference between bytes and characters isn't just the difference between a single number and an associated character. If you happen to be dealing with the multi-byte characters—common in many Asian languages—then your strings can have many more bytes than characters.

4. This was not always the case. In pre-1.9 versions of Ruby, strings did have an each method that iterated over—wait for it—lines! This somewhat less than intuitive method disappeared in 1.9.

5. The code is slightly edited to fit on the page.

If making text safe for XML seems a bit pedestrian, consider the inflection code in Rails. Rails uses the **inflection** facility to figure out that the class contained within current_employee.rb should be CurrentEmployee and the database table associated with CurrentEmployee is current_employees. Although this sounds sophisticated in a very AI way, it's all done with simple string processing.

The key data structure behind the Rails inflections is a set of rules, where each rule consists of a pattern and a replacement. The easiest inflection rules to understand are ones that handle the irregular cases, like pluralizing 'person' into 'people'. Here's the code that creates a bunch of special pluralizing cases:

```
inflect.irregular('person', 'people')
inflect.irregular('man', 'men')
inflect.irregular('child', 'children')
inflect.irregular('sex', 'sexes')
```

And how does Rails actually apply those rules? With a call to gsub[6]:

```
inflections.plurals.each do |(rule, replacement)|
  break if result.gsub!(rule, replacement)
end
```

The inflections code is one of the things that gives Rails its wonderful human-centered feeling, and it's all built around gsub.

Staying Out of Trouble

Ruby strings are mutable. Since this aspect of the language takes many newcomers by surprise, let me say it again: Ruby strings are mutable. Like the collections, it is perfectly possible to change a Ruby string out from under code that is expecting the string to remain stable. Keep in mind that if you have these two strings:

```
first_name = 'Karen'
given_name = first_name
```

---

6. Again, the code is edited to fit on the page.

In fact you only have *one* string: Modify `first_name`:

```
first_name[0] = 'D'
```

And you have also changed `given_name`. You should treat Ruby strings like any other mutable data structure. Get in the habit of saying this:

```
first_name = first_name.upcase
```

Instead of this:

```
first_name.upcase!
```

Finally, you can sometimes make your string code more comprehensible by taking advantage of the flexibility that Ruby gives you between those string indexing brackets. You can, for example, use negative numbers to index from the end of the string, with –1 being the last character in the string, so that you can turn this:

```
first_name[first_name.size - 1]
```

Into

```
first_name[-1]
```

You can also use ranges to index into your strings so that `"abcde"[3..4]` will evaluate to `"de"`.

Wrapping Up

As with the collection classes, Ruby strings are a good news/bad news proposition. The good news is that strings are very powerful objects that allow you to do all sorts of interesting things. You have a range of string literal forms to choose from, everything from `'simple quoted strings'` to `%Q{much more exotic forms}`. The bad news is that strings are very powerful objects *that you have to learn how to use.* The programming power that flows out of really mastering the string API is well worth the effort—especially when you couple your strings to regular expressions, which is where we turn next.

CHAPTER 5

Find the Right String with Regular Expressions

I'd like to pose a problem for you: Imagine that you have some text stored in a string, and somewhere in that text hides a time, something like 09:24 AM. You need to write a program that will locate the time. How do you do it? You might, using the methods we talked about in the last chapter, scan the string for a digit and then check to see whether it is followed by another digit and then see whether *that* is followed by a colon, then two more digits . . . well, you get the picture. Doing all this with the String methods is certainly possible. Tedious, but possible.

Sometimes a problem speaks to you. This time-finding problem is trying to tell you that you are using the wrong tool. The tool this problem is crying out for is the regular expression. The idea behind the regular expression—that you construct a pattern that either will or will not match some string—is as simple as regular expressions are powerful. Unfortunately, regular expressions have a reputation for being complex and obscure, and many engineers shy away from them. But shying away from regular expressions is not really an option: As we saw in the last chapter, Ruby programs do a lot of string processing, and where you find strings you will find regular expressions. To help with the shyness, we'll spend the first half of this chapter going over the regular expression basics before turning to their use in Ruby code. As usual, we will finish with a look at some real-world uses for regular expressions as well as some of the sharp edges that you would do well to avoid.

Matching One Character at a Time

Although whole books[1] have been written about regular expressions, the basics of this very useful tool are not very complex. For example, in a regular expression, letters and numbers match themselves. Thus:

- The regular expression x will match x.

- The regular expression aaa will match three a's all in a row.

- The regular expression 123 will match the first three numbers.

- The regular expression R2D2 will match the name of a certain sci-fi robot.

By default, case is important in regular expressions, so the last expression will *not* match r2d2 nor will it match R2d2.[2]

Unlike letters and numbers, most of the punctuation characters—things like . and *—have special meanings in regular expressions. For example, the period or dot character matches *any* single character.[3] Thus:

- The regular expression . will match any single-character string including r and % and ~.

- In the same way, two periods (..) will match any two characters, perhaps xx or 4F or even [!, but won't match Q since it's one, not two, characters long.

You use a backslash to turn off the special meanings of the punctuation characters. Thus:

- The regular expression \. will match a literal dot.

- 3\.14 will match the string version of PI to two decimal places, complete with the decimal point: 3.14

- Mr\. Olsen will match exactly one thing: Mr. Olsen

---

1. See the Appendix for the names of a couple of books on regular expressions.

2. As we will see in a bit, you can turn off regular expression case sensitivity.

3. Well, any single character except a newline character, but keep reading.

One of the beauties of regular expressions is that you can combine the different kinds of expressions to build up more complex patterns. For example:

- The regular expression `A.` will match any two-character string that starts with a capital `A`, including `AM`, `An`, `At`, and even `A-`.

- Similarly, `...X` will match any four-character string that *ends* with an `X`, including `UVWX` and `XOOX`.

- The regular expression `.r\. Smith` will match both `Dr. Smith` as well as `Mr. Smith` but not `Mrs. Smith`.

It's easy to see how the dot, with its talent for matching any single character, extends the reach of regular expressions. But what if you want to match something less than any? What if you want to write an expression that would match only the letters, or only the vowels, or maybe just the numbers?

Sets, Ranges, and Alternatives

Enter the **set**. Sets match any one of a bunch of characters. To create a regular expression set, you wrap the characters in square brackets: Thus the regular expression `[aeiou]` will match any single lowercase vowel. The key word there is *single*: Although `[aeiou]` will match the single character `a` or the single character `i`, it will not match `ai`, since `ai` is two characters long. Similarly:

- The regular expression `[0123456789]` will match any single digit.

- `[0123456789abdef]` will match any single hexadecimal digit,[4] like `7` or `f`.

Once you understand how sets work, you can start to build up some fairly complex regular expressions. For example:

- The regular expression `[Rr]uss [Oo]lsen` will match my name, with or without leading capitals.

- More practically, you could use `[0123456789abcdef][0123456789abcdef]` to pick out a two-digit hexadecimal number like `3e` or `ff`.

---

4. As long as the letter, if there is one, is lowercase.

- You can also use [aApP][mM] to match am or PM and anything in between, like aM or Pm.

There is one problem with simple sets: They don't scale well at the keyboard. No one wants to type [0123456789abcdef], let alone [abcdefghijklmnopqrstuvwxyz] or [abcdefghijklmnopqrstuvwxyz0123456789]. Fortunately, there is a special regular expression syntax for building just this sort of large set of continuous characters: the range.

As the name suggests, you define a **range** by specifying the beginning and end of a sequence of characters, separated by a dash. So the range [0-9] will match exactly what you expect: any decimal digit. Similarly, [a-z] will match any lowercase letter. You can also combine several ranges together and mix them with the regular set notation, so that:

- [0-9abcdef] will match a single hexadecimal digit.
- [0-9a-f] will also match a single hexadecimal digit.
- [0-9a-zA-Z_] will match any letter, number, or the underscore character.

If even [0-9] seems like too much work, there are some shorter shortcuts for common sets:

- \d will match any digit, so that \d\d will match any two digit number from 00 to 99.
- \w, where the w stands for "word character," will match any letter, number or the underscore.
- \s will match any white space character including the vanilla space, the tab, and the newline.

Another way to extend the power of your regular expressions is by using alternatives. If you separate the different parts of your expression with the vertical bar character |, the expression will match either the thing before the bar *or* the thing after it:

- A|B will match either A or B.
- AM|PM will match either AM or PM.
- Batman|Spiderman will match the name of one of the two superheros.

The sky is the limit with alternatives: You can specify as many choices as you like. Thus `A\.M\.|AM|P\.M\.|PM` will match `A.M.` or `AM`, or `P.M.` or `PM`. You can also surround your alternatives in parentheses to set them off from the rest of the pattern, so that:

```
The (car|boat) is red
```

Will match both `The car is red` as well as `The boat is red`.

Pull all of this together and you have enough regular-expression moxie to solve the time-finding problems that we opened this chapter with:

```
\d\d:\d\d (AM|PM)
```

Translated into English, the expression above says "Any string that starts with two digits, followed by a colon, followed by two more digits, followed by a space, followed by either `AM` or `PM`."

The Regular Expression Star

Now that we have the basics of regular expressions down it's time to move on to the interesting part: the asterisk. In regular expressions, an asterisk (`*`) matches zero or more of the thing that came just before it. Pause and think that through for a minute . . . zero or more of the thing that came just before the asterisk. What this means is that `A*` will match zero or more `A`'s. The `A` is the thing that came before the star, so the pattern will match zero or more `A`'s. Similarly:

- `AB*` will match `AB`—that's an `A` followed by one `B`.

- `AB*` will also match `ABB` as well as `ABBBBBBBB`—remember, it's an `A` followed by any number of `B`'s.

- Don't forget that `AB*` will also match plain old `A`—any number of `B`'s includes no `B`'s at all.

Although our examples so far have the star at the end of the expression, you can put it anywhere: It can be up at the front, so that `R*uby` means any number of `R`'s followed by `uby`. So `uby`, `Ruby`, `RRuby`, and `RRRRRRRuby` all match. The star can also be in the middle of your expression, so that you can use `Rub*y` to match `Ruy`, `Ruby`, as well as `Rubbbbbbbbbby`. There's also no limit to the number of stars that you can use in a regular expression so that `R*u*by` will match any number of R's followed by any number of u's followed by `by`.

You can also use the star in combination with sets, so that:

- The expression `[aeiou]*` will match any number of vowels: The whole `[aeiou]` set is the thing that came before the star.

- Likewise, the expression `[0–9]*` will match any number of digits.

- And `[0-9a-f]*` will match any number of hexadecimal digits.

Finally, we can combine the idea of a dot matching any single character and the `*` matching zero or more of the thing that came before into one of the most widely used of all regular expressions:

```
.*
```

This little gem—just a dot followed by an asterisk—will match any number of any characters, or to put it another way, *anything*. This works because the star matches any number of what came before, so that `.*` is the same as `.` and `..` and `...` and so on. But `.` matches any single character, while `..` matches any two characters, and so on. So `.*` will match anything.

Frequently you combine `.*` with other regular expression bits to make extremely elastic patterns. For example:

- The regular expression `George.*` will match the full name of anyone whose first name is `George`.

- In contrast, `.*George` will match the name of anyone whose last name is `George`.

- Finally `.*George.*` will match the name of anyone who has `George` in his name somewhere.

Regular Expressions in Ruby

In Ruby, the regular expression, or `Regexp` for short,[5] is one of the built-in data types, with its own special literal syntax. To make a Ruby regular expression you encase your pattern between forward slashes. So in Ruby our time regular expression would be:

---

5. `Regexp` is the name of the Ruby regular expression class.

```
/\d\d:\d\d (AM|PM)/
```

You use the =~ operator to test whether a regular expression matches a string. Thus, if we wanted to match the regular expression above with an actual time we would run:

```
puts /\d\d:\d\d (AM|PM)/ =~ '10:24 PM'
```

Which would print out:

```
0
```

That zero is trying to tell us a couple of things. First, it is saying that the regular expression matched, starting at index zero. Second, the zero is telling us is that when you match a regular expression, Ruby scans along the string, searching for a match *anywhere* in the string. We can see the scanning in action with this next example:

```
puts /PM/ =~ '10:24 PM'
```

Run the code shown here and it will print:

```
6
```

That six is an indication that the Regexp did match, but only after Ruby scanned well into the string. If there is no match, then you will get a nil back for your trouble, so that this:

```
/May/ =~ 'Sometime in June'
```

Will return a nil. Since =~ returns a number when it finds a match and nil if it doesn't, you can use regular expression matches as booleans:

```
the_time = '10:24 AM'
puts "It's morning!" if /AM/ =~ the_time
```

The =~ operator is also ambidextrous: It doesn't matter whether the string or the regular expression comes first, so we could rephrase the last example as:

```
puts "It's morning!" if '10:24 AM' =~ /AM/
```

As I mentioned earlier, regular expressions are by default case sensitive: /AM/ will not match 'am'. Fortunately, you can turn that case sensitivity off my sticking an i on the end of your expression, so that this:

```
puts "It matches!" if /AM/i =~ 'am'
```

Will print something.

Aside from their more or less stand-alone use with the =~ operator, regular expressions also come into play in the string methods that involve searching. Thus, you can pass a regular expression into the string gsub method, perhaps to blot out all of the times in the content of a document:

```
class Document
  # Most of the class omitted...

  def obscure_times!
    @content.gsub!( /\d\d:\d\d (AM|PM)/, '**:** **' )
  end
end
```

Taken together, strings and regular expressions make for a very powerful text-processing toolkit.

Beginnings and Endings

The fact that the =~ operator scans for a match anywhere in the string raises an interesting question: What if you only want your regular expression to match at the beginning of the string? For example, what if you were looking for the words Once upon a time? No problem: Simply cook up a straightforward regular expression:

```
/Once upon a time/
```

But what if you were looking specifically for fairy tales, which typically *start* with those immortal words? Again, there's a special regular expression for that, \A. Thus:

```
/\AOnce upon a time/
```

Will match a string only if it *begins* like a fairy tale. Note that the \A doesn't match the first *character*. Instead, it matches the unseen leading edge of the string. Similarly, \z (note the lower case) matches the end of the string, so that:

```
/and they all lived happily ever after\z/
```

Will only match a string that *ends* like a classic fairy tale.

Multiline strings, the ones full of embedded newlines, present some interesting challenges when you are doing this sort of work. Imagine that our alleged fairy tale is stored in a multiline string like this:

```
content = 'The Princess And The Monkey

Once upon a time there was a princess...
...and they all lived happily ever after.

The End'
```

Now *you* know, and *I* know, this is a fairy tale, but how do we write a regular expression that will know it? Our previous try, /\AOnce upon a time/ isn't going to work because the string above doesn't *start* with the right words. Instead, inside of the string is a *line* that starts with the magic words. Fortunately, there a Regexp for that too: the circumflex ^. The circumflex character matches two things: the beginning of the string *or* the beginning of any line within the string. Just the thing to ferret out a fairy tale:

```
puts "Found it" if content =~ /^Once upon a time/
```

Similarly, the dollar sign $ matches the end of the string *or* the end of any line within the string, so that we could also say:

```
puts "Found it" if content =~ /happily ever after\.$/
```

Multiline strings pose one more challenge to regular expressions, specifically to the dot: By default, the dot will match any character *except* the newline character. So if we were trying to match the whole text of fairy tale, less the title and The End, we might try:

```
/^Once upon a time.*happily ever after\.$/
```

But this attempt is doomed because the .* won't match across the lines . . . unless we simply turn off this behavior by adding an m to our expression:

```
/^Once upon a time.*happily ever after\.$/m
```

And then they did live happily ever after.

In the Wild

You can find a great example of the practical use of regular expressions in the time.rb file, which comes with your Ruby installation. The code in time.rb knows how to parse a string containing a date and time in any of a number of standard formats[6] and turn it into an instance of the Time class. Unlike the simple example that kicked off this chapter, time.rb needs to deal with all of the glorious complexities of real dates and times. Early on in the file you will find the zone_offset method, which attempts to parse the time zone section of a date and time string, figuring out if this string is supposed to represent 12:01 AM in Greenwich or Green Bay or Greenland. Among other things, the method needs to be able to understand time zones expressed as names like 'UTC', or in numeric offsets like '-07:00'.

The zone_offset method starts out by switching the whole zone string to upper-case, mixing in a pinch of simplicity right there at the start:

```
def zone_offset(zone, year=self.now.year)
  # ...
  zone = zone.upcase
  # ...
```

Next the code tests the zone against a number of regular expressions, trying to figure out if the zone is one of the numeric forms:

```
if /\A([+-])(\d\d):?(\d\d)\z/ =~ zone
```

This expression makes use of a regular expression feature that we haven't seen yet: Similar to the asterisk, the question mark matches zero or *one* of the things that came

---

6. It can also go the other way, from the Time object to a string.

before. Thus `:?` allows the regular expression to match zone offsets with or without a colon.

If the regular expression doesn't match, the `zone_offset` method goes on to do some plain old string comparison-based processing, looking for things like `'GMT'` or `'EST'`, all of which are stored in the `ZoneOffset` collection:

```
elsif ZoneOffset.include?(zone)
```

The `zone_offset` method takes a wonderfully pragmatic approach to an annoyingly complex problem: It uses regular expressions where they work best and the simple string methods where they work best.

Staying Out of Trouble

There are a couple of easy-to-make but also easy-to-avoid mistakes that you can perpetrate when working with regular expressions. The first is to write something like this:

```
puts /abc*/ == "abccccc"
```

The problem with this code is that I've let my fingers do the thinking as well as the typing. The regular expression `/abc*/` will never, ever be equal to `"abccccc"`, at least according to the `==` operator. Remember that the regular expression match operator is `=~` and not `==`. The correct way to say it is:

```
puts /abc*/ =~ "abccccc"
```

The second boneheaded thing that you can do, particularly if your background includes C or C++,[7] is to look at the output of the last example:

```
0
```

And decide that there was no match. Zero always seems so negative to C++ programmers. What the result is trying to tell you is that the regular expression matched the string starting at the beginning, or the zero-th index of the string. As we saw earlier, regular expression matches return `nil` when there is no match.

---

7. As does mine, so I know the bonehead of which I speak.

Wrapping Up

When it comes to serious string processing, there is only one word for regular expressions, and that word is *gift*. Regular expressions, with their stars, dollar signs, and little hat characters, can be intimidating, but the fundamental ideas are well within the reach of any coder.

CHAPTER 6

Use Symbols to Stand for Something

I have to admit that I tend to be a bit anthropomorphic about the technologies I work with. I just can't help but think of all those complex piles of software as somehow alive, each with its own personality—sometimes friendly, sometimes not. Early in my career I imagined FORTRAN as a grouchy old camel—capable of carrying a huge load, but fairly ugly and not a creature you would want to turn your back on. Later on I had this mental image of the -> operator in the C programming language (it dereferences pointers) as an arrow in flight: also very powerful, also nothing to mess with. These days, the colon that precedes every Ruby symbol always makes me think of the eyes peering out from the tilted head of a confused but friendly dog. The key word here is confused—symbols probably have the dubious distinction of being the one bit of syntax that perplexes the greatest number of new Ruby programmers.

In this chapter I am going to try to stamp out all of that confusion and show symbols for what they really are: very simple, useful programming language constructs that are a key part of the Ruby programming style. So let's get started and see why symbols are such handy little mutts to have around.

The Two Faces of Strings

Sometimes a good way to explain a troublesome topic is to engage in a little creative fiction. You start out with an oversimplified explanation and, once that has sunk in a bit, you work your way from there back to the real world. In this spirit, let's start our exploration of symbols with a slight simplification: Symbols are really just strings. This is not as far fetched as it sounds: Think about the string "dog" and its closest symbolic cousin, :dog. The thing that hits you in the face about these two objects is that they both are essentially three characters: a "d", an "o", and a "g".

Strings and symbols are also reasonably interchangeable in real life code: Take this familiar example of some ActiveRecord code, which finds all of the records in the books table:[1]

```
book = Book.find(:all)
```

The argument to the find method is simply a flag, there to tell find that we want all of the records in the books table—not just the first record, not just the last record, but all of them. The actual value that we pass into Book.find doesn't really matter very much. We might imagine that if we had the time and motivation, we could go into the guts of ActiveRecord and rewrite the code so that we could use a string to signal that we wanted *all* the books:

```
book = Book.find('all')
```

So there is my simplified explanation of symbols: Other than the fact that typing :all requires one less keystroke than typing 'all', there is not really a lot to distinguish a symbol from a string. So why does Ruby give us both?

Not Quite a String

The answer is that we tend to use strings of characters in our code for two rather different purposes: The first, and most obvious, use for strings is to hold some data that we are processing. Read in those Book objects from the database and you will very likely have your hands full of string data, things like the title of the book, the author's name, and the actual text.

The second way that we use strings of characters is to represent things in our programs, things like wanting to find *all* of the records in a table. The key thing about

---

1. If you are not familiar with ActiveRecord, don't worry. In ActiveRecord there is a class for each database table. In our example we have the (unseen) Book class that knows about the books table. Every ActiveRecord table class has a class method called find, which takes various arguments telling the method for what it should search.

`:all` in our `Book` ActiveRecord example is that ActiveRecord can recognize it when it sees it—the code needs to know which records to return, and `:all` is the flag that says it should return every one. The nice thing about using something like `:all` for this kind of "stands for" duty is that it also makes sense to the humans: You are a lot more likely to recognize what `:all` means when you come across it than 0, or -1, or even (heaven forbid!) `0x29ef`.

These two uses for strings of characters—for regular data processing tasks on the one hand and for internal, symbolic, marker-type jobs on the other—make very different demands on the objects. If you are processing data, you will want to have the whole range of string manipulation tools at your fingertips: You might want the first ten characters of the title, or you might want to get its length or see whether it matches some regular expression. On the other hand, if you are using some characters to stand for something in your code, you probably are not very interested in messing with the actual characters. Instead, in this second case you just need to know whether this thing is the flag that tells you to find all the records or just the first record. Mainly, when you want some characters to stand for something, you simply need to know if *this* is the same as *that*, quickly and reliably.

Optimized to Stand for Something

By now you have probably guessed that the Ruby `String` class is optimized for the data processing side of strings while symbols are meant to take over the "stands for" role—hence the name. Since we don't use symbols for data processing tasks, they lack most of the classic string manipulation methods that we talked about in Chapter 4. Symbols do have some special talents that make them great for being symbols. For example, there can only ever be one instance of any given symbol: If I mention `:all` twice in my code, it is always exactly the same `:all`. So if I have:

```
a = :all
b = a
c = :all
```

I know that a, b, and c all refer to exactly the same object. It turns out that Ruby has a number of different ways to check whether one object is equal to another,[2] but

---

2. For more on object equality, see Chapter 12.

with symbols it doesn't matter: Since there can only be one instance of any given symbol, :all is always equal to itself no matter how you ask:

```
# True! All true!

a == c
a === c
a.eql?(c)
a.equal?(c)
```

In contrast, every time you say "all", you are making a brand new string. So if you say this:

```
x = "all"
y = "all"
```

Then you have manufactured two different strings. Since both the strings happen to contain the same three characters, the two strings are equal in some sense of the word, but they are emphatically not identically the same object. The fact that there can only be one instance of any given symbol means that figuring out whether *this* symbol is the same as *that* symbol is not only foolproof, it also happens at lightning speeds.

Another aspect of symbols that makes them so well suited to their chosen career is that symbols are immutable—once you create that :all symbol, it will be :all until the end of time.[3] You cannot, for example, make it uppercase or lob off the second 'l'. This means that you can use a symbol with confidence that it will not change out from under you.

You can see all these issues at play in hashes. Since symbol comparison runs at NASCAR speeds and symbols never change, they make ideal hash keys. Sometimes, however, engineers want to use regular strings as hash keys:

```
author = 'jules verne'
title = 'from earth to the moon'
hash = { author => title }
```

---

3. Or at least until your Ruby interpreter exits.

So what would happen to the hash if you changed the key out from underneath it?

```
author.upcase!
```

The answer is that nothing will happen to the hash, because the Hash class has special defenses built in to guard against just this kind of thing. Inside of Hash there is special case code that makes a copy of any keys passed in if the keys happen to be strings. The fact that the Hash class needs to go through this ugly bit of special pleading precisely to keep you from coming to grief with string keys is the perfect illustration of the utility of symbols.

In the Wild

In practice, the line between symbols and regular strings is sometimes a bit blurry. It is, for example, trivially easy to turn a symbol into a string: You just use the ubiquitous to_s method:

```
the_string = :all.to_s
```

To go in the reverse direction, you can use the to_sym method that you find on your strings:

```
the_symbol = 'all'.to_sym
```

The blurriness between symbols and strings sometimes also extends into the minds of Ruby programmers. For example, every object in Ruby has a method called public_methods, which returns an array containing the names of all of the public methods on that object. Now, you might argue that method names are the poster children for objects that stand for something (in this case a bit of code), and therefore the public_methods method should return an array of symbols. But call public_methods in a pre-1.9 version of Ruby, like this:

```
x = Object.new
pp x.public_methods
```

And you will get an array of strings, not symbols:

```
["inspect",
 "pretty_print_cycle",
 "pretty_print_inspect",
 "clone",
 ...
 ]
```

Is there something wrong with our reasoning? Apparently not, because in Ruby 1.9 `public_methods` does indeed return an array of symbols:

```
[:pretty_print,
 :pretty_print_cycle,
 :pretty_print_instance_variables,
 :pretty_print_inspect,
 :nil?,
 ...
 ]
```

The lesson here is that if you find symbols a bit confusing, you seem to be in very good company.

Staying Out of Trouble

Given the curious relationship between symbols and strings, it probably will come as no surprise that the best way to screw up with a symbol is to use it when you wanted a string, and vice versa. As we have seen, you want to use strings for data, for things that you might want to truncate, turn to uppercase, or concatenate. Use symbols when you simply want an intelligible thing that stands for something in your code.

The other way to go wrong is to forget which you need at any given time. This seems to happen a lot when using symbols as the keys in hashes. For example, take a look at this code fragment:

```
# Some broken code

person = {}
person[:name] = 'russ'
```

```
person[:eyes] = 'misty blue'

# A little later...

puts "Name: #{person['name']} Eyes: #{person['eyes']}"
```

The code here is broken, but you might have to look at it a couple of times to see that the keys of the person hash are symbols, but the puts statement tries to use strings. What you really want to say here is:

```
puts "Name: #{person[:name]} Eyes: #{person[:eyes]}"
```

This kind of mistake is common enough that Rails actually provides a Band-Aid for it in the form of the HashWithIndifferentAccess class. This convenient, but somewhat dubious bit of code is a subclass of Hash that allows you to mix and match strings and symbols with cheerful abandon.

Wrapping Up

In this chapter we have looked at symbols and saw that they exist purely to stand for something in your code. Symbols and garden variety strings have a lot in common—both are mostly just a stretch of characters. Unlike strings, symbols are specially tuned to their "stands for" purpose: Symbols are both unique—there can only ever be one :all symbol in your Ruby interpreter—and immutable, so that :all will never change. The good news is that once you understand that symbols and strings are like two siblings—related, but with different talents—you will be able to take advantage of the things that each does best.

CHAPTER 7

Treat Everything Like an Object—Because Everything Is

Early in my career I worked with a mainframe operating system that had a variety of file types. That old OS supported text files for your documentation, source files for your code, executable files for your programs, and data files for your output. Actually, "supported" is not really the right word. "Imposed with an iron fist" would be more accurate. Creating new files involved specifying the file type using a complex and arcane syntax. You needed to use one command for copying data files and a similar, but subtlety different, command for copying source files. Converting from one file type to another was a task worthy of a Ph.D. I'm sure that the designers of that ancient system had originally set out to make life easier for their users by imposing some order on the everyday complexities of computing. Along the way, however, they lost sight of something important: Sometimes—like when you are trying to make a copy—a file is just a file.

Ruby is an object oriented programming language, which means that the world of Ruby is a world of objects, instances of `Date` and `String` and `Document` and a thousand other classes. As different as all these objects are bound to be, at some level they are all just objects. In the pages that follow we will focus on the things that all Ruby objects have in common. We will start by doing a quick tour of the Ruby object system and then look at how pervasive objects are in Ruby. Next we will look at the methods common to all Ruby objects, the basic toolkit that every object inherits, and at how you can control access to methods. We will round out the chapter by looking at how classes and methods play a key role in the infrastructure of Ruby itself and at some avoidable potholes lurking in the land of the object.

A Quick Review of Classes, Instances, and Methods

On the surface, Ruby is a very conventional, almost boring, object oriented language. Every Ruby object is an instance of some class. Classes mainly earn their keep by providing two key things: First, classes act as containers for methods:

```
class Document

  # Most of the class omitted...

  # A method

  def words
    @content.split
  end

  # And another one

  def word_count
    words.size
  end
end
```

Second, classes are also factories, factories for making instances:

```
doc = Document.new( 'Ethics', 'Spinoza', 'By that which is...' )
```

Once you have an instance, you can call methods on it using the more or less universal object oriented syntax of instance.method_name:

```
doc.word_count
```

During a method call, Ruby sets self to the instance that you called the method on, so that if you added this to Document:

```
class Document
  # Most of the class on holiday...

  def about_me
    puts "I am #{self}"
    puts "My title is #{self.title}"
    puts "I have #{self.word_count} words"
  end
end
```

And then ran `doc.about_me`, you would see something like:

```
I am #<Document:0x8766ed4>
My title is Ethics
I have 4 words
```

Ruby treats `self` as a sort of default object: When you call a method without an explicit object reference, Ruby assumes that you meant to call the method on `self`, so that a call to plain old `word_count` gets translated to `self.word_count`. You should rely on this assumption in your code: Don't write `self.word_count` when a plain `word_count` will do.[1]

Every class—except one—has a superclass, someplace that the class can turn to when someone calls a method that the class doesn't recognize. If you don't specify a superclass when you are defining a new class, the new class automatically becomes a direct subclass of `Object`. Our `Document` class, for example, is a direct subclass of `Object`. Alternatively, you can specify a different superclass:

```
# RomanceNovel is a subclass of Document,
# which is a subclass of Object

class RomanceNovel < Document
  # Lot's of steamy stuff omitted...
end
```

---

1. You Python programmers know who I'm talking to!

The Ruby technique for resolving methods is straight out of the object oriented handbook: Look for the method in the class of the object. If it is there, call it and you are done. If not, move on to the superclass and try there. Repeat until you either find the method or run out of superclasses.[2]

Objects All the Way Down

While Ruby's basic object system is not the most original bit of technology, it does have something very powerful going for it: consistency. You can see just how consistent Ruby's object oriented philosophy is by computing the absolute value of a number:

```
-3.abs            # Returns 3
```

Nothing very exciting there ... except for the syntax. Why is it -3.abs and not abs(-3)? The answer is both simple and profound: In Ruby the number -3 is an object. When you say -3.abs, you are calling the abs method on an object, an object that goes by the name -3. It's not just the numbers either. In Ruby, strings and symbols and regular expressions are all objects, objects that come equipped with their very own methods:

```
# Call some methods on some objects

"abc".upcase
:abc.length
/abc/.class
```

In fact, virtually everything you come across in Ruby is an object. You might, for example, think that true and false are a couple of special Ruby language constructs. Not so—they're just objects:

```
# Call some methods on a couple of familiar objects

true.class        # Returns Trueclass
false.nil?        # False is close, but not nil
```

---

2. Ruby does add some cool twists to its fairly vanilla object model, twists that we are going to explore in Chapters 13, 16, and 24.

So are the classes:

```
true.class.class # Returns Class
```

Even our old buddy—and sometimes nemesis—`nil` is an object:

```
nil.class          # Returns NilClass
nil.nil?           # Yes, finally true!
```

In Ruby, if you can reference it with a variable, it's an object.

The Importance of Being an Object

Actually, if you can reference it with a variable it's probably not just an object, but an *Object*, an instance of the `Object` class.[3] Since virtually all Ruby objects can trace their ancestry back to `Object`, virtually all Ruby objects have a set of methods in common: the ones they inherit from `Object`. So the next time you call `class` or `instance_of?` to see just what sort of object you have, thank the `Object` class for supplying those methods. The `Object` class is also the source of the well-worn `to_s` method, which returns a string representation of your object. It's the `to_s` method that `puts` relies on to turn its arguments into printable strings.[4] Like a lot of `Object` methods, you can rely on the default implementation of `to_s`. So if you ran this:

```
doc = Document.new( 'Emma', 'Austin', 'Emma Woodhouse, ...' )
puts doc
```

You would see something like:

```
#<Document:0x8767120>
```

---

3. The reason I hedge is that Ruby 1.9 added the `BasicObject` class, as the new superclass of `Object`. `BasicObject` instances are, however, few and far between and tend to be used in a way that masks their true identity. All these mysteries will be explained in Chapter 22.

4. This is a bit of a simplification, but not much. Many of the `Object` methods actually live in the `Kernel` module, which is mixed into the `Object` class, a process that we will explore in Chapter 16. For most practical purposes this is a distinction without a difference.

Alternatively, you can override to_s for your own purposes:

```
class Document
  # Mostly omitted...

  def to_s
    "Document: #{title} by #{author}"
  end
end
```

With the class above, our documents would print out something like:

```
Document: Emma by Austin
```

Instances of Object also inherit some more esoteric talents. For example, the eval method, defined by Object, takes a string and executes the string *as if it were Ruby code*. The possibilities with eval are literally limitless: Having eval around means that every Ruby programmer has the entire Ruby language available at a moment's notice. You can, to take an easy example, create a quick riff on irb with nothing more than eval and a handful of other Object supplied methods:[5]

```
while true
  print "Cmd> "
  cmd = gets
  puts( eval( cmd ) )
end
```

Run the code above and you will find yourself in a very irb-like loop:

```
Cmd> 2 + 2
4
Cmd> puts "hello world"
hello world
```

---

5. The print method prints what you tell it to, without mixing in any additional newline characters the way that puts does. The gets method is the inverse of puts: It reads a string.

The `Object` class also supplies a set of reflection-oriented methods, methods that let you dig into the internals of an object. We met one of these in the last chapter: the `public_methods` method, which returns an array of all the method names available on the object. There is also `instance_variables`, which will pull out the names of any instance variables buried in the object. So, if you run this:

```
pp doc.instance_variables
```

You will see:

```
[:@title, :@author, :@content]
```

In all, `Object` bestows about fifty methods on its children.

Public, Private, and Protected

Like a lot of object oriented programming languages, Ruby lets you control the visibility of your methods. Methods can either be public—callable by any code anywhere, or private, or protected. Ruby methods are public by default, so up to now all of our `Document` methods have been public.

You can make your methods private by adding `private` before the method definition:

```
class Document
  # Most of the class omitted

  private  # Methods are private starting here

  def word_count
    return words.size
  end
end
```

Or by making them private after the fact:

```
class Document
  # Most of the class omitted
```

```
def word_count
  return words.size
end

private :word_count
end
```

Ruby's treatment of private methods is a bit idiosyncratic. The rule is that you cannot call a private method with an explicit object reference. So if word_count was indeed private, then this:

```
n = doc.word_count
```

Will throw an exception, since we tried to use an explicit object reference (doc) in the call. By restricting the way that private methods can be called, Ruby ensures that private methods can only be called from inside the class that defined them. Thus the call to word_count in the print_word_count method that follows will work:

```
class Document
  # Most of the class omitted...

  def word_count
    return words.size
  end

  private :word_count

  # This method works because self is the right thing,
  # the document instance, when you call it.
  def print_word_count
    n = word_count
    puts "The number of words is #{word_count}"
  end
end
```

Note that in Ruby, private methods are callable from subclasses. Think about it: You don't need an explicit object reference to call a superclass method from a subclass. Thus, this is a perfectly functional bit of code:

```
# RomanceNovel is a subclass of Document,
# which is a subclass of Object

class RomanceNovel < Document
  def number_of_steamy_words
    word_count / 4      # Works: self is a Document instance!
  end
end
```

The rules for protected methods are looser and a bit more complex: Any instance of a class can call a protected method on any other instance of the class. Thus, if we made word_count protected, any instance of Document could call word_count on any other instance of Document, including instances of subclasses like RomanceNovel.

There are a couple of things to keep in mind about private and protected methods in Ruby. The first is that while Ruby's system of controlling method visibility is perfectly respectable, it doesn't get a lot of use. For example, if you look at the Ruby standard library you will find nearly 200,000 lines of code. In that huge pile of software, private appears just over 1000 times and protected only about fifty times. Second, remember that just because the rules say that you can't call some private or protected method, well, you can still call it. Among the methods that every object inherits from Object is send. If you supply send with the name of a method and any arguments the method might need, send will call the method, visibility be damned:

```
n = doc.send( :word_count )
```

The Ruby philosophy is that the programmer is in charge. If you want to declare some method private, fine. Later, if someone, perhaps you, wants to violate that privacy, fine again. You are in charge and presumably you know what you are doing.

In the Wild

One thing that takes a while to sink in when learning Ruby is just how central the idea of methods and method calls are to the fundamental infrastructure of the language. Certainly there are lots of of things that go on in Ruby that are *not* method calls. Assigning a value to a local variable is not a method call. An if statement is not a method call. Neither is a while loop. Once, however, you get beyond the lowest layer of basic infrastructure, a surprising number of things you might consider to be part of the language are, in fact, just calls to methods. For example, you can't get much more fundamental than method visibility. Nevertheless, `private`, the magic word that makes Ruby methods private, is not really magic at all: It's just a method, albeit one that is implemented inside the Ruby interpreter. The same is true of `private`'s buddies, `public` and `protected`.

The Ruby interpreter also defines another method, one that takes the name of a file, reads the contents of the file, and executes those contents as Ruby code. This method maintains a list of the files it has already processed and won't re-execute a file that it has already seen. We call that *method* `require`:[6]

```
require 'date'    # A Call to a method
```

Another set of methods that play the part of language keywords are the `attr_accessor` family:

```
class Person
  attr_accessor :salary  # A method call
  attr_reader :name      # Another method call
  attr_writer :password  # And another
end
```

Not only are `attr_accessor` and friends just methods, but they are within the reach of mortal programmers. In Chapter 26 we are going to build our own versions of `attr_reader` and `attr_writer`. Stay tuned!

Staying Out of Trouble

The good news is that virtually all Ruby objects[7] inherit about fifty methods from the `Object` class, methods that allow you to do all sorts of useful things. The bad news is that those inherited methods also represent about fifty opportunities to have a name collision. Take this innocent-looking addition to the `Document` class:

```
class Document
  # Most of the class omitted...
```

---

6. The `require` method can also handle loading native libraries.

7. Except for those `BasicObject` oddballs.

```
    # Send this document to off via email
    def send( recipient )
      # Do some interesting SMTP stuff...
    end
  end
```

Innocent, except that we have just overridden the `Object` supplied send method. Know your `Object` class, if for no other reason than to stay out of its way.

Another way to go wrong is to intentionally override a method from `Object`—and to get it wrong. Recall that earlier in the chapter we overrode the `to_s` method so that it would produce a better description of our document. Make a mistake in the `to_s` method, perhaps like this:

```
class Document
  # Mostly omitted...

  def to_s
    "#{title} by #{aothor}"    # oops!
  end
end
```

And you will no longer be able to print `Document` instances via `puts`.

Finally, programmers new to the language will sometimes forget how uniform the Ruby object model is and invent special cases where none actually exist, perhaps like this:

```
if the_object.nil?
  puts 'The object is nil'
elsif the_object.instance_of?( Numeric )
  puts 'The object is a number'
else
  puts "The object is an instance of #{the_object.class}"
end
```

When they could get away with the much simpler:

```
puts "The object is an instance of #{the_object.class}"
```

The single line of code here will work with virtually any object in your Ruby interpreter: Feed it a string and it will tell you that you have a `String`. Feed it a number and you might see that you have an instance of `Fixnum` or `Float`. Feed it `nil` and it will tell you that you have an instance[8] of `NilClass`. This example illustrates a more general and very pleasant side effect of Ruby's uniform object system: Since Ruby's `nil` is a real object, it is generally much less toxic than the equivalent constructs in other programming languages. When I'm coding in Ruby I don't have to be quite as paranoid that this object I have might just be `nil`. Remember, a great way to avoid broken code is to have less of it. The code that you never write will work forever.

Wrapping Up

If you remember anything from this chapter, remember this: Virtually everything in Ruby is an object, and virtually all of those objects inherit a basic set of methods from the `Object` class. In a very real way, the `Object` class is the glue that binds Ruby together and lends the language its simple elegance. Given how fundamental the `Object` class is to Ruby, it shouldn't come as much of a surprise that we aren't done with it. In chapters to come, we will look at how you can use the framework provided by the `Object` class to define your own operators, to create objects with their own ideas of equality, to rewire your inheritance tree, and to handle calls to methods that you haven't written.

For the moment, however, we will turn our attention to a different question. In this chapter we have focused on the things that all Ruby objects have in common: At their core, the dates and strings and documents floating around in our programs are all the same. But they are also all different: Outside of its `Object` core, a `Date` instance is very different from a `String` instance. The question for the next chapter is simple: How do you keep all of these different objects straight?

---

8. The only instance!

CHAPTER 8

Embrace Dynamic Typing

How? Why? These are the two questions that every new Ruby coder—or at least those emigrating from the more traditional programming languages—eventually gets around to asking. How can you possibly write reliable programs without some kind of static type checking? And why? Why would you even want to try? Figure out the answer to those two questions and you're on your way to becoming a seasoned Ruby programmer. In this chapter we will look at how dynamic typing allows you to build programs that are simultaneously compact, flexible, and readable. Unfortunately, nothing comes for free, so we will also look at the downsides of dynamic typing and at how the wise Ruby programmer works hard to make sure the good outweighs the bad.

This is a lot for one chapter, so let's get started.

Shorter Programs, But Not the Way You Think

One of the oft-repeated advantages of dynamic typing is that it allows you to write more compact code. For example, our `Document` class would certainly be longer if we needed to state—and possibly repeat here and there—that `@author`, `@title`, and `@content` are all strings and that the `words` method returns an array. What is not quite so obvious is that the simple "every declaration you leave out is one bit less code" is just the down payment on the code you save with dynamic typing. Much more significant savings comes from the classes, modules, and methods that you never write at all.

To see what I mean, let's imagine that one of your users has a large number of documents stored in files. This user would like to have a class that looks just like a

Document,[1] but that will delay reading the contents of the file until the last possible moment: In short, the user wants a lazy document. You think about this new requirement for a bit and come up with the following: First you build an abstract class that will serve as the superclass for both the regular and lazy flavors of documents:

```ruby
class BaseDocument

  def title
    raise "Not Implemented"
  end

  def title=
    raise "Not Implemented"
  end

  def author
    raise "Not Implemented"
  end

  def author=
    raise "Not Implemented"
  end

  def content
    raise "Not Implemented"
  end

  # And so on for the content=
  # words and word_count methods...

end
```

Then you recast `Document` as a subclass of `BaseDocument`:

```ruby
class Document < BaseDocument
  attr_accessor :title, :author, :content
```

---

1. Again, to keep things simple we are going to start over here with the very minimal functionality of the original Document class of Chapter 1.

```ruby
  def initialize( title, author, content )
    @title = title
    @author = author
    @content = content
  end

  def words
    @content.split
  end

  def word_count
    words.size
  end
end
```

Finally, you write the LazyDocument class, which is also a subclass of BaseDocument:

```ruby
class LazyDocument < BaseDocument

  attr_writer :title, :author, :content

  def initialize( path )
    @path = path
    @document_read = false
  end

  def read_document
    return if @document_read
    File.open( @path ) do | f |
      @title = f.readline.chomp
      @author = f.readline.chomp
      @content = f.read
    end
    @document_read = true
  end

  def title
    read_document
    @title
  end
```

```
    def title=( new_title )
      read_document
      @title = new_title
    end


    # And so on...
  end
```

The `LazyDocument` class is a typical example of the "leave it to the last minute" technique: It looks like a regular document but doesn't really read anything from the file until it absolutely has to. To keep things simple, `LazyDocument` just assumes that its file will contain the title and author of the document on the first couple of lines, followed by the actual text of the document.

With the classes above, you can now do nice, polymorphic things with instances of `Document` and `LazyDocument`. For example, if you have a reference to one or the other kind of document and are not sure which:

```
  doc = get_some_kind_of_document
```

You can still call all of the usual document methods:

```
    puts "Title: #{doc.title}"
    puts "Author: #{doc.author}"
    puts "Content: #{doc.content}"
```

In a technical sense, this combination of `BaseDocument`, `Document`, and `LazyDocument` do work. They fail, however, as good Ruby coding. The problem isn't with the `LazyDocument` class or the `Document` class. The problem lies with `BaseDocument`: It does nothing. Even worse, `BaseDocument` takes more than 30 lines to do nothing. `BaseDocument` only exists as a misguided effort to provide a common interface for the various flavors of documents. The effort is misguided because Ruby does not judge an object by its class hierarchy.

Take another look at the last code example: Nowhere do we say that the variable `doc` needs to be of any particular class. Instead of looking at an object's type to decide whether it is the correct object, Ruby simply assumes that if an object has the right methods, then it is the right kind of object. This philosophy, sometimes called **duck** typing,[2] means that you can completely dispense with the `BaseDocument` class and redo the two document classes as a couple of completely independent propositions:

```
class Document
  # Body of the class unchanged...
end

class LazyDocument
  # Body of the class unchanged...
end
```

Any code that used the old related versions of `Document` and `LazyDocument` will still work with the new unrelated classes. After all, both classes support the same set of methods and that's what counts.

There are two lessons you can take away from our `BaseDocument` excursion. The first is that the real compactness payoff of dynamic typing comes not from leaving out a few `int` and `string` declarations; it comes instead from all of the `BaseDocument` style abstract classes that you never write, from the interfaces that you never create, from the casts and derived types that are simply irrelevant. The second lesson is that the payoff is not automatic. If you continue to write static type style base classes, your code will continue to be much bulkier than it might be.

Extreme Decoupling

Compact code is a great thing, but compact code is by no means the only advantage of dynamic typing. There is also the free and easy flexibility that flows from writing code sans type declarations. For example, let's imagine that the editorial department of your company also has an enhancement request. It seems that the folks over at editorial are putting in a more formal system to keep track of authors and publications. In particular, they have invented a couple of new classes:

```
class Title
  attr_reader :long_name, :short_name
  attr_reader :isbn
```

2. As in, "If it walks like a duck and quacks like a duck, then it must be a duck."

```
  def initialize(long_name, short_name, isbn)
    @long_name = long_name
    @short_name = short_name
    @isbn = isbn
  end
end

class Author
  attr_reader :first_name, :last_name

  def initialize( first_name, last_name )
    @first_name = first_name
    @last_name = last_name
  end
end
```

The editorial department would like you to change the Document class so that they can use Title and Author instances instead of strings as the @title and @author values in Document instances, like this:

```
two_cities = Title.new( 'A Tale Of Two Cities',
                        '2 Cities', '0-999-99999-9' )
dickens = Author.new( 'Charles', 'Dickens' )
doc = Document.new( two_cities, dickens, 'It was the best...' )
```

Being a nice person and a consummate professional you immediately agree to undertake this task. And then you do nothing. Absolutely nothing. You do nothing because the Document class already works with Title and Author instances. There are no interfaces to extract, no declarations to change, no class hierarchies to adjust, nothing. It just works.

It works because Ruby's dynamic typing means that you don't declare the classes of variables and parameters. That means that your classes are not frozen together in a rigid network of type relationships. In Ruby, any two classes that *can* work together *will* work together. Flexibility is a huge advantage when it comes to constructing programs. In our example, the Document class does not really do anything with @title and @author other than carry them around; the Document class therefore has absolutely no opinion as to what the class of these objects should be.

Even if `Document` did make some demands on `@title` and `@author`, perhaps like this:

```
class Document
  # Most of the class omitted...

  def description
    "#{@title.long_name} by #{@author.last_name}"
  end
end
```

Then we will have increased the coupling between `Document` and the `@author` and `@title` objects just a bit. With the addition of the `description` method, `Document` now expects that `@title` will have a method called `long_name` and `@author` will have a `last_name` method. But the bump in coupling is as small as it can be. `Document` will, for example, accept any object that has a `long_name` method for `@title`.

Taking advantage of the loose coupling offered by dynamic typing is easy: As you can see from this last example, it is right there for you—unless you go out of your way to mess it up. Programmers new to Ruby will sometimes try to cope with the loss of static typing by adding type-checking code to their methods:

```
def initialize( title, author, content )
  raise "title isn't a String" unless title.kind_of? String
  raise "author isn't a String" unless author.kind_of? String
  raise "content isn't a String" unless content.kind_of? String
  @title = title
  @author = author
  @content = content
end
```

This kind of pseudo-static type checking combines all the disadvantages of the two camps: It destroys the wonderful loose coupling of dynamic typing. It also bloats the code while doing little to improve reliability. Don't do this.

This last example illustrates another, more subtle advantage to dynamic typing. Programming is a complex business. Writing a tricky bit of code is like that old circus act where the performer keeps an improbably large number of plates spinning atop vertical sticks, except that here it's the details of your problem that are spinning and it's all happening in your head. When you are coding, anything that reduces the number of revolving mental plates is a win. From this perspective, a typing system that you can sum up in a short phrase, "The method is either there or it is not," has some definite appeal. If the problem is complexity, the solution might just be simplicity.

Required Ceremony Versus Programmer-Driven Clarity

One thing that variable declarations do add to code is a modicum of documentation. Take the `initialize` method of our `Document` class:

```
def initialize( title, author, content )
```

Considerations of code flexibility and compactness aside, there is simply no arguing with the fact that a few type declarations:

```
# Pseudo-Ruby! Don't try this at home!

def initialize( String title, String author, String content )
```

Would make it easier to figure out how to create a `Document` instance. The flip side of this argument is that not all methods benefit—in a documentation sense—from type declarations. Take this hypothetical `Document` method:

```
def is_longer_than?( n )
  @content.length > n
end
```

Even without type declarations, most coders would have no trouble deducing that `is_longer_than?` takes a number and returns a boolean. Unfortunately, when type declarations are required, you need put them in your code whether they make your code more readable or not—that's why they call it *required*. Required type declarations inevitably become a ceremonial part of your code, motions you need to go through just to get your program to work. In contrast, making up for the lost documentation value of declarations in Ruby is easy: You write code that is painfully, blazingly obvious. Start by using nice, full words for class, variable, and method names:

```
def is_longer_than?( number_of_characters )
  @content.length > number of characters
end
```

If that doesn't help, you can go all the way and throw in some comments:

```
# Given a number, which needs to be an instance of Numeric,
# return true if the number of characters in the document
# exceeds the number.
def is_longer_than?( number_of_characters )
  @content.length > number_of_characters
end
```

With dynamic typing, it's the programmer who gets to pick the right level of documentation, not the rules of the language. If you are writing simple, obvious code, you can be very minimalistic. Alternatively, if you are building something complex, you can be more elaborate. Dynamic typing allows you to document your code to exactly the level you think is best. It's your job to do the thinking.

Staying Out of Trouble

Engineering is all about trade-offs. Just about every engineering decision involves getting something, but at a price, and there is a price to be paid for dynamic typing. Undeniably, dynamic typing opens us up to dangers that don't exist in statically typed languages. What if we missed the memo saying that the Document class now expects the @title to have a long_name method? We might just end up here:

```
NoMethodError: undefined method `long_name' for "TwoCities":String
```

This is the nightmare scenario that virtually everyone who comes to Ruby from a statically typed language background worries about. You think you have one thing, perhaps an instance of Author, when in fact you actually have a reference to a String or a Time or an Employee and you don't even know it. There is just no getting around the fact that this kind of thing can happen in Ruby code.

What's a Ruby programmer to do? My first bit of advice is to simply relax. The experience that has accumulated over the past half century of dynamic language use is that horrible typing disasters are just not all that common. They are, in fact, downright rare in any carefully written program. The best way to avoid mixing your types, like metaphors, is to write the clearest, most concise code you can, which explains why Ruby programmers place such a high premium on (wait for it!) clear and concise code. If it's easy to see what's going on, you will make fewer mistakes.

Fewer mistakes, but not zero mistakes. Inevitably you are going to experience a type-related bug now and then. Unsurprisingly, you are also going to have non-type-related bugs as well. The Ruby answer to both kinds of bugs is to write automated tests, lots and lots of automated tests. In fact, automated tests are such a core part of writing good Ruby code that the next chapter is devoted to them.

You should also keep in mind that there is a difference between concise and cryptic. Ruby allows you to write wonderfully expressive code, code that gets things done with a minimum of noise. Ruby also allows you to write stuff like this:

```ruby
class Doc
  attr_accessor :ttl, :au, :c

  def initialize(ttl, au, c)
    @ttl = ttl; @au = au; @c = c
  end

  def wds;  @c.split; end
end
```

In any language, this kind of "damn the reader" terseness, with its cryptic variable and method names, is bad. In Ruby it's a complete disaster. Since bad Ruby code does not have the last resort crutch of type declarations to lean on, bad Ruby code can be very bad indeed. The only solution is to not write bad Ruby code. Try to make your code speak to the human reader as much as it speaks to the Ruby interpreter. It comes down to this: Ruby is a language for grown-ups; it gives you the tools for writing clear and concise code. It's up to you to use them.

In the Wild

A good example of the Ruby typing philosophy of "if the method is there, it is the right object" is as close as your nearest file and string. Every Ruby programmer knows that if you want to open a Ruby file, you do something like this:[3]

---

3. Actually, most Ruby programmers would call `File.open` with a block, but that is beside the point here.

```
open_file = File.open( '/etc/passwd' )
```

Sometimes, however, you would like to be able to read from a string in the same way that you read from a file, so we have `StringIO`:

```
require 'stringio'
open_string = StringIO.new( "So say we all!\nSo say we all!\n" )
```

The idea is that you can use `open_file` and `open_string` interchangeably: Call `readchar` on either and you will get the next character, either from the file or the string. Call `readline` and you will get the next line. Calling `open_file.seek(0)` will put you back at the beginning of the file while `open_string.seek(0)` will put you at the beginning of the string.

Surprisingly, the `File` and `StringIO` classes are completely unrelated. The earliest common ancestor of these two classes is `Object`! Apparently reading and writing files and strings is different enough that the authors of `StringIO` (which was presumably written after `File`) decided that there was nothing to gain—in terms of implementation—from inheriting from `File`, so they simply went their own way. This is fairly typical of Ruby code, where subclassing is driven more from practical considerations—"Do I get any free implementation from inheriting from this class?"—than a requirement to make the types match up.

You can find another interesting example of the "don't artificially couple your classes together" thinking in the source code for the `Set` class, which we looked at briefly in Chapter 3. It turns out that you can initialize a `Set` instance with an array, like this:

```
five_even = [ 2, 4, 6, 8, 10 ]
five_even_set = Set.new( five_even )
```

In older versions of `Set`, the code that inserted the initial values into the new `Set` instance looked like this:[4]

```
enum.is_a?(Enumerable) or raise ArgumentError, "not enumerable"
enum.each { |o| add(o) }
```

---

4. I did take some liberties with this code to make it fit within the formatting restrictions of this book.

These early versions of `Set` first checked to see if the variable `enum`, which held the initial members of the set, was an instance of `Enumerable`—arrays and many other Ruby collections are instances of `Enumerable`—and raised an exception if it wasn't. The trouble with this approach is that the requirement that `enum` be `Enumerable` is completely artificial. In the spirit of dynamic typing, all that `Set` should really care about is that `enum` has an `each` method that will iterate through all of the elements. Apparently the maintainers of the `Set` class agree, because the `Enumerable` check has disappeared from the current version of `set.rb`.

Wrapping Up

So how do you take advantage of dynamic typing? First, don't create more infrastructure than you really need. Keep in mind that Ruby classes don't need to be related by inheritance to share a common interface; they only need to support the same methods. Don't obscure your code with pointless checks to see whether *this* really is an instance of *that*. Do take advantage of the terseness provided by dynamic typing to write code that simply gets the job done with as little fuss as possible—but also keep in mind that someone (possibly you!) will need to read and understand the code in the future.

Above all, write tests. . . .

CHAPTER 9

Write Specs!

The past few decades have seen the software world argue endlessly about the best way to develop reliable programs: Should our languages be procedural or object oriented or functional? Should we build things top down or bottom up or inside out? When we code, should we be rational, agile, or simply pragmatic? Out of all this discussion, one simple idea has emerged: If you want to know that your code works, you need to test it. You need to test it early, you need to test it often, and you certainly need to test it whenever you change it. It turns out that with programs, seeing is believing.

Unless you want to spend all your waking hours running tests manually, you need a test framework, a framework that will let the computer exercise the code for you. Although the whole programming world has awakened to the need for automated tests, few language communities have embraced the concept with the passion of the Ruby community. A key part of the Ruby style of programming is that no class, and certainly no program, is ever done if it lacks automated tests.

In this chapter we are going to take a look at two different Ruby testing frameworks, starting with the very traditional Test::Unit and moving on to the very popular—and very nontraditional—RSpec. We'll also look at some of the do's and don'ts for writing tests, no matter what framework you use. Finally, we will also look at how the RubySpec project is using an RSpec-like approach to specifying the Ruby programming language itself.

Test::Unit: When Your Documents Just Have to Work

We are going to open our look at Ruby testing frameworks by starting with the familiar: Test::Unit. Test::Unit comes packaged with Ruby itself and is a member of the so-called XUnit family of testing frameworks, so called because there is a similar one for virtually every programming language out there.

The very simple idea behind Test::Unit is to exercise your code in a series of individual tests, where each test tries out one aspect of the program. In Test::Unit, each test is packaged in a method whose name needs to begin with test_. Here, for instance, is a little test that checks to make sure that the Document class can do the very basic thing that documents need to do, namely, to hold onto text:

```ruby
def test_document_holds_onto_contents
  text = 'A bunch of words'
  doc = Document.new('test', 'nobody', text)
  assert_equal text, doc.content
end
```

There is not really a lot going on in this test: We make a document with some text, and then we check, using assert_equal, that the document does indeed still have the text. If the two arguments to assert_equal are not, in fact, equal, the test fails. One stylistic thing that his test does well is to have a nice descriptive name. If we do this testing thing right we are going to have a lot of test methods, and the last thing we want is to have to dig through the test code to see just what test_that_it_works or test_number_four is all about. In the same spirit, we could improve our use of assert_equal by adding the third, optional description parameter:

```ruby
assert_equal text, doc.content, 'Contents are still there'
```

Along with assert_equal, Test::Unit also allows you to assert that some arbitrary condition is true with the assert method. Thus we might check that our words method is returning what it should with:

```ruby
assert doc.words.include?( 'bunch' )
```

To really use Test::Unit you need to roll your tests up in a class, a subclass of Test::Unit::TestCase. Inside the class you can have any number of test methods:

```ruby
require 'test/unit'
require 'document.rb'

class DocumentTest < Test::Unit::TestCase
  def test_document_holds_onto_contents
    text = 'A bunch of words'
    doc = Document.new('test', 'nobody', text)
    assert_equal text, doc.content, 'Contents are still there'
  end

  def test_that_doc_can_return_words_in_array
    text = 'A bunch of words'
    doc = Document.new('test', 'nobody', text)
    assert doc.words.include?( 'A' )
    assert doc.words.include?( 'bunch' )
    assert doc.words.include?( 'of' )
    assert doc.words.include?( 'words' )
  end

  def test_that_word_count_is_correct
    text = 'A bunch of words'
    doc = Document.new('test', 'nobody', text)
    assert_equal 4, doc.word_count, 'Word count is correct'
  end
end
```

Kicking off a Test::Unit test is about as easy as it comes: Just run the file containing the test class with Ruby:[1]

```
ruby document_test.rb
Loaded suite document_test
Started
...
Finished in 0.000261 seconds.

3 tests, 3 assertions, 0 failures, 0 errors
```

---

1. I'd like to invite you to stop for a minute and think about how this could possibly work. How do those tests get run when you just feed your test class declaration into the Ruby interpreter with no main program? I'm afraid you will have to wait until Chapter 20 for the answer.

Note that if one of the test methods does happen to fail, Test::Unit will keep soldiering along, running all the other tests. This is generally a good thing, since if there are multiple broken tests it allows you to survey all the wreckage after a single test run.

One problem with the document test is that it contains a fair bit of redundant code: We keep creating that Document instance over and over. To deal with this kind of thing, Test::Unit provides the setup method along with its friend, the teardown method. The setup method gets called before each test method is run; it's your opportunity to do what needs to be done to get ready for your tests. In our example we would probably just create the document:

```ruby
class DocumentTest < Test::Unit::TestCase
  def setup
    @text = 'A bunch of words'
    @doc = Document.new('test', 'nobody', @text)
  end

  def test_that_document_holds_onto_contents
    assert_equal @text, @doc.content, 'Contents are still there'
  end

  def test_that_doc_can_return_words_in_array
    assert @doc.words.include?( 'A' )
    assert @doc.words.include?( 'bunch' )
    assert @doc.words.include?( 'of' )
    assert @doc.words.include?( 'words' )
  end

  def test_that_word_count_is_correct
    assert_equal 4, @doc.word_count, 'Word count is correct'
  end
end
```

In the same way, the teardown method gets called after each test method gets run. The teardown method is great for closing database connections, deleting temporary files, or any other general post-test tidying up. Note that setup and teardown get called around *each* test method, not before, and after all of the tests in the class get run.

A Plethora of Assertions

So far our tests have only needed to check that something is true with `assert` or that one thing is equal to something else with `assert_equal`. These two methods are certainly not the only assertions in the Test::Unit toolkit. To go with `assert` and `assert_equal` we have `assert_not_equal` as well as `assert_nil` and `assert_not_nil`, each of which does about what you would expect.

If you are dealing with a lot of strings, Test::Unit has a handy `assert_match`, which will fail if a string does not match a given regular expression:

```
assert_match /times.*/, 'times new roman'
```

You can also check that an object is an instance of some class:

```
assert_instance_of String, 'hello'
```

And you can assert that some code raises an exception:

```
assert_raise ZeroDivisionError do
  x = 1/0
end
```

Or doesn't raise (or throw, as the name of the assertion would have it) an exception:

```
assert_nothing_thrown do
  x = 1/2
end
```

In all, Test::Unit tests can call on about twenty different assertions.

Don't Test It, Spec It!

Clearly Test::Unit is a workmanlike chunk of testing support, and if you are only going to write an occasional bit of test code it would probably do. The trouble is that if you are doing the Ruby thing right, you are not just writing the occasional test. A good Ruby application comes with lots of tests, tests that try out everything that can be tried out.

Unfortunately, much of the code of a Test::Unit test is about the *test* and not about the code that you are testing. Take another look at `DocumentTest`: You will see that we have methods that do this and assert that result, but if you are reading the `DocumentTest` code, you need to *infer* what `Document` behavior is being tested from the test code.

In a more perfect world, the test would focus on the behavior itself, so that the test would read something like this:

> About the `Document` class: When you have a document instance, it should hang onto the text that you give it. It should also return an array containing each word in the document when you call the `words` method. And it should return the number of words in the document when you call the `word_count` method.

Rspec, possibly the Ruby world's favorite testing framework, tries to get us to that more perfect world. Here is the same set of `Document` tests expressed in RSpec:

```
describe Document do
  it 'should hold on to the contents' do
    text = 'A bunch of words'
    doc = Document.new( 'test', 'nobody', text )
    doc.content.should == text
  end

  it 'should return all of the words in the document' do
    text = 'A bunch of words'
    doc = Document.new( 'test', 'nobody', text )
    doc.words.include?( 'A' ).should == true
    doc.words.include?( 'bunch' ).should == true
    doc.words.include?( 'of' ).should == true
    doc.words.include?( 'words' ).should == true
  end

  it 'should know how many words it contains' do
    text = 'A bunch of words'
    doc = Document.new( 'test', 'nobody', text )
    doc.word_count.should == 4
  end
end
```

RSpec tries to weave a sort of pseudo-English out of Ruby: The code above isn't a test, it's a description. The description says that the `Document` class should hold on to the contents. We don't assert things; we say that they should happen. Thus, we don't assert that `word_count` returns 4; instead, we say that `word_count` should equal 4. Like Test::Unit assertions, RSpec `should`s come in a wide variety of forms. We could, for example, simplify the code above by using `should include`, turning this:

```
doc.words.include?( 'bunch' ).should == true
```

Into:

```
doc.words.should include( 'bunch' )
```

Similarly, there is `should match` for those times when a plain `==` will not do:

```
doc.content.should match( /A bunch.*/ )
```

If you are feeling negative you can resort to `should_not`.[2]

```
doc.words.should_not include( 'Excelsior' )
```

By convention, your RSpec code—generally just called a **spec**—goes in a file called `<<class name>>_spec.rb`, so the previous example would be best stored away in `document_spec.rb`. You can run the spec by using the `spec` command:[3]

```
spec document_spec.rb
```

Do that and you should see something like this:

```
...

Finished in 0.016846047 seconds

3 examples, 0 failures
```

---

2. You can find out all about RSpec—including all the ways that you can say what should happen—at www.rspec.info.

3. Note that spec is an operating system command, along the lines of `ls` or `dir`, not something you would say in Ruby.

A very handy feature of the `spec` command is its ability to hunt down all of the spec files in a whole directory tree, assuming that you follow the `<<class name>>_spec.rb` convention. All you need to do is supply the path to a directory instead of a file to the `spec` command. So if you run:

```
spec .
```

RSpec will run all of the specs that live in the current directory and any of its subdirectories.

A Tidy Spec Is a Readable Spec

As it stands right now, our new document spec has the same problem as the original Test::Unit based `DocumentTest`: It has a lot of redundant code in it. Like the original test, each little chunk of the specification—called an **example** in RSpec parlance—creates the same document with the same text. RSpec deals with this problem the same way that Test::Unit does, by allowing you to supply code that is executed before each example. Here is a somewhat shorter-winded version of our spec:

```ruby
require 'document'

describe Document do
  before :each do
    @text = 'A bunch of words'
    @doc = Document.new( 'test', 'nobody', @text )
  end

  it 'should hold on to the contents' do
    @doc.content.should == @text
  end

  it 'should know which words it has' do
    @doc.words.should include( 'A' )
    @doc.words.should include( 'bunch' )
    @doc.words.should include( 'of' )
    @doc.words.should include( 'words' )
  end
```

```
it 'should know how many words it contains' do
  @doc.word_count.should == 4
end

end
```

There is also an `after`, which is the RSpec cousin of `teardown` and allows you to get code executed after each example. The `:each` parameter means to run the code supplied before (or after) each example. Alternatively, you can use `before(:all)` and `after(:all)` to have some code run before or after any of the examples are run.

Easy Stubs

One of the banes of unit testing flows from the fact that an ideal test exercises exactly one class at a time. Doing this means that when the test fails we know there is something wrong with the class we are testing and not some other class that just happened to get dragged along. The trouble is that most classes will not function without other classes to help them: Programs tend to be complicated ecosystems, with the majority of classes relying on the kindness of other classes. It's this supporting software that is a problem for tests: How do you test just the one class when that class needs an entourage of other classes to work?

What you need are stubs and mocks. A **stub** is an object that implements the same interface as one of the supporting cast members, but returns canned answers when its methods are called. For a concrete example, imagine that we've created a subclass of our `Document` class, a subclass that supports printing. Further, suppose that the real work of printing is done by a printer class, which supports two methods. Method one is called `available?`, and it returns true if the printer is actually up and running. Method two is `render`, which actually causes paper to come spewing out of a real printer. With the printer class in hand, getting our document onto paper is pretty easy:

```
class PrintableDocument < Document
  def print( printer )
    return 'Printer unavailable' unless printer.available?
    printer.render( "#{title}\n" )
    printer.render( "By #{author}\n" )
    printer.render( content )
```

```
        'Done'
      end
    end
```

The idea of the `print` method is that we pass it a printer object and it will print the document—but only if the printer is actually running.

The question here is, how do we test the `print` method without having to get involved with a real printer? Conceptually this is easy: You just create a stub printer class, a sort of stand-in class that has the same `available?` and `render` methods of the real printer class but doesn't actually do any printing. In practice, coding stubs by hand can be tedious and, if you are testing a complex class with a lot of dependencies, tedious and error prone.

The RSpec `stub` method is there to reduce the pain of creating stubs. To use the `stub` method, you pass in a hash of method names (as symbols) and the corresponding values that you want those methods to return. The `stub` method will give you back an object equipped exactly with those methods, methods that will return the appropriate values. Thus, if you called `stub` like this:

```
stub_printer = stub :available? => true, :render => nil
```

You would end up with `stub_printer` pointing at an object with two methods, `available?` and `render`, methods that return `true` and `nil` respectively. With `stub` there are no classes to create, no methods to code; `stub` does it all for you. Here's an RSpec example that makes use of `stub_printer`:

```
describe PrintableDocument do
  before :each do
    @text = 'A bunch of words'
    @doc = PrintableDocument.new( 'test', 'nobody', @text )
  end

  it 'should know how to print itself' do
    stub_printer = stub :available? => true, :render => nil
    @doc.print( stub_printer ).should == 'Done'
  end

  it 'should return the proper string if printer is offline' do
    stub_printer = stub :available? => false, :render => nil
```

```
        @doc.print( stub_printer ).should == 'Printer unavailable'
    end
end
```

Along with stub, RSpec also provides the stub! method, which will let you stub out individual methods on any regular object you might have lying around. Thus, if we need a string that claimed to be a million characters long, we could say:

```
apparently_long_string = 'actually short'
apparently_long_string.stub!( :length ).and_return( 1000000 )
```

What all of this means is that with RSpec you will never have to write another class full of stubbed-out methods again.

. . . And Easy Mocks

Stubs, with their ability to quietly return canned answers, are great for producing the boring infrastructure that you need to make a test work. Sometimes, however, you need a stublike object that takes more of an active role in the test. Look back at our last printing test (the one with the stub) and you will see that the test doesn't verify that the print method ever called render. It's a sad printing test that doesn't check to see that something got printed.

What we need here is a **mock**. A mock is a stub with an attitude. Along with knowing what canned responses to return, a mock also knows which methods should be called and with what arguments. Critically, a disappointed mock will fail the test. Thus, while a stub is there purely to get the test to work, a mock is an active participant in the test, watching how it is treated and failing the test if it doesn't like what it sees.

In a boring bit of consistency, RSpec provides a mock method to go with stub. Here again is our PrintableDocument spec, this time enhanced with a mock:

```
it 'should know how to print itself' do
  mock_printer = mock('Printer')
  mock_printer.should_receive(:available?).and_return(true)
  mock_printer.should_receive(:render).exactly(3).times
  @doc.print( mock_printer ).should == 'Done'
end
```

In the code shown here we create a mock printer object and then set it up to expect that, during the course of the test, `available?` will be called at least once and render will be called exactly three times. As you can see, RSpec defines a little expectation language that you can use to express exactly what should happen. In addition to declaring that some method will or will not be called, you can also specify what arguments the method should see, RSpec will check these expectations at the end of each example, and if they aren't met the spec will fail.

These examples really just scratch the surface of what you can do with RSpec. Take a look at http://rspec.info for the full documentation.

In the Wild

Given the intense interest of the Ruby community in testing, it's not surprising that there are a lot of Ruby testing frameworks and utilities around. For example, if you decide to use Test::Unit, you might want to look into shoulda.[4] The shoulda gem defines all sorts of useful utilities for your Test::Unit tests, including the ability to replace those traditional test methods with RSpec-like examples:

```ruby
require 'test/unit'
require 'shoulda'
require 'document.rb'

class DocumentTest < Test::Unit::TestCase
  context 'A basic document class' do
    def setup
      @text = 'A bunch of words'
      @doc = Document.new('a test', 'russ', @text)
    end

    should 'hold on to the contents' do
      assert_equal @text, @doc.content, 'Contents still there'
    end

    # Rest of the test omitted...
  end
end
```

---

4. http://github.com/thoughtbot/shoulda

Test::Unit users should also look into mocha,[5] which provides mocking facilities along the same lines as RSpec.

If you have settled on RSpec, a great place to look for examples of specs is the RubySpec[6] project. The fine folks behind RubySpec are trying to build a complete Ruby language specification in RSpec format. The beauty of this approach is that when they are done we will not only have a full specification of the Ruby language that people can read, but we will also have an executable specification, one that you can run against any Ruby implementation.

For our purposes, RubySpec is a great place to find real world, but nevertheless easy to understand specs. For example, here is a spec which makes sure that if statements work as advertised:

```ruby
describe "The if expression" do
  it "evaluates body if expression is true" do
    a = []
    if true
      a << 123
    end
    a.should == [123]
  end

  it "does not evaluate body if expression is false" do
    a = []
    if false
      a << 123
    end
    a.should == []
  end

  # Lots and lots of stuff omitted
end
```

And here is a spec for the Array.each method:

```ruby
describe "Array#each" do
  it "yields each element to the block" do
```

5. http://mocha.rubyforge.org
6. http://rubyspec.org

```
    a = []
    x = [1, 2, 3]
    x.each { |item| a << item }.should equal(x)
    a.should == [1, 2, 3]
  end


  # Lots of stuff omitted
end
```

There's a bit of irony in looking at the RubySpec project for tips on how to use RSpec given that RubySpec does not actually use RSpec. Instead, the RubySpec project uses a mostly compatible RSpec offshoot called MSpec. Although MSpec is close enough to RSpec for our "find me an example" purposes, it differs from RSpec in ways that are important if you are trying to test the whole Ruby language.

Finally, if you would like to do RSpec style examples but don't want to go to the trouble of installing the RSpec gem, you might consider Minitest, which is included in Ruby 1.9. MiniTest is a complete rewrite of Test::Unit, and it also sports MiniSpec, an RSpec like framework. Did I mention that Ruby people like testing?

Staying Out of Trouble

Simply having a set of automated tests is as close to a magical elixir for software quality as you are likely to find in this life. There are, however, a number of things you can do to ensure that you are getting the maximum testing magic for your effort. For example, unit tests, the ones that developers run as they develop, should be quick. Ideally the tests for your whole system should run in at most a few minutes. Think about it: Unit tests that take an hour to run will be run at most once per hour. Who am I kidding? Given the level of patience displayed by the average developer, unit tests that take an hour to run will get run once or twice a week if you are lucky. If you want developers to run your unit tests as often as they should, they gotta go quick.

Don't get me wrong—longer running tests are fine; in fact, they are great. Longer-running tests that pound away at the database, that require all the servers to be running, that stress the heck out of the system are great. They are just not unit tests. Unit tests should run quick with the setup that every developer has. They are your first line of defense, and in order to be any good they must be run often.

Another thing that your tests should be is *silent*. When you run a test you want a simple answer to a simple question: Does it work or does it not work? You don't want to know how many elements are in the list, that you are now entering this method or leaving that method, and you certainly don't need help with today's date. If the test fails, and it tells you clearly that it failed, then you can pull out your tools and start looking at the problem. Until then, quiet please.

Tests also need to be independent of one another: You want to carefully avoid having one test rely on the output of a previous test. Don't create a file in one test (or RSpec example) and then expect it to be there in another. In particular, use RSpec's `before(:any)` in preference to `before(:all)`.

Do make sure that your tests will actually fail. It is all too easy to create a test that looks right but doesn't actually test anything worthwhile. For example, imagine that we implemented the `clone` method on `Document`. The `clone` method is another method that every object gets from the `Object` class: Call `clone` and you get a copy of your object. The default `clone` implementation makes a shallow copy; you get a second object from `clone`, but the instance variables of both the original and the clone will point at identically the same objects. We don't, however, have to live with the default: Here's a `Document` `clone` method that does a deep copy, duplicating `@title`, `@author`, and `@content` along with the `Document` instance:

```
class Document

  # ...

  def clone
    Document.new( title.clone, author.clone, content.clone )
  end
end
```

Having taken the advice of this chapter to heart, we make sure that we have a spec for our new `clone`. Here it is:

```
describe Document do
  it 'should have a functional clone method' do
    doc1 = Document.new( 'title', 'author', 'some stuff' )
    doc2 = doc1.clone
```

```
      doc1.title.should == 'title'
      doc1.author.should == 'author'
      doc1.content.should == 'some stuff'
    end
  end
```

The trouble with this last spec is that it is an impostor: It does indeed make a cloned copy of the document, but then it goes on to test the original (doc1) instead of the copy (doc2). The bottom line is that an important part of writing a test is making sure that it actually tests what you think it tests.

Let me also add a personal bit of testing heresy. Although the ideal set of unit tests will cover all of the significant features of your code, sometimes you just can't get to the ideal. Sometimes you can't get anywhere near it: The bug fix needs to go out, or the release is late, or your coworkers are just not into the whole testing thing. What to do? Well, write whatever unit tests you can. As an absolute minimum, just write a unit test that exercises the code a little, with no asserts at all. For example, look at this seemingly worthless spec:

```
require 'document'

describe Document do
  it 'should not catch fire when you create an instance' do
    Document.new( 'title', 'author', 'stuff' ).should_not == nil
  end
end
```

While far, far from ideal, this spec actually does more than you might think. If it runs successfully you will know:

- Document is a class.[7]

- The Document class is indeed found in the document.rb file.

- The document.rb file doesn't contain any really egregious Ruby syntax errors.

- Document.new will take three arguments.

---

7. Or at least it acts like a class.

- `Document.new` actually returns something.

- `Document.new` doesn't throw an exception.

Not bad for a few lines of code. At the risk of repeating myself, let me say it again: Write really, really good tests if you can. Write OK ones if that is all you can do. If you can't do anything else, at least write some tests that exercise your code, even just a little bit.

Given that you are going to have tests, or specs, there is also the question of *when* to write your tests. A large segment, perhaps a majority, of Ruby programmers adhere to the test-first philosophy of programming: Never, ever, add a feature to your code without first adding a test. Start out by writing a test that fails, the test-firsters say, and then write the code that makes the test pass. Repeat until you have the Great American Program, complete with a full suite of tests. The test-firsters make the very valid point that if you never write any code without first having a test for whatever that code is supposed to do, you will automatically write testable programs.

I have to say that I like the idea of test-first development, and I frequently practice it. But not—and here is the rub—always. There are times when I can be more productive by simply writing the code and then going back and adding the tests. When I hit those times I leave the tests for the end. Test-first development is a great idea, but we in the software industry have a habit of messing up really good ideas by deciding they are not just good but absolutely universal. And required. The take-away here is that you are not finished until you have both the software and the tests or specs to go with it. Write the tests first, or second, or third. But write the darned tests.

Wrapping Up

Let me say it again: Write the tests. Although I've tried to make the case in this chapter that Test::Unit is a fine, traditional testing framework and that RSpec, with its readable examples and easy mocking, is a great testing framework, the real message is that you need to write the tests. You will never know whether your code works unless you write the tests. Write thoroughly comprehensible tests if you can, write sketchy tests if you must, but write the tests.

PART II

Classes, Modules, and Blocks

CHAPTER 10

Construct Your Classes from Short, Focused Methods

Let's face it: Despite shelves full of books on software architecture, enough UML diagrams to fill an art museum, and design meetings that seem to last longer than the pyramids, building software mostly comes down to writing one method after another.

An important, but frequently ignored question is, how exactly should we break our classes up into those methods? Although the question of "How should I write my methods?" is not really one that a programming language can answer, programming languages do tend to encourage one style over another. In this chapter we are going to look at how Ruby programmers tend to write methods. We will see that most Ruby programmers favor very short methods, methods that stick to doing one thing and doing it well. We will see that breaking your code up into many short, single-purpose methods not only plays to the strengths of the Ruby programming language but also makes your whole application more testable.

Compressing Specifications

Imagine that you just landed a job working for the Universal Software Specification Repository. You and your colleagues are tasked with archiving every software spec that has ever been written. Since the industry has spewed out a lot of specs over the years, the plan is to compress the documents before they are stored. Your job is to implement

117

the heart of the compression algorithm, which will take in a text string and produce two arrays, which will then be stored in the archive. The first array will contain all the unique words in the original text. Thus, if you start with this text:

```
This specification is the specification for a specification
```

Then the first array would contain all the words found in the text, with no repeats, like this:

```
["This", "specification", "is", "the", "for", "a"]
```

The second array will contain integer indexes. There will be one index in this second array for each word in the original document. In our example, the second array would contain this:

```
[0, 1, 2, 3, 1, 4, 5, 1]
```

We can use these two data structures to reproduce the original sequence of words by running through the index array, looking up each word in the unique words array as we go. Thus we can tell that the fourth word of our text is `"the"`, since the fourth index is 3 and `"the"` is the word at index 3 in the unique words array. This technique is the sort of thing you might do when you want to compress some text that contains a lot of long, repeated words—which is more or less the definition of a software specification.

Doing a passable job of taking some text apart and compressing it into the two arrays is not difficult. Here's our first stab:

```
class TextCompressor
  attr_reader :unique, :index

  def initialize( text )
    @unique = []
    @index = []

    words = text.split
    words.each do |word|
      i = @unique.index( word )
      if i
        @index << i
```

```
      else
        @uniquo << word
        @index << unique.size - 1
      end
    end
  end
end
```

Using the `TextCompressor` class is simplicity itself: You just supply some text to the constructor:

```
text = "This specification is the spec for a specification"
compressor = TextCompressor.new( text )
```

And then you can get at the arrays of unique words and the word indexes, presumably for storage elsewhere:

```
unique_word_array = compressor.unique
word_index = compressor.index
```

From many points of view, the code here is just fine: It does work,[1] and it is fairly simple. The trouble with this first attempt is that the code itself doesn't do a very good job of speaking to the humans who need to maintain it. The next programmer who tries to understand `TextCompressor` will need to spend some time looking hard at the `initialize` method. It would be nice if the code, along with working, would also do a better job of explaining itself to the next engineer.

Let's see if we can't make the code a little more articulate:

```
class TextCompressor
  attr_reader :unique, :index

  def initialize( text )
    @uniquc = []
    @index = []
```

---

1. Well, it does lose all the white space in the text and won't react well to punctuation. Close enough for an example.

```ruby
    words = text.split
    words.each do |word|
      i = unique_index_of( word )
      if i
        @index << i
      else
        @index << add_unique_word( word )
      end
    end
  end

  def unique_index_of( word )
    @unique.index(word)
  end

  def add_unique_word( word )
    @unique << word
    unique.size - 1
  end
end
```

What we have done in this second pass is to pull out the code that looks up a word in the unique array into the `unique_index_of` method. We have also pulled out the code that adds a new word to the `@unique` array into the `add_unique_word` method.

This second version is definitely an improvement: At least the names of the new methods give us a clue as to what's going on in the `initialize` method. But we are not done yet: Our new `initialize` method is still fairly obtuse and, worse, it seems a bit unbalanced. On the one hand `initialize` is acting like a "don't bother me with the details" boss by delegating work to `unique_index_of` and `add_unique_word`, but then it turns around and gets involved in the dirty details of managing the `@index` array.

Let's take one more shot at it:

```ruby
class TextCompressor
  attr_reader :unique, :index

  def initialize( text )
    @unique = []
    @index = []
```

```
        add_text( text )
    end

    def add_text( text )
      words = text.split
      words.each { |word| add_word( word ) }
    end

    def add_word( word )
      i = unique_index_of( word ) || add_unique_word( word )
      @index << i
    end

    def unique_index_of( word )
      @unique.index(word)
    end

    def add_unique_word( word )
      @unique << word
      unique.size - 1
    end
  end
```

We've done a number of things with this latest version: The `initialize` method now foists the task of doing the compression onto the `add_text` method, which itself mostly delegates to `add_word`. In addition, by cutting down on the clutter, it became apparent that we could collapse the original "is the word there or not?" if statement into an or[2] expression, which ends up in the `add_word` method.

Composing Methods for Humans

What we have just done to our `TextCompressor` class is to apply the **composed method** technique to it. The composed method technique advocates dividing your class up into methods that have three characteristics. First, each method should do a single thing—focus on solving a single aspect of the problem. By concentrating on one thing, your methods are not only easier to write, they are also easier to understand.

---

2. That's or as in ||.

Second, each method needs to operate at a single conceptual level: Simply put, don't mix high-level logic with the nitty-gritty details. A method that implements the business logic around, say, currency conversions, should not suddenly veer off into the details of how the various accounts are stored in a database.

Finally, each method needs to have a name that reflects its purpose. Nothing new here; we have all heard endless lectures about picking good method names. The time to listen to all of that haranguing is when you are creating lots of little methods that you are trying to pull together into a functional whole. Done right, the method names guide you through the logic of the code.

Take another look at the final version of the compression code and you will see that it follows all three maxims. There's a method to add some text, one to add a single word, and one to find the index of a word that's already there. A little more subtly, the code in each of the new methods is at a single conceptual level: Some methods, `add_unique_word` for example, are down in the weeds dealing with the messy details of array indexes, while other methods, particularly `add_text`, operate at a higher conceptual level. Aside from being compact and focused, each of our methods also has a carefully chosen name, a name that tells the reader exactly what the method does.

Why is building small, well-named methods that do one thing such a good idea? It's not about writing better code for the computer, because the computer doesn't care. You can code the same algorithm in a handful of large methods or in a myriad of little methods and, as long as you've gotten the details right, the computer will give you exactly the same answer. The reason you should lean toward smaller methods is that all those compact, easy-to-comprehend methods will help *you* get the details right.

Composing Ruby Methods

People have been writing short, coherent methods in a whole range of programming languages for years. The reason we are talking about it here is that, like testing, the Ruby community has taken to composing their methods with a vengeance. Look at a class, and if it contains a lot of short, pointed methods it just feels like Ruby.

Nor is this simply a cultural phenomenon: The composed method way of building classes is particularly effective in Ruby because Ruby is such a "low ceremony" language. In Ruby, the cost of defining a new method is very low: just an additional `def` and an extra `end`. Since defining a new Ruby method adds very little noise to your code, in Ruby you can get the full composed method bang for a very modest code overhead buck.

Having many fine-grained methods also tends to make your classes easier to test. Consider that with the original version of `TextCompressor`, the only thing you could test was, well, everything. You fed some text into the class and that monolithic `initialize` method took over. Contrast that with our latest version that allows us to test all sorts of things:

```
describe TextCompressor do

  it "should be able to add some text" do
    c = TextCompressor.new( '' )
    c.add_text( 'first second' )
    c.unique.should == [ 'first', 'second' ]
    c.index.should == [ 0, 1 ]
  end

  it "should be able to add a word" do
    c = TextCompressor.new( '' )
    c.add_word( 'first' )
    c.unique.should == [ 'first' ]
    c.index.should == [ 0 ]
  end

  it "should be able to find the index of a word" do
    c = TextCompressor.new( 'hello world' )
    c.unique_index_of( 'hello' ).should == 0
    c.unique_index_of( 'world' ).should == 1
  end

  # ...
end
```

By decomposing your class into a lot of small methods, you provide a much larger number of sockets into which you can plug your tests.

One Way Out?

Short, easily comprehended methods also have some secondary advantages as well. Take the old bit of coding advice that every method should have exactly one way out, so that all of the logic converges at the bottom for a single return. Suppose, for example, we needed a method to rate the text in a document, based on the number of pretentious or slangy words in the document. If we construct a single, longish method and sprinkle returns here and there, we end up with code that is definitely hard to follow:

```ruby
class Document

  # Most of class omitted...

  def prose_rating
    if pretentious_density > 0.3
      if informal_density < 0.2
        return :really_pretentious
      else
        return :somewhat_pretentious
      end
    elsif pretentious_density < 0.1
      if informal_density > 0.3
        return :really_informal
      end
      return :somewhat_informal
    else
      return :about_right
    end
  end

  def pretentious_density
    # Somehow compute density of pretentious words
  end

  def informal_density
    # Somehow compute density of informal words
  end

end
```

The code above is not horrible, but I suspect you would have to stare at it awhile to really get a feeling for the flow. Now take a look at a single-return rewrite of the same method:

```ruby
def prose_rating
  rating = :about_right
```

```
      if pretentious_density > 0.3
        if informal_density < 0.2
          rating = :really_pretentious
        else
          rating = :somewhat_pretentious
        end
      elsif pretentious_density < 0.1
        if informal_density > 0.3
          rating = :really_informal
        else
          rating = :somewhat_informal
        end
      end

      rating
    end
```

It's not that dramatic, but the single-exit version does seem more comprehensible—you don't find yourself scanning every line trying to figure out if the method is suddenly going to exit right there on you. So, problem solved, right?

Not really. The real problem is that the first version of the prose_rating method goes on and on for way too long. The second version is marginally better, but only just. A better fix is to attack the "hard to understand" problem head-on with some composed methods:

```
def prose_rating
  return :really_pretentious if really_pretentious?
  return :somewhat_pretentious if somewhat_pretentious?
  return :really_informal if really_informal?
  return :somewhat_informal if  somewhat_informal?
  return :about_right
end

def really_pretentious?
  pretentious_density > 0.3 && informal_density < 0.2
end

def somewhat_pretentious?
  pretentious_density > 0.3 && informal_density >= 0.2
end
```

```
def really_informal?
  pretentious_density < 0.1 && informal_density > 0.3
end


def somewhat_informal?
  pretentious_density < 0.1 &&  informal_density <= 0.3
end


def pretentious_density
  # Somehow compute density of pretentious words
end


def informal_density
  # Somehow compute density of informal words
end
```

Now that we have broken `prose_rating` into something more digestible, it really doesn't matter whether it has one return or whether—as in this last version—it is made up entirely of returns. Once you can take in the whole method in single glance, then the motivation for the single-return rule goes away.

Staying Out of Trouble

The key to preventing your composed methods from turning on you is to remember that every method should have two things going for it. First, it should be short. And second, it should be coherent. In plain English, your method should be compact but it should also *do something*. Unfortunately, since short is so much easier to remember than coherent, programmers will sometimes go too far in breaking up their methods. For example, we might set out to decompose the `add_unique_word` method even further and end up with this:

```
class TextCompressor
  # ...

  def add_unique_word( word )
    add_word_to_unique_array( word )
    last_index_of_unique_array
  end


  def add_word_to_unique_array( word )
```

```
        @unique << word
    end

    def last_index_of_unique_array
        unique.size - 1
    end
end
```

The two new methods do add something to the class. Unfortunately, the word for this addition is *clutter*. Taken to the dysfunctional extreme, it's possible to compose method yourself into a diffuse cloud of programming dust. Don't do that.

In the Wild

Getting into the habit of writing the short, pointy methods technique takes time and effort. As you go through the process, it's easy to get frustrated and decide that it's just impossible to get anything done with such tiny chunks of logic. But like a lot of conclusions born of frustration, this one is just not correct. If you need a good role model to motivate your forays into composed method land, consider `ActiveRecord::Base`.

If you are a Rails programmer, then you know that it is `ActiveRecord::Base` that turns this:

```
class Employee < ActiveRecord::Base
end
```

Into a functionally rich interface to a database table. Yet a quick look at `base.rb`, which defines the core of the `ActiveRecord::Base` class, turns up about 1800 non-comment lines that define about 200 methods. Do the math and you have an average of about nine lines of code per method. Here, for example is the key `find` method, all 11 non-blank lines of it:

```
def find(*args)
    options = args.extract_options!
    validate_find_options(options)
    set_readonly_option!(options)

    case args.first
    when :first then find_initial(options)
```

```
    when :last   then find_last(options)
    when :all    then find_every(options)
    else              find_from_ids(args, options)
    end
  end
```

Not only are the `ActiveRecord::Base` methods generally short, but they also follow the other composed method recommendation: They sport very descriptive names. Care to venture a guess as to what the `find_last` or `find_every` methods in the code above do? `ActiveRecord::Base` is the existence proof for the postulate that you can get something done—in this case, quite a lot done—with short, focused methods.

Wrapping Up

In this chapter we have looked at the composed method technique, which advocates building short, focused methods. While the composed method technique is not technically part of the Ruby programming language, it is a key tool that Ruby programmers use to construct code. Building your methods this way really comes down to writing short, focused methods, each with a name that tells the reader exactly what it does. Not only will these short methods be easier to understand, they will also be easier to test.

CHAPTER 11

Define Operators Respectfully

In the history of programming languages, operator overloading—the ability to put your own code behind built-in operators like + and *—has had a somewhat checkered career: The very minimalistic C programming language had no room for programmer-defined operators. By contrast, the very expansive C++ embraced operator overloading and included some fairly elaborate facilities to support it. Programmer-defined operators vanished again when Java entered the scene, only to rematerialize again with Ruby.

All of this to-ing and fro-ing betrays a certain ambivalence about programmer-defined operators on the part of language designers. In this chapter we will look at how you define operators for your Ruby classes and how they might be useful. Along the way we will look into some of the deep pits that wait for you on the road to building your own operators and perhaps gain a little insight into why this is one of those features that falls in and out of vogue. Most importantly, we will talk at some length about how you can dodge those black pits by knowing when *not* to define an operator.

Defining Operators in Ruby

One of the nice things about Ruby is that the language keeps very few secrets from its programmers. Many of the tools used to construct the basic workings of the Ruby programming language are available to the ordinary Joe Programmer. Operators are a good example of this: If you were so inclined, you could implement your own Float class and—at least as far as operators like +, -, *, and / are concerned—your hand-crafted `Float` would be indistinguishable from the `Float` class that comes with Ruby.

The Ruby mechanism for defining your own operators is straightforward and based on the fact that Ruby translates every expression involving programmer-definable operators into an equivalent expression where the operators are replaced with method calls. So when you say this:

```
sum = first + second
```

What you are really saying is:

```
sum = first.+(second)
```

The second expression sets the variable `sum` to the result of calling the + method on `first`, passing in `second` as an argument. Other than + being a strange-looking method name (it is, however, a perfectly good Ruby method name), the second expression is a simple assignment involving a method call. It is also exactly equivalent to the first expression. The Ruby interpreter is clever about the operator-to-method translation process and will make sure that the translated expression respects operator precedence and parentheses, so that this:

```
result = first + second * (third - fourth)
```

Will smoothly translate into:

```
result = first.+(second.*(third.-(fourth)))
```

What this means is that creating a class that supports operators boils down to defining a bunch of instance methods, methods with names like +, -, and *.

To make all of this a little more concrete, let's add an operator to our `Document` class. Documents aren't the most operator friendly of objects, but we might think of adding two documents together to produce a bigger document:

```
class Document
  # Most of the class omitted...

  def +(other)
    Document.new( title, author, "#{content} #{other.content}" )
```

```
    end
  end
```

With this code we can now sum up our documents, so that if we run:

```
doc1 = Document.new('Tag Line1', 'Kirk', "These are the voyages")
doc2 = Document.new('Tag Line2', 'Kirk', "of the star ship ...")

total_document = doc1 + doc2
puts total_document.content
```

We will see the famous tag line:

```
These are the voyages of the star ship ...
```

A Sampling of Operators

Of course, + is not the only operator you can overload. Ruby allows you to define more than twenty operators for your classes. Among these are the other familiar arithmetic operators of subtraction (-), division (/), and multiplication (*), along with the modulo operator (%). You can also define your own version of the bit-oriented and (&) or (|), as well as the exclusive or (^) operator.

Another widely defined operator is the bitwise left shift operator, <<. This operator is not popular because Ruby programmers do a lot of bit fiddling; it's popular because it has taken on a second meaning as the concatenation, or "add another one," operator:

```
names = []
names << 'Rob'      # names.size is now 1
names << 'Denise'   # names.size is now 2
```

Along with binary operators like << and *—which do their thing on a pair of objects—Ruby also lets you define single object, or **unary**, operators. One such unary operator is the ! operator. Here's a somewhat silly unary operator definition for the ! operator:[1]

---

1. This will not work in versions earlier than Ruby 1.9, which greatly expanded the number of operators you can define.

```
class Document
  # Stuff omitted...

  def !
    Document.new( title, author, "It is not true: #{content}")
  end
end
```

This code enables us to have a tongue-in-cheek argument with ourselves. Start with this:

```
favorite = Document.new( 'Favorite', 'Russ', 'Chocolate is best')
```

And !favorite will have a content of:

```
It is not true: Chocolate is best
```

One interesting aspect of the ! operator is that it sits right on the cusp between the operator-defining facilities available to the Ruby programmer and what is built into the language. Although you can override ! and make it do anything you want, you can't override the nearly synonymous not. The not operator, along with and, or, ||, and &&, are built in to Ruby, and their behavior is fixed.

The + and − operators are interesting in a different way: They can be both binary and unary. It's easy to see the dual role of + and − with numeric expressions. In the expression -(2+6), the minus sign is a unary operator that simply changes the sign of the final result while the plus sign is a binary operator that adds the numbers together. But rewrite the expression as +(2-6) and the operator roles are reversed. We saw earlier that defining the + method on your class defines the binary addition operator. To create the unary operator, you need to define a method with the special (and rather arbitrary) name +@. The same pattern applies to −: The plain old − method defines the binary operator while -@ defines the unary one. Here, for example, are some silly unary operator definitions for our Document class:

```
class Document
  # Most of the class taking a break...

  def +@
    Document.new( title, author, "I am sure that #{@content}" )
  end
```

```
    def -@
      Document.new( title, author, "I doubt that #{@content}" )
    end
  end
```

Which lets us do this:

```
  favorite = Document.new('Favorite', 'Russ', 'Chocolate is best')
  unsure = -(+favorite)
```

So we end up with a document containing this wonderful statement of dietary angst:

```
  I doubt that I am sure that Chocolate is best
```

Ruby programmers can also define a couple of methods that will make their objects look like arrays or hashes: [] and []=. Although technically these bracketed methods are not operators, the Ruby parser sprinkles some very operator-like syntactic sugar on them: When you say foo[4] you are really calling the [] method on foo, passing in four as an argument. Similarly, when you say foo[4] = 99, you are actually calling the []= method on foo, passing in four and ninety-nine.

You might, for example, define a [] method on the Document class, a method that will make Document instances look like an arrays of words:

```
class Document
  # Most of the class omitted...

  def [](index)
    words[index]
  end
end
```

If you do add the bracket methods to your object, you will probably also want to put in a size method too, otherwise your users won't be able to tell when they are running off the end of the pseudo-array.

Operating Across Classes

One nice thing about the unary operators is that you only need to deal with one object—and one class—at a time. Coping with two objects doesn't present much of a challenge if you are dealing with two objects of the same class, but binary operators that work across classes can be one of those "seems simple until you try it" kind of jobs. Take our `Document` addition method:

```
def +(other)
  Document.new( title, author, "#{content} #{other.content}" )
end
```

Methods don't get much simpler than this: It just does the Ruby thing and assumes that the other operand is a `Document`—or at least an object with a `content` method that returns some text—and lets it go at that.[2] It would be nice, however, if we could add a string to a document, so that if we did this:

```
doc = Document.new( 'hi', 'russ', 'hello')
new_doc = doc + 'out there!'
```

We would end up with a document containing `'hello out there!'` There's not much to making this happen:

```
def +(other)
  if other.kind_of?(String)
    return Document.new( title, author, "#{content} #{other}")
  end
  Document.new( title, author, "#{content} #{other.content}" )
end
```

Great! Now we can add a document and a string together to get ever larger documents. Unfortunately, we missed something. If we reverse the expression and add a document to a string:

---

2. You could argue that this method is a bit too simple. After all, we just throw away the author and title of the second document. This is fine for an example, but it is perhaps an issue in real life.

```
'I say to you, ' + doc
```

We end up with a very unpleasant error:

```
#<TypeError: can't convert Document into String>
```

The trouble is that this expression calls the + method on the *String* class, which blows up in our face because `String` doesn't know about the `Document` class. The bottom line is that if you want to define binary operators that work across classes, you need to either make sure that both classes understand their responsibilities—as `String` does not in this example—or accept that your expressions will be sensitive to the order in which you write them.[3]

Staying Out of Trouble

So when should you define operators for your classes and when should you just stick to ordinary methods? Like most software engineering questions, the answer to this one is a resounding "It depends." Mainly it depends on the kind of object you are defining and the specific operations it supports.

The easiest case is where you find yourself building a class that has some natural, intuitive operator definitions. Envy the authors of the Ruby `Matrix` and `Vector` classes: The answer to the question of whether to have a + operator—and what that operator should do—is as close as the nearest linear algebra textbook. Similarly, the built-in `Set` class very logically maps the boolean | and & operators to the union and intersection operations. If you find yourself in a similar situation—you are building a class that has a natural, well-understood meaning for the operators—then count yourself lucky and start coding.

Another easy case is where you are building a class that, although it doesn't come with a whole set of universally understood operators, does have a few operator targets of opportunity. If you are writing some kind of collection class, it's an easy decision to add an << operator. In the same vein, if your class has some natural indexing tendencies, then defining [ ] and perhaps [ ]= may not be a bad idea.

---

3. Don't get the idea that all is lost with making String cooperate with our Document class. As we will see in Chapter 24, we can teach an old String some new tricks.

Finally, there's the case where, even though there are no widely accepted operators in the domain you are modeling, you realize that many of the methods on your class behave in a way that parallels the ordinary arithmetic operators. Perhaps you are modeling organizational structures and you realize that when you put two employees together you can get a department:

```
department = employee_1 + employee_2
```

And combining two departments will give you a division:

```
division = department_1 + department_2
```

What you can do is invent your very own operator-based object calculus, with a hierarchy of increasingly complex organizational types and a rich set of operators . . .

Actually, what you can do is pull back from the brink. Assigning arbitrary, farfetched meanings to the common operators is one thing that gives programmer-defined operators a bad name. Remember, the goal is clear and concise code. Code that requires me to recall that I get a department when I add two employees together, but that a department minus an employee is still a (smaller) department, is going to be anything but clear. If you find that your operators are starting to take on a life of their own, then perhaps you have gone a little too far. In any event, it is always a good idea to provide ordinary method names as aliases for your fancy operators as a sort of escape valve, just in case other programmers fail to appreciate the elegance of adding two departments together.

You also need to have proper respect for the generally accepted meanings of the common operators. Operators are nice because they are an easy way of firing off a complicated set of ideas in the head of anyone reading your program. Write this very simple code:

```
a + b
```

And you have, with a single character, conjured up a whole cloud of ideas in your readers' heads, a cloud that goes by the name *addition*. Very convenient, but also a bit dangerous. The danger lies in knowing just how big the cloud is and exactly where its boundaries are. For example, if the users of your class are thinking about plain old elementary school addition, then they will be sure that the + operator is commutative, that adding a to b will produce the same result as adding b to a. On the other hand, if they are thinking about higher math—or strings—they might not be so certain. In the same vein, we saw earlier that people do tend to assume that if a + b is defined, then b + a will also be defined. If you define an operator that doesn't quite live up to its symbol—if b + a throws an exception or you define a multiplication operator that isn't commutative or a subtraction that is—then you owe it to the next engineer to at least document the fact.

Sometimes even documentation isn't enough: There are some assumptions that are absolutely core. Show me this expression:

```
c = a + b
```

And then tell me that this code changes the value b, and I will be inclined to throw you out of a window. The mental cloud of ideas around every operator holds some absolutely unshakable assumptions—and woe to you if you violate them.

In the Wild

A good example of an operator that might be commutative—but isn't—is the + operator for instances of the Time class. Get yourself an instance of Time, perhaps like this:

```
now = Time.now
```

And you can roll the clock forward by simply adding some seconds:

```
one_minute_from_now = now + 60
```

Unfortunately, since Fixnum does't know about Time, you can't write the expression the other way around:

```
one_minute_from_now = 60 + now  # Bang!
```

Your Ruby installation also has some more exotic operator specimens. Exhibit A is the string formatting operator, %. The formatting operator is great when you need to construct a string and you need more control than the usual Ruby "string #{interpolation}" gives you. A very simple formatting example would look something like this:

```
"The value of n is %d" % 42
```

This will result in `"The value of n is 42"`—the `%d` in the string signals that this is the place where the value on the right side of the `%` operator should be inserted. If that were all there was, you would probably be better off with plain old string interpolation. The beauty of the format operator is that it gives you very fine control over how the values get inserted into the string. For example, imagine you have the components of a date in three separate variables:

```
day = 4
month = 7
year = 1776
```

Now imagine that you need to format these three date components into a string suitable for use as a filename. You could get there very easily with:

```
file_name = 'file_%02d%02d%d' % [ day, month, year ]
```

Run the code shown here and you will end up with a convenient zero-filled string: `file_04071776`. A nice thing about the formatting operator is that if `%` does not shout "Format!" to you, you can use the equivalent `sprintf` method,[4] which is defined on all Ruby objects.

If you do find the `%` formatting operator a little odd, then you will need to fasten your seat belt for our final example. Think back to Chapter 9 where we discussed specifying program behavior with RSpec. Recall that with RSpec, instead of writing an assertion that some condition is true, you write code that looks like this:

```
x.should == 42
```

Let's pass over the details of what the `should` method does and focus on the `==` operator. RSpec has turned the meaning of the `==` operator completely inside out. The garden variety `==` method is there to answer a question—"Are these two things equal?" But the RSpec version of `==` is more like an enforcer: If the two values are equal, nothing much happens; but if they are not equal, the test fails. The cool thing about RSpec is that its authors managed to find an alternative meaning for `==` that not only works in Ruby but also in the squishy computer between your ears. Quite a trick, but not one that is easy to repeat.

---

4. As all the former C programmers sit up and take notice.

Wrapping Up

In this chapter we have looked at the ups and downs of defining your own Ruby operators. The up part is that the actual mechanics of defining Ruby operators is very easy—you define a method with the right name. The down part is actually getting that operator to work the way your users might expect it to work. This turns out to be harder for operators than with garden-variety methods because people have some strong built-in expectations of what a given operator should do. The wise coder tries to respect those expectations.

So much for the Ruby operators. Almost. I have deliberately ignored one set of operators in this chapter: those having to do with equality. The reason I have ignored the familiar == and the somewhat less commonplace === operators is that equality is an entire topic in itself, one that we'll tackle in the next chapter.

CHAPTER 12

Create Classes That Understand Equality

Have you ever noticed that it's smallest words that have the longest entries in the dictionary? My copy of *Webster*'s dismisses a ten-dollar word like *cryptozoology* with a single three-line definition.[1] In contrast, although we all would like to think that we know right from wrong, the word *right* consumes almost two pages and sports no less than 58 separate definitions. Fortunately, software engineers don't usually have to wrestle with the finer points of moral philosophy while coding. We do, however, have something almost as difficult: We have object equality. Like right and wrong, object equality is a much tougher question than it appears on first blush.

Since understanding object equality is one of the keys to creating well-behaved Ruby objects, we are going to spend this chapter looking at the various Ruby definitions of equality. We will see that there are a lot of different ways that Ruby objects can be equal, and that all these definitions of equality are rooted firmly in helping you make your objects behave the way you want them to behave.

An Identifier for Your Documents

To see just how slippery object equality can be, let's return again to our documents and imagine that everyone likes your Document class so much that they've been creating

---

1. It's the study of animals like the Loch Ness Monster and Yeti, animals that may or may not exist. Probably not.

more and more of them at a furious pace. There are now so many documents that managing them has become a problem, so your company has started a second project, a project aimed at building a system to store and manage all of those documents. To this end, you decide that you will need some kind of identifier object for your documents, a key that will allow you to pick a given document out of a crowd. And thus is born the `DocumentIdentifier` class:

```ruby
class DocumentIdentifier
  attr_reader :folder, :name

  def initialize( folder, name )
    @folder = folder
    @name = name
  end
end
```

The idea behind `DocumentIdentifier` is very simple: The management system assigns each document a (presumably unique) name and groups the documents into folders. To locate any given document you need both the document name and its folder, which is exactly the information that `DocumentIdentifier` instances carry around. You release the `DocumentIdentifier` class to the group that is building the document management system and then lean back and put your feet up on the desk.

Sadly, your "not much to that job" feeling does not survive the afternoon. Your colleagues are back, and they have a complaint: As it stands, there is no easy way to compare two instances of `DocumentIdentifier` to see whether they actually point at the same document. They want you to enhance your class so that they can tell whether one document identifier is equal to another.

An Embarrassment of Equality

The question is, equal in what sense? It turns out that Ruby's `Object` class defines no less than four equality methods. There is `eql?` and `equal?` as well as `==` (that's two equal signs), not to mention `===` (that's three equal signs). For a language that prides itself on simplicity and conciseness, that's an awful lot of ways of saying nearly the same thing. Nearly, but not exactly the same.

The good news is that we can dismiss one of these equality methods, `equal?`, right up front. Ruby uses the `equal?` method to test for object identity. In other words, the only way that this:

```
x.equal?(y)
```

Should ever return true is if x and y are both references to identically the same objects. If x and y are different objects, then `equal?` should always return false, no matter how similar x and y might be. This brings us to the reason why `equal?` is unlikely to cause you any problems: Ruby is really good at figuring out when two objects are the same object. In fact, Ruby—in the form of the implementation of `equal?` found in `Object` class—is so good at this that there is no need for you to override `equal?`. Ever.

Double Equals for Everyday Use

Which brings us to the next version of Ruby equality, the `==` or double-equals operator. Since the `==` operator is the one that Ruby programmers habitually reach for when they are coding, this is probably the one we need to fix in our `DocumentIdentifier` class. Our problem is that the default implementation of `==`, the one that `DocumentIdentifier` inherits from `Object`, does the same thing as `equal?`—it tests for object identity. For example, if you do this:

```
first_id = DocumentIdentifier.new( 'secret/plans', 'raygun.txt' )
second_id = DocumentIdentifier.new('secret/plans', 'raygun.txt' )

puts "They are equal!" if first_id == second_id
```

You will see, well, nothing. Left to its own devices, the `==` method will behave just like `equal?` and will only return true if the objects being compared are identically the same object. Unlike the `equal?` method, testing for object identity is just the default behavior for the `==` method: You are free to implement any kind of "same value" comparison that makes sense for your object. The way to do this is to implement your own `==` method:

```
class DocumentIdentifier
  attr_reader :folder, :name
```

```
    def initialize( folder, name )
      @folder = folder
      @name = name
    end

    def ==(other)
      return false unless other.instance_of?(self.class)
      folder == other.folder && name == other.name
    end
end
```

The logic behind the == method shown here is pretty mundane: First, it makes sure that the other object is in fact an instance of DocumentIdentifier. If it is, the method goes on to check that the other object has the same folder and name. Notice that there is no need for a special check for nil: Ruby's nil is just another object, in this case an object that will fail the instance_of? test.

One addition we might make is to check whether the other object is in fact identically the same as this object:

```
class DocumentIdentifier

  # ...

  def ==(other)
    return true if other.equal?(self)
    return false unless other.instance_of?(self.class)
    folder == other.folder && name == other.name
  end
end
```

This kind of check can speed up your equality comparisons quite a bit and might be worth doing if you think you are going to being using the == method a lot.

With our newly enhanced code, the most common of the Ruby equality methods now works for our document identifiers so that this:

```
puts "They are equal!" if first_id == second_id
```

will indeed print something.

Broadening the Appeal of the == Method

One problem with our current == implementation is that it takes a very narrow view of what it means to be equal. That instance_of? test at the beginning means that the other object must be an instance of a DocumentIdentifier—no subclasses allowed. We can loosen the rules a bit by using kind_of?, which will return true if the object is an instance of DocumentIdentifier or a subclass of DocumentIdentifier:

```
class DocumentIdentifier
  # ...

  def ==(other)
    return true if other.equal?(self)
    return false unless other.kind_of?(self.class)
    folder == other.folder && name == other.name
  end
end


class ContractIdentifier < DocumentIdentifier
end
```

Now, if we make an instance of each:

```
doc_id =  DocumentIdentifier.new( 'contracts', 'Book Deal' )
con_id =  ContractIdentifier.new( 'contracts', 'Book Deal' )
```

And then compare the two, we will find that doc_id == con_id is indeed true, since the two objects are carrying around the same data and ContractIdentifier is a subclass of DocumentIdentifier.

You may be feeling that all this worry about classes and subclasses has a distinctly un-Ruby feel to it. Didn't we say that Ruby programmers frown on attaching too much importance to the class of an object? Can't we do something a little more in the spirit of Ruby's dynamic typing?

We can indeed. The following code defines DocumentPointer, a class completely unrelated to DocumentIdentifier:

```
class DocumentPointer
  attr_reader :folder, :name

  def initialize( folder, name )
    @folder = folder
    @name = name
  end

  def ==(other)
    return false unless other.respond_to?(:folder)
    return false unless other.respond_to?(:name)
    folder == other.folder && name == other.name
  end
end
```

The DocumentPointer class dispenses with the class check and instead pays attention to whether the other object has the right methods: Using the respond_to? method, the DocumentPointer class asks if this other object has a name method and a folder method. If so, then it might be an equal. Using this approach, instances of DocumentPointer will accept an instance of a completely unrelated class—Document-Identifier for example—as an equal:

```
doc_id = DocumentIdentifier.new( 'secret/area51', 'phone list' )
pointer = DocumentPointer.new( 'secret/area51', 'phone list' )

pointer == doc_id   # True!!
```

Well-Behaved Equality

Unfortunately we still have some problems. Both the kind_of? as well as the respond_to? based implementations of == suffer from the "different classes may have different points of view" problem that we came across in the last chapter. For example, in the last section we were happy because by relying on kind_of?, we had managed to make the DocumentIdentifier recognize the equality of subclasses, so that we got some output from:

```
doc_id =  DocumentIdentifier.new( 'contracts', 'Book Deal' )
con_id =  ContractIdentifier.new( 'contracts', 'Book Deal' )

puts "They are equal!" if doc_id == con_id
```

The trouble starts when we try to reverse the order of the expression. This:

```
puts "They are equal!" if con_id == doc_id
```

Will print nothing. The problem is that although `ContractIdentifier` is a subclass of `DocumentIdentifier`, the reverse is not true, and when you say `con_id == doc_id`, you are really calling the `==` method on the `ContractIdentifier` instance.

We have a similar disconnect between `DocumentIdentifier` and the `DocumentPointer` classes. In the last section we put the `respond_to?` logic into `DocumentPointer` so that `pointer == identifier` comes out true. Unfortunately, since we didn't put the same smarts into the `DocumentIdentifier` class, `identifier != pointer`.

As I say, this sad situation is an example of exactly the kind of muddled operator definition that we talked about back in Chapter 11. The problem is that we have defined equality relationships that violate the principal of **symmetry**: People tend to expect that if `a == b` then `b == a`.

There really is no magic elixir that will fix an asymmetrical equality relationship: You can either change the `==` methods on both classes so that they agree, or you can simply live with (and perhaps document) a less-than-intuitive, asymmetrical equality.

Asymmetry is also not the extent of our woes. Another built-in assumption we have about equality is that if `a == b` and `b == c`, then surely `a == c`. This **transitive property** is another expectation that is all too easy to violate. To see how, imagine that our document management system starts storing multiple of versions of each document. We might then build a subclass of `DocumentIdentifier` that knows about the versions and tries to be smart doing equality comparisons:

```
class VersionedIdentifier < DocumentIdentifier
  attr_reader :version

  def initialize( folder, name, version )
    super( folder, name )
```

```
      @version = version
  end

  def ==(other)
    if other.instance_of? VersionedIdentifier
      other.folder == folder &&
      other.name == name &&
      other.version == version
    elsif other.instance_of? DocumentIdentifier
      other.folder == folder && other.name == name
    else
      false
    end
  end
end
```

This == method does something that seems very sensible: If the other object is a
VersionedIdentifier, then it does a full comparison including the version. Alternatively, if the other object is a plain old DocumentIdentifier, then the method looks
only at the folder and name fields. The trouble is that this == method is not transitive.
To see why, think about these objects:

```
versioned1 = VersionedIdentifier.new( 'specs', 'bfg9k', "V1" )
versioned2 = VersionedIdentifier.new( 'specs', 'bfg9k', "V2" )
unversioned = DocumentIdentifier .new('specs', 'bfg9k')
```

All three point to the same basic document, but the two versioned identifiers
point at different versions of the document. Since the plain DocumentIdentifier
class doesn't know about the versions, and the VersionedIdentifier class deliberately ignores the version when dealing with a plain identifier, both of these expressions
are true:

```
versioned1 == unversioned    # True!
unversioned == versioned2    # True!
```

Unfortunately, this expression is very definitely not true:

```
versioned1 ==   versioned2    # Not true!
```

In our efforts to do something sensible we have managed to create a situation where (a == b) and (b == c) but (a != c).

There are a couple of ways around this conundrum. One is to dispense with trying to deal with both `VersionedIdentifier` instances and regular `DocumentIdentifier` instances in the `VersionedIdentifier` == method. Instead, add a method to `VersionedIdentifier` that returns the plain old document identifier:

```
def as_document_identifier
  DocumentIdentifier.new( folder, name )
end
```

You can then compare the resulting document identifier, serene in the knowledge that you know exactly what is going on.

The other way out is to ask yourself whether you really need to use the == operator for everything. It is easy enough to add your own specialized comparison method to `VersionedIdentifier`:

```
def is_same_document?(other)
  other.folder == folder && other.name == name
end
```

The `is_same_document?` method here simply ignores the versions and will return true if the two identifiers point at the same document.

Triple Equals for Case Statements

The next contestant in our equality sweepstakes is the triple equals operator ===. The main use for === is in `case` statements.

So why do we need yet another operator just for `case` systems? Why not just use == in `case` statements? It turns out that this is another example of Ruby pragmatism in pursuit of[2] clean and concise code. Take strings and regular expressions for example. Strings are not regular expressions and regular expressions are not strings, so we certainly would not want a string to be equal to a regular expression according to == even if they do match:

---

2. Wait for it!

```
/Roswell.*/ =~ 'Roswell' # Yes!
/Roswell.*/ == 'Roswell' # No!
```

However, pattern matching regular expressions against strings in `case` statements does make for tidy-looking code:

```
location = 'area 51'

case location
when /area.*/
  # ...
when /roswell.*/
  # ...
else
  # ...
end
```

To this end, the `Regexp` class has a `===` method that does pattern matching when confronted with a string.

By default, `===` calls the double equals method, so unless you specifically override `===`, wherever you send `==`, `===` is sure to follow. It's probably a good idea to leave `===` alone unless doing so results in really ugly case statements.

Hash Tables and the eql? Method

Finally, we have the `eql?` method. Since you don't typically call `eql?` directly, you might never know you need it—until you try to use your object as a key in a hash. To see where the trouble lies, imagine that you store a document in a hash table with a `DocumentIdentifier` as the key:

```
hash = {}
document = Document.new( 'cia', 'Roswell', 'story' )
first_id = DocumentIdentifier.new( 'public', 'CoverStory' )

hash[first_id] = document
```

Initially, things seem to work. You have no trouble getting your document out of the hash with the identifier, so `hash[first_id]` will indeed return your document.

The problem is that if you try fetching your document out of the hash with a second instance of `DocumentIdentifier`, like this:

```
second_id = DocumentIdentifier.new( 'public', 'CoverStory' )
the_doc_again = hash[second_id]
```

You will end up with `the_doc_again` set to `nil`. To see what the problem is, we need to dive into the workings of the `Hash` class.

The idea behind a hash is to build a thing that works a lot like an array, but an array on performance-enhancing drugs. The feature that makes hashes special is that they can take things other than just numbers as indexes. Now there is a spectacularly simple way to get this behavior: You build a class that stores all the keys and values in a simple list. When you need to find a value by its key, you simply do a linear search down that list, looking at each key until you find the one you want. The trouble with this simple implementation is that performance falls off in direct proportion to the number of entries in the table. If you have ten entries in your simple table, then on average you'll have to look at five entries[3] before you hit the key that you want, which isn't too bad. Unfortunately, if you have 1,000 entries you'll probably have to look at 500 entries before you get lucky, and if you have 10,000 entries . . . Well, you get the picture.

Real hash tables improve the performance of this simple model with a divide-and-conquer strategy. Instead of maintaining a single key/value list, a typical hash table implementation maintains a number of lists, or **buckets**. By spreading out the stuff that's stored in the table across a number of buckets, a hash table can do things dramatically faster. Take that 10,000 entry table: If you spread the 10,000 entries over 100 different buckets, instead of having to look at 5,000 entries to find the one you want, you only need to search through about 50.[4]

The challenging thing with this scheme is picking the right bucket: If you are saving a new key/value pair, which bucket do you use? Later, when you go looking for that same key, how do you know which bucket you picked originally? Answering the

---

3. Remember, on average you are only going to have to search down half the list before you find what you are looking for.

4. Starting in version 1.9, Ruby hashes have a list superimposed atop the whole bucket structure, a list that keeps track of the order of the hash keys, because the natural workings of a hash will randomize the keys very thoroughly.

"which bucket" question is where the hash part of a hash table comes in. The idea goes like this: You define a method on all of your objects, a method which returns a hash value. The **hash value** is a more or less random number somehow generated from the value of the object. When you need to store a key/value pair in your hash table, you pull the hash value from the key. You then use that number to pick a bucket—typically by using the modulo operator (hash_code % number_of_buckets)—and you store your key/value pair in that bucket. Later on when you are looking to retrieve the value associated with some key, you get the hash code for the key again and use it to pick the right bucket to search.

Hash codes need to have a couple of properties to make this all work. First, they need to be stable over time: If a key generates one hash code now and a different one later, we are inevitably going to end up looking in the wrong bucket. Hash codes also need to be consistent with the value of the key: If two keys are equal—if they should return the same value out of the hash table—then, when asked, they must return the same hash code.

Building a Well-Behaved Hash Key

All of this theory translates pretty directly into Ruby: The Hash class calls the aptly named hash method (another one of those methods that you inherit from Object) to get the hash code from its keys. The Hash class uses the eql? method to decide if two keys are in fact the same key. The default implementations of hash and eql? from the Object class, like the default implementations of == and ===, are based on object identity: The default eql? returns true only if the other object is identically the same as this object. The default hash method returns the object_id of the object, which is guaranteed to be unique. This is why, in the example, our second DocumentIdentifier instance failed to find anything in the hash.

There is, however, no rule saying that your class needs to accept the default implementation. As long as you follow the hash Prime Directive—that if a.eql?(b) then a.hash == b.hash—you are free to override these two methods. Devising an implementation of eql? and hash that will work together is really not that difficult. You just need to make sure that any field that has a vote in the hash code also has a vote in equality.

Going back to the DocumentIdentifier example, our eql? should obviously take both the folder and the name fields into account. Given this, we want to make sure that both fields have a say in the hash code. So here is what we do:

```
class DocumentIdentifier

  # Code omitted...

  def hash
    folder.hash ^ name.hash
  end

  def eql?(other)
    return false unless other.instance_of?(self.class)
    folder == other.folder && name == other.name
  end
end
```

In the code above, the `hash` method combines the hash codes from the two fields using the exclusive or operator `^`: Doing this is a simple way of creating a very thorough mishmash of the two numbers, which is exactly what we are looking for in a hash. The other thing to notice in this code is that the `eql?` method takes a very restrictive view of equality. According to the `eql?`, only other instances of `DocumentIdentifier` can be equal: Getting your objects to work as hash table keys is no time to be imaginative about cross-class equality.

Staying Out of Trouble

Making equality work can be painful. There are, however, things that you can do to minimize the pain. The best thing is to avoid the suffering all together. Given how easy it is to screw up when you start messing with object equality, your first rule should be: If it ain't broke—or used—don't fix it. Many objects will never find themselves in the middle of an equality expression or be called upon to be a hash key. If you have an object like this, then just leave its equality methods alone.

Even if you do need to implement some or all of the equality methods, you might be able to lean on someone else's work.[5] If you're defining a class that is mostly a wrapper for some other object, consider borrowing the equality methods from that other object. For example, if you are building a class that wraps an array, you just might be able to delegate to the array's equality methods:

---

5. According to the American screenwriter Aaron Sorkin, good writers borrow from other writers. Great writers steal from them outright. Apparently Sorkin stole this line from Oscar Wilde.

```ruby
class DisArray

  attr_reader :my_array

  def initialize
    @my_array = []
  end

  def ==(other)
    return false unless other.kind_of?(DisArray)
    @my_array == other.my_array
  end

  def eql?(other)
    return false unless other.kind_of?(DisArray)
    @my_array.eql?( other.my_array )
  end

  def hash
    @my_array.hash
  end

  # Rest of the class omitted...
end
```

Finally, if you do need to write your own equality methods, do the simplest thing that will work. If you don't have to support equality across different classes, then don't. A limited, but working implementation is better than an elaborate and subtly broken one.

In the Wild

Ruby's built-in numeric classes do a bit of equality slight of hand right under your nose. A little exploration will show that integers (that is, instances of Fixnum or Bignum) will accept instances of Float as equals, at least according to the == method. Thus, if you run:

```ruby
puts 1 == 1.0     # A Fixnum and a Float
```

You will see that 1 is in fact == to 1.0. Ruby does this by converting the Fixnum to a Float before doing the comparison.

Classes like Float and Fixnum, classes whose instances have a natural ordering, can add one additional twist to the equality saga in the form of the <=> operator. The expression:

```
a <=> b
```

Should evaluate to –1 if a is less than b, 0 if they are equal, and 1 if a is greater than b. The <=> is a boon when you are trying to sort a collection of objects. If you find yourself needing to implement <=>, keep in mind that <=> should be consistent with ==. That is, if a <=> b evaluates to zero, then a == b should be true. The good news is that Ruby actually supplies a mixin module (see Chapter 16 for more on mixin modules) to help you keep all of this straight. If you define a <=> operator for your class, and include Comparable, like this:

```
class RomanNumerals
  include Comparable


  # Actual guts of the class omitted...

  def <=>(other)
    # Return -1, 0, or 1...
  end
end
```

Then Comparable will not only add a == method to your class, but also <, <=, >=, and >, all of which will rely on your <=> method to come up with the right answer.

Ruby classes—those objects that are instances of Class—have their own twist on the triple equality method: Classes treat the === method as an alias for kind_of?. This is so that you can pick out the class of an object with a case statement, like so:

```
the_object = 3.14159

case the_object
when String
  puts "it's a string"
```

```
when Float
  puts "It's a float"

when Fixnum
  puts "It's a fixnum"

else
  puts "Dunno!"
end
```

This is yet another asymmetric relationship: Although `Float === 1.0` is true, `1.0 === Float` is not.

Wrapping Up

I sometimes think that you can divide software engineers into two classes: the optimists and those who have tangled with object equality. In my more optimistic moments I realize that while getting object equality right can be trying, it is certainly doable. The key to getting it right is to keep in mind that Ruby has a fairly fine-grained model of equality—we have the `equal?` method, strictly for object identity. We have the everyday equality method, `==`, and we also have the `===` method, which comes out mostly for `case` statements. We also have `eql?`, and its friend `hash`, to cope with hash tables. Getting object equality right is all about understanding the differences between all those methods and overriding the right ones.

CHAPTER 13

Get the Behavior You Need with Singleton and Class Methods

Much of programming is about building models of the world. Social networking systems model the relationships between people. Accounting systems model the flow of money. Flight simulations model airplanes in flight (or slamming into the ground if I'm at the controls). You can, in fact, look at all of object oriented programming as a support system for this kind of modeling. We build classes to describe groups of similar things, and we have instances to represent the things themselves.

Usually, the class/instance approximation works fine: You define a class called American, and you define methods that indicate instances of this class like hamburgers and baseball. The problem is that the class/instance approximation is exactly that, an approximation. I am, for example, an American who does indeed like the occasional burger, but I can't tell you the last time I willingly sat through a baseball game.

What do you do when the central approximation of object oriented programming breaks down, when your instance does not want to follow the rules laid down by its class? In this chapter we will look at Ruby's answer to this question: the singleton method. We will see how singleton methods allow you to produce objects with an independent streak, objects whose behavior is not completely controlled by their class. We will also see how class methods are actually just singleton methods by another name.

A Stubby Puzzle

Let's start with a question. Recall that back in Chapter 9 we saw how RSpec made it easy to create stub objects, those stand-ins for real objects that make writing tests less of a pain. We saw that if, inside of a spec, you did something like this:

```
stub_printer = stub :available? => true, :render => nil
```

You would end up, in the form of stub_printer, with an object having two methods, available? and render:

```
stub_printer.available?   # Always returns true
stub_printer.render       # Always returns nil
```

We also saw in Chapter 9 that RSpec doesn't limit you to one stub object at a time, so you could easily conjure up a second stub, perhaps for a font:

```
stub_font = stub :size => 14, :name => 'Courier'
```

Now for the question: If you look at the classes of these two stub objects:

```
puts stub_printer.class
puts stub_font.class
```

You will discover that they are one and the same:

```
Spec::Mocks::Mock
Spec::Mocks::Mock
```

How is this possible? After all, the printer object supports different methods than the font object. How could they both be of the same class?

The answer is that the available? and render methods on the printer instance, as well as the size and name methods on the font instance, are singleton methods. In Ruby, a **singleton method** is a method that is defined for exactly one object instance.[1]

---

1. Let me also hasten to add that the term "singleton" as it is used here has nothing to do with the Singleton Pattern of design patterns fame. It's just an unfortunate collision of terminology. If you feel a bit put out by this, consider the plight of the guy who wrote the Ruby design patterns book.

It's as though Ruby objects can declare independence from their class and say, "Yeah, I know that no other `Spec::Mocks::Mock` instance has an `available?` method, but I'm special."

You can hang a singleton method on just about any object at any time.[2] The mechanics of defining singleton methods are really pretty simple: Instead of saying `def method_name` as you would to define a regular garden-variety method, you define a singleton method with `def instance.method_name`. If, for example, you wanted to create your own stub printer by hand, you could say this:

```
hand_built_stub_printer = Object.new

def hand_built_stub_printer.available?
  true
end

def hand_built_stub_printer.render( content )
  nil
end
```

You could then call `hand_built_stub_printer.available?` and `render`. Singleton methods are in all respects ordinary methods: They can accept arguments, return values, and do anything else that a regular method can do. The only difference is that singleton methods are stuck to a single object instance.

Singleton methods override any regular, class-defined methods. For example, if you run the (admittedly more fun than useful) code shown here:

```
uncooperative = "Don't ask my class"

def uncooperative.class
  "I'm not telling"
end

puts uncooperative.class
```

---

2. Well, any object except for instances of the numeric classes and symbols, neither of which supports singleton methods.

You will see:

```
I'm not telling
```

There is also an alternative syntax for defining singleton methods, one that can be less bulky if you are creating a lot of methods:

```ruby
hand_built_stub_printer = Object.new

class << hand_built_stub_printer
  def available?          # A singleton method
    true
  end

  def render              # Another one
    nil
  end
end
```

Either way you say it, you end up with the same singleton methods.

A Hidden, but Real Class

So how does Ruby pull off the singleton method trick? The key is that every Ruby object carries around an additional, somewhat shadowy class of its own. As you can see in Figure 13-1, this more or less secret class—the **singleton** class—sits between every object and its regular class.[3] The singleton class starts out as just a methodless shell and is therefore pretty invisible.[4] It's only when you add something to it that the singleton class steps out of the shadows and makes its existence felt.

Since it sits directly above the instance, the singleton class has the first say on how the object is going to behave, which is why methods defined in the singleton class will win out over methods defined in the object's regular class, and in the superclasses.

---

3. Singleton classes are also known as metaclasses or eigenclasses. Although terminology is mostly in the ear of the beholder, I like the more descriptive and less pretentious "'singleton."

4. In fact, since the average Ruby object never uses its singleton class, Ruby implementations will typically delay creating the singleton classes until they are actually needed. This is, however, just an implementation issue. If you do look, the singleton class will always be there for you.

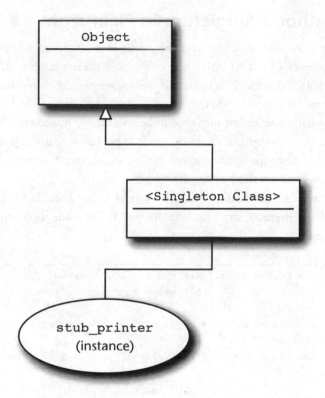

Figure 13-1 The singleton class

Don't think that the singleton class is just a convenient fiction, either. There really is an actual Ruby class hidden in there. You can even get hold of the singleton class, like this:

```
singleton_class = class << hand_built_stub_printer
  self
end
```

The code shown here may look bizarre, but it is straightforward: When you do the `class << hand_built_stub_printer`, you change context so that `self` is the singleton class. Since class definitions, like most Ruby expressions, return the last thing they evaluate, simply sticking `self` inside the class definition causes the whole class statement to return the singleton class.

Class Methods: Singletons in Plain Sight

A common programmer reaction when bumping into singleton methods for the first time is to dismiss them as an interesting but mostly useless feature. After all, outside of a few specialized cases such as stubs and mocks, why bother building classes of consistent behavior only to override that behavior with a singleton method? In fact, this sensible, pragmatic assessment turns out to be completely mistaken. There is one particular application of singleton methods that is so pervasive that it is practically impossible to build a Ruby program without it. We even have a special name for these ubiquitous singleton methods, **class methods**.

To see how class methods are actually singleton methods in disguise, let's build another singleton method, this time one that prints out some interesting information about its host object:

```
my_object = Document.new('War and Peace', 'Tolstoy',
                          'All happy families...')

def my_object.explain
  puts "self is #{self}"
  puts "and its class is #{self.class}"
end

my_object.explain
```

Run the code above and you will get output that looks something like this:

```
self is #<Document:0xb7bc2ca0>
and its class is Document
```

No surprise here, we are just traveling over ground that we covered earlier. Next, however, comes the twist: What if, instead of an instance of Document, we defined the explain method on the Document class itself?

```
my_object = Document

def my_object.explain
  puts "self is #{self}"
```

```
    puts "and its class is #{self.class}"
  end

  my_object.explain
```

Do that and you will get the following output:

```
  self is Document
  and its class is Class
```

Since my_object is just a reference to Document, we can also call the explain method like this:

```
  Document.explain
```

We can also define the explain method on Document explicitly:

```
  def Document.explain
    puts "self is #{self}"
    puts "and its class is #{self.class}"
  end
```

If the code above looks familiar, it should, since it is a typical Ruby class method definition. It is also a singleton method definition! If you think about it, this all makes sense: Any given class, say, Document, is an instance of Class. This means that it inherits all kinds of methods from Class, methods like name and superclass. When we want to add a class method, we want that new method to exist only on the one class (Document in the example), not on *all* classes. Since the object that goes by the name of Document is an instance of Class, we need to create a method that exists only on the one object (Document) and not on any of the other instances of the same class. What we need is a singleton method.

Once you get used to the idea that a class method is just a singleton method on an instance of Class, a lot of things that you learned in Ruby 101 start to make sense. For example, you will sometimes see the following syntax used to define class methods:

```
  class Document
    class << self
      def find_by_name( name )
```

```
      # Find a document by name...
    end

    def find_by_id( doc_id )
      # Find a document by id
    end
  end
end
```

This code only makes sense in light of the *class method = singleton method* equation: It is simply the `class << some_object` syntax applied to the `Document` class.

In the Wild

Class methods abound in real Ruby programs. Class methods are the perfect home for the code that is related to a class but independent of any given instance of the class. For example, we've seen that each ActiveRecord model class is associated with a particular table in the database. So that if you had this:

```
class Author < ActiveRecord::Base
end
```

You would have a class that is associated with a database table. Which table? For that, you need to ask the *class*, not an instance:

```
my_table_name = Author.table_name
```

A common use for class methods is to provide alternative methods for constructing new instances. The Ruby library `Date` class, for example, comes with a whole raft of class methods that create new instances. You can, for example, get a date from the year, the month, and the day:

```
require 'date'
xmas = Date.civil( 2010, 12, 25 )
```

Or by the year and the day of that year:

```
xmas = Date.ordinal( 2010, 359 )
```

Or by the day, the week number, and the day of the week:

```
xmas = Date.commercial( 2010, 51, 6 )
```

If you have many different ways that you might create an object, a set of well-named class methods is generally clearer than making the user supply all sorts of clever arguments to the new method.

Plain, nonclass singleton methods are as rare as class methods are common. In fact, their main use in real code is the one we explored earlier in this chapter, building mocks and stubs for testing frameworks. Both RSpec and the Mocha framework that we looked at briefly in Chapter 9 use singleton methods to do their mocking magic. But don't take my word for it, look for yourself:

```
describe "Singleton methods in stubs" do
  it "is just a demonstration of stubs as singleton methods" do
    stub_printer = stub :available? => true, :render => nil
    pp stub_printer.singleton_methods
  end
end
```

This RSpec example creates our familiar stubbed-out printer and then uses `singleton_methods`—part of the arsenal of every Ruby object—to print out a list of the names of all of the singleton methods. Run this spec and you will see:

```
[:available?, :render]
```

If you do the same kind of thing with the mocks and stubs created by the Mocha gem, you will discover that they too rely on singleton methods.

Staying Out of Trouble

Most of the problems you are likely to encounter with singleton methods, particularly in their role as class methods, will likely stem from simple confusion. Easiest to deal with is confusion over scope. Remember, when you define a class method, it is a method attached to a class. The instances of the class will not know anything about that method. Thus, if you define a class method on `Document`:

```
class Document
  def self.create_test_document( length )
    Document.new( 'test', 'test', 'test ' * length )
  end

  # ...
end
```

Then you can call that method via the class:

```
book = Document.create_test_document( 10000 )
```

But Document instances are completely ignorant of the Document class methods, so that this:

```
longer_doc = book.create_test_document( 20000 )
```

Will give you this:

```
NoMethodError: undefined method `create_test_document'
  for #<Document:0xb7cd7c6c>
```

Well, perhaps not completely ignorant, since instances do know all about their classes:

```
longer_doc = book.class.create_test_document( 20000 )
```

A bit more subtle is the confusion over the value of self during the execution of a class method when you mix classes, subclasses, and class methods. To see what I mean, consider this simple pair of classes:

```
class Parent
  def self.who_am_i
    puts "The value of self is #{self}"
  end
end

class Child < Parent
end
```

Now, clearly, if you run `Parent.who_am_i` you would expect the following output:

```
The value of self is Parent
```

But what happens if you run `Child.who_am_i`? The answer is that `self` is always the thing before the period when you called the class method:

```
The value of self is Child
```

While this behavior can be a bit unsettling, it is actually the secret behind some very powerful Ruby metaprogramming techniques, techniques that we will take up in Chapter 26.

Wrapping Up

In this chapter we took a tour of singleton methods and learned how they work. We saw that singleton methods are great for those times when you need an object with some unique behavior. We saw that singleton methods are hidden inside the more or less secret singleton class that is part of most Ruby objects. We saw that the singleton class is a real class, one that you can actually get hold of. We saw how singleton methods can really shine in testing, where they make it easy to construct stub and mock objects. But we also saw that the most common use of singleton methods is for class methods, which are just singleton methods defined on the instances of `Class`.

## CHAPTER 14

Use Class Instance Variables

In the last chapter we saw how you can add methods to your classes, methods that concern themselves with the issues that affect a class as a whole. But wherever you have code, you're going to want to have data, which raises the question of where to store your class-level data. In this chapter we will look at the two alternatives that Ruby gives us for storing class-level data, the class variable, and the class instance variable.

We are going to start by looking at class variables, those Ruby things that start with @@ and seem to be the easy answer to storing your class-related information. Sadly, we will discover that class variables behave in some unfortunate ways, making them less of a solution and more of a problem. For a real solution to the problem of class-level data we will turn to a class instance variable, a slightly less obvious but much more practical solution.

A Quick Review of Class Variables

Imagine that we decide that our Document class needs some defaults.[1] We want to be able to set a default paper size, either the U.S. letter-size paper that is popular in the United States or the similar A4 size that is in vogue almost everywhere else. Since any given user will consistently use either U.S. letter or A4, we want to be able to set the

---

1. Also imagine that, as usual, we have reset the Document class back to its primordial, Chapter 1 form.

paper size at the Document class level and have any document created from then on default to using that paper size. So how do you store information associated with a Ruby class?

The obvious answer is to use a class variable. Class variables start with two @'s instead of one and are associated with a class instead of an ordinary instance. So here is Document enhanced to use class variables to track its default paper size:

```ruby
class Document

  @@default_paper_size = :a4

  def self.default_paper_size
    @@default_paper_size
  end

  def self.default_paper_size=(new_size)
    @@default_paper_size = new_size
  end

  attr_accessor :title, :author, :content
  attr_accessor :paper_size

  def initialize(title, author, content)
    @title = title
    @author = author
    @content = content
    @paper_size = @@default_paper_size
  end

  # Rest of the class omitted...
end
```

Our new document class starts out by setting the class variable `@@default_paper_size` to `:a4`. Since class variables are not visible to the outside world, we also supply a pair of accessor methods. A nice thing about class variables is that they *are* visible to instances of the class, so inside the `initialize` method we can pick up the value of `@@default_paper_size` as the paper size for the new document. On the surface, the class variable seems like an ideal solution to our problem. But all is definitely not well.

Wandering Variables

To understand the problem with class variables, we need to look at how they are resolved. As the name suggests, a class variable is one that is associated with a class. But which class? Therein lies a tale: When you say `@@default_paper_size = :a4`, Ruby needs to figure out which class will provide the home for the `@@default_paper_size` variable. Ruby starts by looking at the current class. Does the current class already have an `@@default_paper_size` class variable? If it does, then the search is over and the `@@default_paper_size` on the current class becomes `:a4`.

Here's where the story gets interesting: If the class variable is not defined in the current class, Ruby will go looking up the inheritance tree for it. So if there is no `@@default_paper_size` in the current class, Ruby will look for one in the superclass and then the super superclass, until it either finds a `@@default_paper_size` defined on one of those classes or runs out of classes. If Ruby does find `@@default_paper_size` somewhere in the inheritance tree, that's the one that gets set. If Ruby runs out of classes without finding `@@default_paper_size`, then it will create a new class variable in the current class. Looking up the value of a class variable works pretty much the same way. Ruby starts with the current class and looks up the inheritance tree; it either finds the variable or runs out of classes and throws a `NameError` exception.

Superficially, this sounds very object oriented and reasonable. The problem is that this method for resolving class variables means they have a tendency to wander from class to class. To see what I mean, let's play out a scenario very similar to our earlier paper size example, but with a very different—and unpleasant—outcome. Imagine your `Document` class has become so popular that a number of groups are building systems that use it. In particular, one group is building an application that helps people write resumes.

Since resumes are a very specific kind of `Document`, the resume group decides they need their own `Document` subclass:

```ruby
class Resume < Document
  @@default_font = :arial

  def self.default_font=(font)
    @@default_font = font
  end
```

```
  def self.default_font
    @@default_font
  end


  attr_accessor :font


  def initialize
    @font = @@default_font
  end

  # Rest of the class omitted...
end
```

The key feature of the resume class is that it defines a default font as a class variable, along with class methods to set and get the default font. Thinking about how class variables work, we know that when `@@default_font = :arial` gets run, Ruby will look at the Resume class, and then at Document, and right on up the inheritance tree. Finding no `@@default_font` defined anywhere, Ruby will set `@@default_font` on the Resume class. All very reasonable.

Now imagine that there is a second group out there, one that is intent on inflicting yet another PowerPoint or KeyNote clone on the world. They too build a subclass of Document, and, since even mundane minds frequently think alike, they also have a default font class variable, although they pick a different font:

```
class Presentation < Document
  @@default_font = :nimbus

  def self.default_font=(font)
    @@default_font = font
  end


  def self.default_font
    @@default_font
  end

  attr_accessor :font
```

```
  def initialize
    @font = @@default_font
  end


  # Rest of the class omitted...
end
```

Again, no problem. When Ruby is confronted with `@@default_font = :nimbus`, it will look at the `Presentation` class (nope), and then at `Document` (no again), and so on, and eventually decide to attach `@@default_font` to the `Presentation` class. Since there are two `@@default_fonts`, one on the `Resume` class and one on the `Presentation` class, the two classes can live side by side in the same application with no problem.

Now for the punch line: Ignorant of the goings on in `Resume` and `Presentation`, you decide to add a `@@default_font` class variable to your `Document` class:

```
class Document
  @@default_font = :times


  # Rest of the class omitted...
end
```

The result of this simple change is that all Hell breaks loose. Here's how: The `Document` class needs to be loaded before `Resume` and `Presentation`—it's the superclass after all. This means the `Document` class `@@default_font` will get set first, which means that whenever either of the subclasses goes looking for `@@default_font`, it will find the one in `Document`. Remember, Ruby looks up the inheritance tree *first*. So your seemingly low-impact change to the `Document` class has changed the behavior of both subclasses. Instead of two separate default font variables, one attached to `Presentation` and the other to `Resume`, there is now only one variable, one that lives up in the `Document` class.

To see how nasty that is, consider that this:

```
require 'document'
require 'resume'        # Load Resume first
require 'presentation'  # then Presentation
```

Sets the default font for all documents to the `Presentation` class's favorite font, `:nimbus`. But if you change the order of the `require` statements:

```
require 'document'
require 'presentation' # Load Presentation first
require 'resume'       # then Resume
```

Then the default font for all documents gets set to `:arial`.

If this "It's my variable!" versus "No! It's mine!" argument sounds familiar, it should. This is exactly the kind of situation we run into with global variables—and is also the reason why coders got out of the global variable business a long time ago. The real problem with class variables is that they are not so much variables attached to a specific class as they are global variables with a slightly restricted realm. In fact, Rubyist David Black calls class variables "vertical global variables," vertical in that they are restricted to a single inheritance tree and global in that they are very visible within that tree.

Getting Control of the Data in Your Class

Clearly, we need an alternative way of associating some data with a class, a technique that is more controllable than class variables. The more controllable alternative to the class variable is the class instance variable. The good news is that class instance variables are not really a new thing. They are in fact garden-variety, single @ instance variables that happen to find themselves attached to a class object.

To see how this might work, recall from the last chapter that inside a class method, `self` is always the class. Now ask yourself this: What would happen if you set an ordinary instance variable inside a class method? Perhaps like this:

```
class Document

  @default_font = :times

  def self.default_font=(font)
    @default_font = font
  end

  def self.default_font
    @default_font
  end
```

```
    # Rest of the class omitted...
end
```

The answer is that since `@default_font = font` always sets an instance variable on `self`, the `default_font=` method above will set the `@default_font` instance variable on the `Document` object. This means that armed with the code above we can now set our document-wide default font:

```
Document.default_font = :arial
```

To get at the `Document` default font, all you need to do is call the right class method, which is exactly what the `Document` `initialize` method does:

```
def initialize(title, author)
  @title = title
  @author = author
  @font = Document.default_font
end
```

Class instance variables are a very Ruby solution to the problem holding onto classwide values. There is no extra syntax and no elaborate special case rules: `@default_font` is simply an instance variable on an object. The only remotely interesting thing here is that the object happens to be a class.

Class Instance Variables and Subclasses

To paraphrase my mother, it's all fun and games until someone starts writing subclasses. Recall that we didn't have any problems with the `@@` class variables until we started messing with subclasses. That was when the class variables started wandering from class to class. Do class instance variables fare any better when the subclasses start flying?

The short answer is that class instance variables do just fine with subclasses. To see how, imagine that we have our `Presentation` subclass and, `Presentation` has its own idea of a default font:

```
class Presentation < Document

  @default_font = :nimbus
```

```
    class << self
      attr_accessor :default_font
    end

    def initialize(title, author)
      @title = title
      @author = author
      @font = Presentation.default_font
    end

    # most of the class omitted...
  end
```

What this code does is create a second class instance variable, this time attached to the `Presentation` class. The `Presentation` `@default_font` is completely separate from the `Document` `@default_font`, and as long as you are careful with which one you are talking about, `Presentation.default_font` or `Document.default_font`, life will be good.

Adding Some Convenience to Your Class Instance Variables

Since class instance variables are just plain old instance variables that happen to be hanging off a class object, we can use all our Ruby trickery to make living with them more pleasant. For example, there is no reason for us to be writing those boring `default_font` getter and setter methods given that Ruby supplies us with the nice `attr_accessor` for just such occasions. So how do you use `attr_accessor` to get at a class instance variable? After all, if you just do this:

```
  class Document
    attr_accessor :default_font
  end
```

You end up being able to get and set an *instance* variable called `default_font`. Fortunately, we already have the answer. Remember that class methods are just singleton methods on a class object. The trick to defining class-level attributes is to make `self` be the `Document` singleton class first:

```
class Document

  @default_font = :times

  class << self
    attr_accessor :default_font
  end

  # Rest of the class omitted...
end
```

Run this code and you will end up with a Document class that has a couple of class methods, one to get the default font and the other to set it.

In the Wild

Examples of class instance variables are easy to find in the Ruby code base. For example, most Rails programmers know how to set up callbacks, methods that get called at particular moments in the life of their ActiveRecord objects. Here, for example, is a class that has arranged for the handle_after_save method to get called just after a Person instance is saved into the database:

```
class Person < ActiveRecord::Base
  after_save :handle_after_save

  def handle_after_save
    # Do something after the record is saved...
  end
end
```

Clearly, the fact that we do want handle_after_save called after each record save is an attribute of the Person class, and that is where ActiveRecord saves this information. Poke around in ActiveRecord and you will find a class instance variable called @after_save_callbacks. Nor is @after_save_callbacks lonely. Dig into ActiveRecord a bit more and you will find a number of similar class instance variables with names like @after_update_callbacks and @after_validation_callbacks.

Despite the amount of space I've used in this chapter to cast aspersions on class variables, people do use them successfully. For example, the URI class that comes with your Ruby install and enables you to make sense of things like "http://russolsen.com" and "sendto:russ@russolsen.com" uses an `@@` variable quite happily. When you say something like this:

```
my_uri = URI.parse('http://www.russolsen.com')
```

The `parse` method will consult `@@schemes`, which is a hash that maps each URI scheme—'http' in this case—to the class that knows how to parse URIs with that scheme. The interesting part of `@@schemes` is the way it gets filled in. Initially, the basic URI code simply sets `@@schemes` to an empty hash:

```
@@schemes = {}
```

Then the classes that know how to parse the different flavors of URIs get loaded. The last thing each of these classes does is add itself to the master list of schemes, so that in `uri/http.rb` you will find:

```
class HTTP
  # Lots of code omitted...
end
@@schemes['HTTP'] = HTTP
```

While in `uri/sendto.rb` you will see:

```
class MailTo
  # Lots of code omitted...
end

@@schemes['MAILTO'] = MailTo
```

One other interesting thing about URI is that `@@schemes` is not actually a class variable—it is in fact a module variable. Ruby modules are a bit like stunted classes, but in the same way that you can hang class variables on classes, you can stick module variables on modules. So if we pull back the camera on the URI code, we see:

```
module URI
  # ...
```

```
      @@schemes = {}

   end

   module URI
     class HTTP
        # Lots of code omitted...
     end

     @@schemes['HTTP'] = HTTP
   end
```

We will be seeing a lot more of modules in Chapters 15 and 16.

Staying Out of Trouble

The URI code avoids ending up in class variable Hell by setting `@@schemes` variable very early on, before any of the individual scheme-parsing code gets loaded. This ensures that there is a single `@@schemes` variable and that it is properly attached to the `URI` module where it belongs. If you must use class variables, then this is a good strategy. A better strategy is to reread the title of this chapter and stick to class instance variables.

Wrapping Up

One of the joys of using Ruby is how well the language adheres to the principal of least surprise: If you are wondering how to do something, there's a good chance that your first guess will be correct. Still no language is perfect, and Ruby does harbor a few unfortunate[2] design decisions. The class variable would get my vote as the most unfortunate Ruby feature of all: Class variables seem designed to trip up newcomers to Ruby and even manage to surprise experienced Ruby developers on occasion. The good news is that class instance variables are just waiting there to fill in.

---

2. Yes, that's the word.

CHAPTER 15

Use Modules as Name Spaces

There comes a time when every successful software project outgrows its shoes: You start with a simple utility, something that fits in one source file and that you can explain in a single elevator ride. Sprinkle in some success in the form of eager—and demanding—users, and before you know it you end up with a mass of code that you couldn't describe on a Washington to Tokyo flight, complete with the stopover in Chicago.

This is why big programs usually look a bit different from little programs. That original, elevator-sized utility needs very minimal defenses against complexity, perhaps a few comments and some well-named methods. It's the massive, trans-Pacific systems that need to pull out every complexity-reducing trick in the book[1] to give the engineers that work on it a fighting chance.

In this chapter we will look at one of those tricks, using modules to organize your classes and constants (and modules) into a nice, human brain-friendly hierarchy.

A Place for Your Stuff, with a Name

Sometimes even the most complicated things can start to seem simple if we hang around them long enough. Take the idea of a class. We generally think of the class as a simple, more or less indivisible thing. Step back a bit and you realize that classes are

---

1. This book, of course.

actually a conglomeration of several different ideas. They are the factories that produce our objects—you say Date.new and the Date class manufactures a new instance for you. But classes are also containers. Most of the effort that goes into creating a new class actually goes into putting things like methods and constants into the class.

A Ruby module is the container part of a class without the factory. You can't instantiate a module, but you can put things inside of a module. Modules can hold methods, constants, classes, and even other modules.

Here, for example, is a module that groups together a couple of related classes:

```ruby
module Rendering
  class Font
    attr_accessor :name, :weight, :size

    def initialize( name, weight=:normal, size=10 )
      @name = name
      @weight = weight
      @size = size
    end

    # Rest of the class omitted...
  end

  class PaperSize
    attr_accessor :name, :width, :height

    def initialize( name='US Let', width=8.5, height=11.0 )
      @name = name
      @width = width
      @height = height
    end
    # Rest of the class omitted...
  end
end
```

Getting at the classes in a module is as simple as pasting the module name on the front of the class name with a couple of colons. To get at that font class above you just say Rendering::Font. Wrapping a module around your classes in this way gives you a couple of advantages. It allows you to group together related classes. Looking at the last example leaves you with no doubt that the Font and PaperSize classes have something to do with `Rendering`. Second, when you put the `Font` class inside of a module, you are dramatically reducing the probability that your `Font` class and someone else's `Font` class will be injured in a name collision.

Modules can also hold constants, so we might add a default font and paper size to our `Rendering` module:

```
module Rendering
  # Font and PaperSize classes omitted...

  DEFAULT_FONT = Font.new( 'default' )
  DEFAULT_PAPER_SIZE = PaperSize.new
end
```

You can access your constants in the same way that you access the classes,[2] so that the default paper size becomes `Rendering::DEFAULT_PAPER_SIZE`. If you get tired of all this `Render::` typing, you can include the module:[3]

```
include Rendering

puts "The default paper height is #{DEFAULT_PAPER_SIZE.height}"
```

Finally, modules can be nested, so that if your rendering module was, say, part of some larger word-processing package, you might have:

```
module WordProcessor
  module Rendering
    class Font
      # Guts of class omitted...
    end

    # and so on...
  end
end
```

---

2. In fact, since class names are constants, it's a very close match.

3. But see the next chapter for the full implications of including a module.

Naturally, if you do nest your modules you will need to dig deeper to find the stuff inside: Nest the `Font` class two modules deep and you will either have to include the `WordProcessor::Rendering` module or utter `WordProcessor::Rendering::Font` in one breath.

A Home for Those Utility Methods

Along with classes and constants and other modules, you can use modules to enclose individual methods. Modules make great homes for those pesky methods that just don't seem to fit anywhere else. For example, the printing business has traditionally used a unit of length called the point, where 72 points will fit into an inch.[4] We can certainly imagine that our document code might need a couple of unit conversion methods to deal with points, and a convenient place to put these might be the `WordProcessor` module:

```
module WordProcessor

  def self.points_to_inches( points )
    points / 72.0
  end

  def self.inches_to_points( inches )
    inches * 72.0
  end

  # Rest of the module omitted
end
```

Notice that we wrote the two conversion methods as module-level methods. Defining them this way—analogous to class-level methods—allows us to call them directly from the module:

```
an_inch_full_of_points = WordProcessor.inches_to_points( 1.0 )
```

---

4. Well, about 72. The actual size of the point has varied with time and geography, but the modern value has settled on 1/72 of an inch or about 0.353 mm.

We can also get at module-level methods with the double-colon syntax (that is `WordProcessor::inches_to_points`), but generally Ruby programmers tend to stick to the period.

Building Modules a Little at a Time

Don't let the `end` at the bottom of a module fool you. As we will see in Chapter 24, nothing is Ruby is ever really done. One of the most visible aspects of this "always open" policy is that you can define your modules in several pieces, spread over a number of source files. The first file defines the module and the rest of the files simply add to it. So, returning to our first, single-level `Rendering` module example, we might have the `Font` class in `font.rb`:

```ruby
module Rendering
  class Font
    # Bulk of class omitted...
  end

  DEFAULT_FONT = Font.new( 'default' )
end
```

And the `PaperSize` class in `paper_size.rb`:

```ruby
module Rendering
  class PaperSize
    # Bulk of class omitted...
  end

  DEFAULT_PAPER_SIZE = PaperSize.new
end
```

If we then pull both files into our Ruby interpreter with suitable `require` statements:

```ruby
require 'font'
require 'paper_size'
```

We will have a single `Rendering` module, complete with fonts and paper sizes.

Treat Modules Like the Objects That They Are

So far we have treated modules as relatively static containers. In our earlier example we created a `Rendering` module and stuck the `Font` class in it. If we wanted to get at `Font` we either spelled out `Rendering::Font` longhand or we explicitly included the `Rendering` module. One key idea in Ruby is that just about everything is an object, and *everything* includes modules. Since modules are just objects, we can treat them like any other object. In particular, we can point a variable at a module and then use that variable in place of the module. For example:

```ruby
the_module = Rendering

times_new_roman_font = the_module::Font.new('times-new-roman' )
```

You can take advantage of the object-ness of modules to swap out whole groups of related classes and constants—and even sub-modules!—at runtime. To see how this might work, imagine that we are trying to cope with two different types of printer, an ink jet printer and a laser printer. Further, let's pretend that we have two classes for each printer type: one class to submit and cancel jobs, and another class that does administrative things such as turning the power off or running diagnostic tests:

```ruby
class TonsOTonerPrintQueue
  def submit( print_job )
    # Send the job off for printing to this laser printer...
  end

  def cancel( print_job)
    # Stop the print job on this laser printer...
  end
end

class TonsOTonerAdministration
  def power_off
    # Turn this laser printer off...
  end

  def start_self_test
    # Test this laser printer...
  end
end
```

```
class OceansOfInkPrintQueue
  def submit( print_job )
    # Send the job off for printing to this ink jet printer...
  end

  def cancel( print_job)
    # Stop the print job on this ink jet printer...
  end
end

Class OceansOfInkAdministration
  def power_off
    # Turn this ink jet printer off...
  end

  def start_self_test
    # Test this ink jet printer...
  end
end
```

The trouble with this code is that we need to manage four classes, two per printer type. We could simplify that by merging the print queue management and administrative methods into a single, massive class for each printer type. This will reduce the number of things we need to manage, but simply jamming things together seems like a bad idea.

A better solution is to package the bits we need for each type of printer into a single module. We can then have a module for the laser printer:

```
module TonsOToner
  class PrintQueue
    def submit( print_job )
      # Send the job off for printing to this laser printer
    end

    def cancel( print_job)
      # Stop!
    end
  end

  class Administration
    def power_off
```

```
        # Turn this laser printer off...
      end

      def start_self_test
        # Everything ok?
      end
    end
  end
end
```

And a second module for the ink jet printer:

```
module OceansOfInk
  class PrintQueue
    def submit( print_job )
      # Send the job off for printing to this ink jet printer
    end
    # Rest omitted...
  end

  class Administration
    #  Ink jet administration code omitted...
  end
end
```

Now for the pay-off: We can set a variable to the correct printer-type module and from then on forget about which kind of printer we are dealing with:

```
if use_laser_printer
  print_module = TonsOToner
else
  print_module = OceansOfInk
end

# Later...

admin = print_module::Administration.new
```

Staying Out of Trouble

So when should you create a name space module and when should you let your classes go naked? An easy rule of thumb is that if you find yourself creating a lot of names that all start with the same word, perhaps `TonsOTonerPrintQueue` and `TonsOTonerAdministration`, then you just may need a `TonsOToner` module.

Most of the dangers involved in actually creating name-space modules are easily avoidable. For example, if you want to enclose stand-alone utility methods in a module, make sure that you define those methods as *module-level* methods. Do this:

```
module WordProcessor

  def self.points_to_inches( points )
    points / 72.0
  end

  # etc...
end
```

Not this:

```
module WordProcessor

  def points_to_inches( points )
    points / 72.0
  end

  # etc...
end
```

The first version of `WordProcessor` creates a module-level method that any code can use. The second version creates a method that might be great when mixed into a class but is useless as a widely available utility method.[5]

Another, more alluring, danger lies in going hog wild with your modules. Think about our original module example:

---

5. We'll be talking about mixing modules into classes in the next chapter.

```
module Rendering
  class Font
    #...
```

This two-level organization is fine, but if you think about it, it is not really complete. After all, a font is a set of glyphs:

```
module Rendering
  module GlyphSet
    class Font
      #...
```

And rendering is just one part of creating output, and creating output is a major subsystem:

```
module Subsystem
  module Output
    module Rendering
      module GlyphSet
        class Font
          #...
```

This is all very logical, but now your users will have to type this monstrosity simply to get to the `Font` class:

```
Subsystem::Output::Rendering::GlyphSet::Font
```

And they will (justifiably) hate you for it. Remember, the goal is clear and concise code.

In the Wild

To underscore the idea that a little bit of module goes a long way, consider DataMapper. DataMapper is a database interface library similar to ActiveRecord. In about 7,500 lines of pretty heavy-duty code, the core of DataMapper uses primarily a three- and occasionally four-level module hierarchy. If DataMapper can limit itself to a very shallow, manageable module structure and still talk to MYSQL, Postgres, and SQLite, chances are pretty good that a modest handful of modules will work for your project too.

In fact, of the larger Ruby projects that do encase themselves in modules, most manage to fit everything very comfortably into a very small number of modules. The code that reads YAML, everyone's favorite XML alternative, consists of exactly four modules, with the vast bulk of the code living right in the YAML module. The URI code that comes with Ruby weighs in at about 2,500 lines of code and consists of a grand total of five modules, again with most of the code concentrated in a single module. Finally, we have RubyGems, all of 14,000 lines and just over a dozen modules.

Wrapping Up

In this chapter we have seen how you can use modules to divide your code into manageable bits and avoid the dreaded name collisions. We saw how you can put classes and constants, individual methods, and even other modules inside of modules, as well as how to access the things inside of a module. We also saw how you can treat a module just like any other object, which can be a boon when you are trying to manage a group of related classes.

We aren't done with modules either. Modules have one other talent that we only touched on in this chapter, a talent that allows Ruby programmers to share code between unrelated classes. But for that, you are going to have to turn the page.

CHAPTER 16

Use Modules as Mixins

I started off the last chapter by pointing out that a class is a combination of two things, a container and a factory. We build classes full of code (that's the container part) and then we use them to manufacture instances. One thing that I glossed over in the last chapter is that along with being containers and factories, Ruby classes can also be *super*: Like classes in most other object oriented programming languages, Ruby classes are arranged in an inheritance tree, so that a key part of constructing a new class is picking its parent, or superclass.

In this chapter we are going to discover that you can also insert, or "mix in," modules into the inheritance tree of your classes. If you haven't come across the idea of a mixin before, let me whet your appetite. Mixins allow you to easily share common code among otherwise unrelated classes. Mixins are custom-designed for those situations where you have a method or six that need to be included in a number of different classes that have nothing else in common. During our tour of mixin modules we'll have a good look at how they work and at how real some real Ruby applications like Rails use mixins.

Better Books with Modules

Let's begin our look at mixins by continuing our quest to improve—or at least measure—the quality of prose entrusted to our Document class. Recall that we've already written a method to measure the average length of the words in our documents. There is, however, more to good writing than modestly sized words. Editors also tend to frown on clichés, those phrases that have been so overused that they've lost all their rhetorical pizzazz. We decide that an array of regular expressions along with a new Document method[1] will do the trick. So we are off and running:

```
class  Document

  CLICHES = [ /play fast and loose/,
              /make no mistake/,
              /does the trick/,
              /off and running/,
              /my way or the highway/ ]

  def number_of_cliches
    CLICHES.inject(0) do |count, phrase|
      count += 1 if phrase =~ content
      count
    end
  end

  # Rest of the class omitted...
end
```

This number_of_cliches method is like much of the code we write—not terribly exciting, but useful nevertheless. So, you release your new Document class and everyone is happy. Unfortunately—at least for you—your employers decide that there might be a world beyond traditional paper books and begin to move into the digital market. To this end, they buy an eBook publishing system, which features its own class hierarchy for representing books:

```
class ElectronicBook < ElectronicText
  # Lots of complicated stuff omitted...
end
```

This is a problem because everyone loves the number_of_cliches method so much that they would like to get it into the new ElectronicBook class. So how do you insert a method into these two, very separate class hierarchies?

---

1. Again, we are starting over with our original Document class.

Your gut reaction—at least if your gut went to the same object oriented programming school as mine—might be to create some sort of common superclass for both `ElectronicBook` and `Document`, maybe `Tome`. This superclass would contain the `number_of_cliches` method, which would then be neatly inherited by both `ElectronicBook` and `Document`. Sensible, but not always doable. Sometimes, especially in cases where you have inherited large bodies of code, it's just not practical to rewire the basic structure of your classes in order to share a few tens of lines of code.[2]

Mixin Modules to the Rescue

The way to solve the problem of sharing code among otherwise unrelated classes is by creating a mixin module. Let's take this step by step: First, you move the `number_of_cliches` method into a module:

```
module WritingQuality

  CLICHES = [ /play fast and loose/,
              /make no mistake/,
              /does the trick/,
              /off and running/,
              /my way or the highway/ ]

  def number_of_cliches
    CLICHES.inject(0) do |count, phrase|
      count += 1 if phrase =~ content
      count
    end
  end
end
```

Note that the `number_of_cliches` method is an ordinary *instance* method in the module, *not* a module-level method. Next, you include the module into the classes that need the method:

---

2. The astute reader will notice that I have passed silently over the possibility of simply copying the code into both classes. We shall speak no more of such an unpleasant alternative.

```ruby
class Document
  include WritingQuality

  # Lots of stuff omitted...
end

class ElectronicBook < ElectronicText
  include WritingQuality

  # Lots of stuff omitted...
end
```

And you are done. When you include a module into a class, the module's methods magically become available to the including class, which means that you can now say this:

```ruby
text = "my way or the highway does the trick"
my_tome = Document.new('Hackneyed', 'Russ', text)
puts my_tome.number_of_cliches
```

As well as this:

```ruby
my_ebook = ElectronicBook.new( 'EHackneyed', 'Russ', text)
puts my_ebook.number_of_cliches
```

The Ruby jargon is that by including a module in a class you have **mixed it in** to the class. We say that the module itself, WritingQuality in this case, is a **mixin module.** A very useful aspect of mixins is that they are not limited by the "one superclass is all you get" rule. You can mix as many modules into a class as you like. For example, if you created ProjectManagement and AuthorAccountTracking modules for your publishing employer, you could include them both in the ElectronicBook class, along with WritingQuality:

```ruby
module ProjectManagement
  # Lots of boring stuff omitted
end
```

```
module AuthorAccountTracking
  # Lots of even more boring stuff omitted
end

class  ElectronicBook < ElectronicText
  include WritingQuality
  include ProjectManagement
  include AuthorAccountTracking

  # Lots of stuff omitted...
end
```

In practice, this means that if you have several unrelated classes that need to share some code, you don't have to resort to restructuring your whole inheritance tree to get at that code. All you need to do is wrap the common stuff in a module and include that module in the classes that need it.

Extending a Module

Sometimes it's the class itself—as opposed to the instances of the class—that needs help from a module. Sometimes you want to pull in a module so that all the methods in the module become *class* methods. You might, for instance, have a module full of methods that know how to locate documents:

```
module Finders
  def find_by_name( name )
    # Find a document by name...
  end

  def find_by_id( doc_id )
    # Find a document by id
  end
end
```

You would like to get the Finders methods into your Document class as *class* methods. One way to get this done is to do this:

```
class Document
  # Most of the class omitted...
```

```
    class << self
      include Finders
    end
  end
```

This code includes the module into the singleton class of `Document`, effectively making the methods of `Finders` singleton—and therefore class—methods of `Document`:

```
  war_and_peace = Document.find_by_name( 'War And Peace' )
```

Including modules into the singleton class is a common enough task that Ruby has a special shortcut for it in the form of `extend`:

```
class Document
  extend Finders

  # Most of the class omitted...
end
```

Run this code and you will end up with class-level `Document.find_by_name` and `find_by_id` methods.

Staying Out of Trouble

Clearly there is something magical going on when you include a module in a class. The key bit of legerdemain is this: When you mix a module into a class, Ruby rewires the class hierarchy a bit, inserting the module as a sort of pseudo superclass of the class. As shown in Figure 16-1, the module gets interposed between the class and its original superclass.

This explains how the module methods appear in the including classes—they effectively become methods just up the inheritance chain from the class.

Although including a module inserts it into the class hierarchy, Ruby is a bit circumspect about this fact: No matter how many modules a class includes, instances of the class will still claim to be, well, instances of the class. So, if `my_tome` is an instance of `ElectronicBook`, then `my_tome.class` will return `ElectronicBook` no matter how many modules the `ElectronicBook` class includes. Module inclusion is not a complete

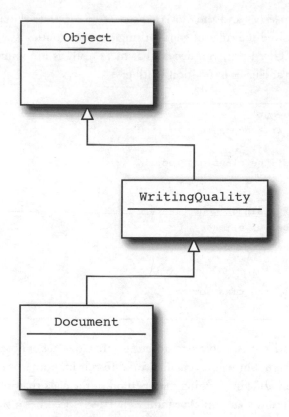

Figure 16-1 A module becomes a pseudo superclass to the class that includes it.

secret, however. You can discover whether the class of an instance includes a given module with the kind_of? method. So if Document includes the WritingQuality module, then my_tome.kind_of?(WritingQuality) will return true. You can also use the ancestors method to see the complete inheritance ancestry—modules included—of a class, so that Document.ancestors might return the following array:

```
[Document, WritingQuality, Object, Kernel, BasicObject]
```

This "insert the module in before the superclass" mechanism is not just some implementation detail that's liable to change at any moment. The way modules work is an integral part of the way that Ruby works. Nor is all of this purely academic— the module inclusion mechanism has some real, practical implications. For example, imagine that your company gets into the business of publishing political tracts such as congressional speeches and the Governor's state of the state statement. Now, where politics are involved the rules of good writing change: Politics is where the clichés go when they die. Given this, you decide that there really is no point in reporting back on the number of clichés in political writing:

```
class Document
  include WritingQuality

  # Rest of the class omitted...
end

class PoliticalBook < Document
  def number_of_cliches
    0
  end

  # Rest of the class omitted...
end
```

This seems like a sensible way to ensure that the `number_of_cliches` method always returns zero, but will it actually work? To put it another way, can you override a method in a module by defining that method in the class that includes the module?

Once you know that a mixin module effectively becomes a superclass when it is included, the answer is easy to come by: Yes. Since we know that the methods in a superclass cannot override the methods in subclasses, we can deduce that no module method can ever override a method in its host class. Call the method and Ruby will look first in the class, find it there, and never go looking in any included modules. So our `PoliticalBook` class above is indeed correct, and we can happily ignore political clichés.

A similar "who wins?" question arises if we have the same method in two modules and include them both in the same class. To see this in action, imagine that we decide to create a slightly tongue-in-cheek writing-quality module especially for political writing:

```
module PoliticalWritingQuality

  # No phrase is too worn out to be a cliché
  # in political writing
```

```
  def number_of_cliches
    0
  end
end
```

Now what happens if we include both the original writing-quality module as well as the political version above in our `PoliticalBook` class?

```
class PoliticalBook < Document
  include WritingQuality
  include PoliticalWritingQuality

  # Lots of stuff omitted...

end
```

Which version of the `number_of_cliches` method will win? Again, the answer flows from the way modules get hooked into the class hierarchy of `PoliticalBook`: Include a module and it becomes the nearest parent "class" of the including class. Include a second module and *it* becomes the nearest parent of the including class, bumping the other module into second place. Have a look at Figure 16-2 to see this graphically. It's the methods in the most recently included module that always win. In our example, the `number_of_cliches` from `PoliticalWritingQuality` would be the one that `PoliticalBook` would end up with.

If you find yourself writing your own mixin module, there is one question that should be uppermost in your mind: What is the interface between my module and its including class? Since mixing in a module sets up an inheritance relationship between the including class and the module, you need to let your users know what that relationship is going to be before they start mixing. You should always add a few concise comments to your creation stating exactly what it expects from its including class:

```
# Methods to measure writing quality.
# Uses the content method of the including class.
module WritingQuality

  # Lots of stuff omitted...

end
```

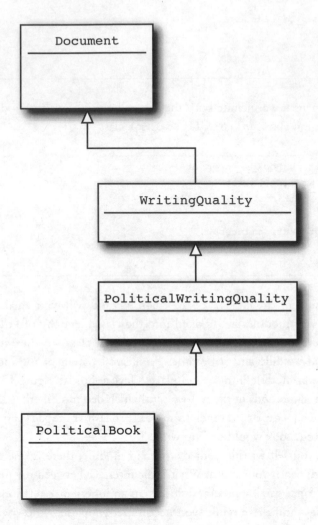

Figure 16-2 Modules get inserted sequentially into the inheritance tree.

A little guidance goes a long way to making your module useful.

In the Wild

Although the examples in this chapter have focused on modules containing a handful of methods, there really is no limit to what you can do with a module. DataMapper[3] is

---

3. DataMapper, which is maintained by a cast of, well, tens, can be found at www.datamapper.org.

a great example of just how far you can take a mixin module. DataMapper is an object relational mapper along the lines of ActiveRecord. Like ActiveRecord, DataMapper's purpose is to make objects persistable in a database. But unlike ActiveRecord, DataMapper does not require that your persistable objects extend any particular class. Instead, it's all done with a module. Here's what our Document class might look like as a DataMapper object:

```ruby
class Document
  include DataMapper::Resource

  property :id, Integer, :serial => true
  property :title, String
  property :content, String
  property :author, String
end
```

By including one module—DataMapper::Resource—your class gains all the equipment it needs to persist itself in a database, and does so without using up the single superclass that Ruby allows for each class.

Rails also makes heavy use of mixin modules, most notably in the form of **helpers**. The Rails helper methods do exactly what their name suggests: They help you. For example, Rails includes a large number of helper methods that ease the pain of creating HTML, methods like label and radio_button, all delivered to your classes courtesy of mixin modules:

```ruby
module ActionView

  # Huge amounts of code and helpful documentation omitted...

  module Helpers
    module FormHelper
      def label(object_name, method, text = nil, options = {})
        # ...
      end

      def radio_button(object_name, method, tag_value,options={})
        # ...
      end
    end
```

```
     end
  end
```

Nor are methods all you can get from a mixin module. Mixin modules are also very convenient places to stash constants. Since including a module in a class inserts the module into the class hierarchy, the including class not only gains access to the module's methods but also to its constants. You can see this at work in the sqlite3 gem, which defines a series of modules full of nothing but constants. For example, there is a module that contains the list of error codes that might come back from sqlite3:[4]

```
module ErrorCode
   OK         = 0    # Successful result
   ERROR      = 1    # SQL error or missing database
   INTERNAL   = 2    # An internal logic error in SQLite
   PERM       = 3    # Access permission denied
   ABORT      = 4    # Callback routine requested an abort
   BUSY       = 5    # The database file is locked
   LOCKED     = 6    # A table in the database is locked

   # Seemingly endless list of remaining error codes omitted...
end
```

Now, as we saw in the last chapter, you can access all of these constants using their fully qualified names by saying things like `ErrorCode::OK` or `ErrorCode::Busy`. This can get tedious if you are doing it a lot; if so, you can drop the qualifying module name by simply including the `ErrorCode` module:

```
class SomeSQLiteApplication
  include ErrorCode

  def print_status_message( status )
    if status == ERROR
      puts "It failed!"
    elsif status == OK
      puts "It worked!"
```

---

4. In real life, the sqlite3 ErrorCode module is buried inside several other modules, which I have omitted here for the sake of brevity.

```
      else
        puts "Status was #{status}"
      end
    end
  end
```

Nothing like being able to insert modules into your class hierarchy to make the workday go faster!

Wrapping Up

In this chapter we have seen how mixin modules solve the problem of code that needs to be shared among classes without using up the one alloted superclass. We have also seen how mixin modules work, how they get drafted into service as a kind of phantom superclass when they are included into a host class. We have also seen that the key issue with mixins is the interface between the host class and the mixin module—what methods does the module provide and what does it expect the class to supply?

For many new Ruby programmers, mixin modules can act as a sort of skeleton key to the whole philosophy behind the language, the elegant way that Ruby tries to help programmers get code to execute where it is needed. Because of this, mixin modules pop up somewhere in most real-world Ruby applications. Nor are we done with them. Mixins will make an encore appearance in Chapter 20 when we look at a slick way to add both instance *and* class methods to a class with a single `include`. For now, however, we will turn to the code block, another way of getting code to where you need it.

CHAPTER 17

Use Blocks to Iterate

For programmers new to Ruby, code blocks are generally the first sign that they have definitely departed Kansas. Part syntax, part method, and part object, the code block is one of the key features that gives the Ruby programming language its unique feel. In fact, code blocks are kind of the Swiss Army Knife of Ruby programming; we use them for everything from initializing objects to building DSLs. In the next few chapters we will take a hard look at code blocks and the things you can do with them. The idea is to get beyond simply passing blocks to other people's methods and move on to squeezing the last bit of utility out of the code blocks that get passed into your own methods.

We're going to kick things off by looking at the most familiar use of code blocks—as iterators. After a quick review of the mechanics of code blocks we will move on to building simple iterators, iterators that can sequence through garden-variety collections. From there we will move on to iterators that run through collections that never actually exist. Next, we will also explore how you can mess up a perfectly good iterator and at how a misbehaving iterator can bring your code to a screeching halt. Finally, we will close by taking a quick tour of the myriad iterating code blocks that you will find in existing Ruby programs.

A Quick Review of Code Blocks

Since code blocks are one of the higher speed bumps on the road to real Ruby fluency, let's take a minute to review the basics. In Ruby you create code blocks by tacking them on to the end of a method call, like this:

```
do_something do
  puts "Hello from inside the block"
end
```

Or this:

```
do_something { puts "Hello from inside the block" }
```

When you tack a block onto the end of a method call, Ruby will package up the block as sort of a secret argument and (behind the scenes) passes this secret argument to the method. Inside the method you can detect whether your caller has actually passed in a block with the block_given? method and fire off the block (if there is one) with yield:

```
def do_something
  yield if block_given?
end
```

Blocks can take arguments, which you supply as arguments to yield, so that if you do this:

```
def do_something_with_an_arg
  yield("Hello World") if block_given?
end

do_something_with_an_arg do |message|
  puts "The message is #{message}"
end
```

You will get:

```
The message is Hello World
```

Finally, like most everything else in Ruby, code blocks always return a value—the last expression that the block executes—which your yielding method can either use or ignore as it sees fit. So if you run this:

```
def print_the_value_returned_by_the_block
  if block given?
    value = yield
    puts "The block returned #{value}"
  end
end

print_the_value_returned_by_the_block { 3.14159 / 4.0 }
```

You will see the value of $\pi/4$:

```
The block returned 0.7853975
```

One Word after Another

The difference between the do_something and do_something_with_an_arg methods and a real iterator method is simple: An iterator method calls its block once for each element in some collection, passing the element into the block as a parameter. For example, we could add an iterator to our Document class, one that runs through all the words in the document:

```
class Document

  # Stuff omitted...

  def each_word
    word_array = words
    index = 0
    while index < words.size
      yield( word_array[index] )
      index += 1
    end
  end
end
```

The Document class, now sports a very respectable-looking Ruby iterator method, one that you can use like any other, so that running this:

```
d = Document.new( 'Truth', 'Gump', 'Life is like a box of ...' )
d.each_word {|word| puts word}
```

Will result in this:

```
Life
is
like
a
box
of
...
```

Although this each_word method is a good, simple illustration of how to build an
iterating method, it does go out of its way to work hard. A real implementation of
each_word would almost certainly take advantage of the existing each method in the
words array:

```
def each_word
  words.each { |word| yield( word ) }
end
```

There's nothing like using the wheel that's already there.

As Many Iterators as You Like

Although so far we have focused on adding *an* iterator to the Document class, a class
can have as many iterator methods as make sense. So along with each_word, the
Document class might also sport an each_character method:[1]

```
class Document
  def each_character
```

---

1. If you are using a pre-1.9 version of Ruby, the each_character method is misnamed since before
   1.9 Ruby strings were just collections of bytes (really just integers), not actual characters. So if
   you are using 1.8.X, the Document each_character method will yield a series of numbers, each
   number the ordinal number of a character in the string. With Ruby 1.9, strings really are strings
   of characters, and the each_character method will yield a series of one-character strings.

```
        index = 0
        while index < @content.size
          yield( @content[index] )
          index += 1
        end
    end
  end
```

You are also free to name your iterator method anything you like, but it does make good sense to follow the Ruby convention and name your most obvious or commonly used iterator each and give any other iterators a name like each_something_else. We might, therefore, decide that words are the key elements of our documents and re-jigger our code to look something like:

```
class Document

  # Stuff omitted

  def each
    # iterate over the words as in our first example
  end

  def each_character
    # iterate over the characters
  end
end
```

Since it's the words that count, we have made the each method run through the document one word at a time while consigning the method that runs through each character a lesser name.

Iterating over the Ethereal

An aspect of iterators that beginners often overlook is that you can write iterators that run through collections that don't actually exist, at least not all at the same time. The simplest example of this sort of thing is the times method that you find on Ruby integers:

```
12.times { |x| puts "The number is #{x}" }
```

This code will print out the first dozen integers, but it will print them without ever assembling a twelve-element collection. Instead, the `times` method produces each number one at a time and feeds it to the block. So far, so obvious. What's not so obvious is that you can use this same trick to build your own iterators. For example, people who are interested in determining the authorship of documents will sometimes gather statistics on which words are likely to appear together in a given document. If you had a document where the word "Mmmm" was frequently followed by the word "donuts," you might guess that the author was Homer Simpson. We can help these authorship-seeking scholars by providing an `each_word_pair` method in the `Document` class:

```ruby
class Document
  # Most of the class omitted...

  def each_word_pair
    word_array = words
    index = 0
    while index < (word_array.size-1)
      yield word_array[index], word_array[index+1]
      index += 1
    end
  end
end
```

Armed with `each_word_pair`, we can write some code to print out every pair of adjacent words in one of the world's great bits of literature:

```ruby
doc = Document.new('Donuts', '?', 'I love donuts mmmm donuts' )
doc.each_word_pair{ |first, second| puts "#{first} #{second}" }
```

Which will produce:

```
I love
love donuts
donuts mmmm
mmmm donuts
```

Notice that we never actually build a four-element array of all the word pairs: We simply generate the pairs on the fly.

Enumerable: Your Iterator on Steroids

As I say, the Ruby convention is to name the main iterator of your class each, and one of the themes of this book is that you should try to stick to the conventions. There is, however, another reason to follow the crowd and name that key iterating method each: Doing so enables you to use the Enumerable module. The Enumerable module is a mixin that endows classes with all sorts of interesting collection-related methods. Here's how Enumerable works: First, you make sure that your class has an each method, and then you include the Enumerable module in your class, like this:

```
class Document
  include Enumerable

  # Most of the class omitted...

  def each
    words.each { |word| yield( word ) }
  end
end
```

The simple act of including Enumerable adds a plethora of collection-related methods to your class, methods that all rely on your each method. So, if you create an instance of the Enumerable-enhanced Document:

```
doc = Document.new('Advice', 'Harry', 'Go ahead make my day')
```

Then you can find out whether your document includes a given word with doc.include?, so that doc.include?("make") will return true, but doc.include?("Punk") will return false. Enumerable also enhances your class with a to_a method that returns an array of all of the items, in our case words, in your collection. The Enumerable module also adds methods that help you find things in your collection, methods with names like find and find_all.

Enumerable also contributes the each_cons method to your class. The each_cons method takes an integer and a block, and will repeatedly call the block, each time

passing in an array of consecutive elements from the collection. So by including
Enumerable in the Document class, the each_word_pair method would reduce down to:

```
def each_word_pair
  words.each_cons(2) {|array| yield array[0], array[1] }
end
```

Along the same lines as each_cons, Enumerable also supplies each_slice, which
simply breaks up the collection in chunks of a given size and passes those into the
block. Finally, if the elements in your collection define the <=> operator, you can use
the Enumerable-supplied sort method, which will return a sorted array of all the elements in your collection. Since strings do indeed define <=>, we can get a sorted list
of the words in our document with doc.sort.[2] In all, Enumerable adds nearly 40
methods to your class—not a bad return on the effort of implementing one or two
methods and mixing in a single module.

Nor are you simply stuck if, as with the latest Document class with its each and
each_character and each_word_pair, you have more than one iterating method.
Along with Enumerable, Ruby also comes with the Enumerator class. If you create an
Enumerator instance, passing in your collection and the name of the iterating method,
what you will get is an object that knows how to sequence through your collection
using that method. For example, if you make a new Enumerator based on a Document
instance and the each_character method:

```
doc = Document.new('example', 'russ', "We are all characters")
enum = Enumerator.new( doc, :each_character )
```

Then you will end up with an object with all of the nice Enumerable methods based
on the each_character method. Thus you can discover the number of characters in
your document text:

```
puts enum.count
```

---

2. Mysteriously, arrays also implement all of these methods. This might lead you to suspect that the
   Array class includes the Enumerable module. You would be right.

Or sort the characters:

```
pp enum.sort
```

To produce:

```
[" ", " ", " ", "W", "a", "a", "a", "a", "c", ...]
```

Although the names are tricky, getting the hang of `Enumerable` and `Enumerator` is well worth the effort.

Staying Out of Trouble

The primary way that an iterator method can come to grief is by trusting the block too much. Remember, the code block you get handed in your iterator method is someone else's code. You need to regard the block as something akin to a hand grenade, ready to go off at any second. We saw one aspect of this when we talked about Ruby's collection classes: What happens if the code block changes the underlying collection? As we saw in Chapter 3, the Ruby collection classes generally throw up their arms and say "Don't do that!" Our `Document` class is, however, made of stronger stuff. Since the `Document each_word` method actually creates a new array before it starts, the document can change any which way while the iteration is going on. The `each_word` method will continue to sequence through the words that were there when the iteration started.

Blocks can also blow up in your face with an exception:

```
doc.each_word do |word|
  raise 'boom' if word == 'now'
end
```

A stray exception will not make much difference to the `each_word` method, but what if your iterator needs to acquire—and get rid of—some expensive resource? What if you have something like:

```
def each_name
  name_server = open_name_server   # Get some expensive resource
  while name_server.has_more?
```

```
      yield name_server.read_name
  end
  name_server.close                 # Close the expensive resource
end
```

Now you have a problem. If the code block decides to raise an exception in mid-yield, then you'll never get a chance to clean up that expensive resource. The answer to this problem is easy:

```
def each_name
  name_server = open_name_server    # Get some expensive resource
  begin
    while name_server.has_more?
      yield name_server.read_name
    end
  ensure
    name_server.close               # Close the expensive resource
  end
end
```

Even an exception-free block is no guarantee that your iterating method will run to completion. Ruby allows applications to call break in mid-block. The idea is to give the code using an iterating method a way to escape early:

```
def count_till_tuesday( doc )
  count = 0
  doc.each_word do |word|
    count += 1
    break if word == 'Tuesday'
  end
  count
```

When called from inside of a block, break will trigger a return out of *the method that called the block*. An explicit return from inside the block triggers an even bigger jump: It causes the method that defined (not called) the block to return. This is generally what you want to simulate breaking out of or returning from a built-in loop. Fortunately, like exceptions, both break and return will trigger any surrounding ensure clauses.

In the Wild

The fact is, you can't swing a dead cat in the Ruby world without hitting some block-based iterators. Iterators in Ruby range from the very mundane to the fairly exotic. At the boring end of the spectrum we have the each method on the `Array` and `Hash` classes that we looked at in Chapter 3. Equally unexciting, but still very useful, is each method on the built-in `Dir` class. The `Dir` each method will iterate over all the files in a given directory:

```
puts "Contents of /etc directory:"
etc_dir = Dir.new("/etc")
etc_dir.each {|entry| puts entry}
```

Slightly more interesting is the each_address method on the `Resolv`[3] class, which is part of the Ruby standard library. The `Resolv` class looks things up in DNS for you. Thus, with the each_address method you can discover all of the IP addresses associated with a given domain name. Run this:

```
require 'resolv'
Resolv.each_address( "www.google.com" ) {|x| puts x}
```

And you will see something like:

```
72.14.204.104
72.14.204.147
72.14.204.99
72.14.204.103
```

At the more esoteric end of the spectrum, we have the each_object method on the standard class `ObjectSpace`. Called without any parameters, `ObjectSpace.each_object` will run through all the objects in your Ruby interpreter[4] (yes, all of them!).

---

3. Yes, without the "e".

4. Do be aware that for performance reasons, JRuby disables ObjectSpace by default. This is one of the few incompatibilities between JRuby and the other Ruby implementations. You can un-disable it, but it is an incompatibility nevertheless.

Call `ObjectSpace.each_object` with a class and it will iterate through all of the instances of that class. For example, to see all of the strings that your Ruby interpreter knows about, run:

```
ObjectSpace.each_object(String) { |the_string| puts the_string }
```

Finally, if your taste in esoteric iterators runs more towards the mathematical, consider the `each` method on the `Prime` class. This method will call your block once for each and every prime number:

```
require 'mathn'

# Warning: According to Euclid, this never stops...

Prime.each {|x| puts "The next prime is #{x}" }
```

Of course, if you want to see all of the prime numbers, you'll need to be patient.

Wrapping Up

In this chapter we looked at the iconic application of code blocks, as iterators. We saw how you can build as many iterator methods as you like for your classes, methods that take a block and call it for each item in some collection. We also saw how you can build iterators that sequence through collections that don't actually exist. As long as you can come up with one element after another, you can build an iterator. We saw how `Enumerable` and `Enumerator` can enhance the iterating chops of your classes by providing most of the methods any collection class could imagine. We also saw how you need to treat the code blocks that get passed to your methods with a certain level of wary respect.

So much for iterators. In the next chapter we will look at a very different use for code blocks, one that turns the idea of an iterator on its head. Iterators are concerned with delivering item after item to a code block. We will see how you can reverse the polarity of code blocks and use them to deliver code to the right spot in your program.

CHAPTER 18

Execute Around with a Block

In the last chapter we looked at using code blocks as iterators. Code blocks do make great iterators, but simply running through a collection one element at a time in no way exhausts what you can do with a code block. In this chapter we will take the next step with code blocks by seeing how we can use them as a science fiction transporter device of sorts, capable of delivering code where it is needed in a shimmering flash of light.[1] Along the way we will examine how you can get data into and out of your code blocks. Finally, we will stumble across yet another reason why carefully chosen method names are worth their weight in gold.

Add a Little Logging

If I had to list my five favorite debugging aids, I'd probably have to ponder the bottom four, but number one would be easy: decent logging. Unglamorous and utilitarian, logging is one of those techniques that we don't talk about a lot, but that is vital in real-world applications. If, for example, we store our documents, keyed by name, in a database, we might write something like this:

---

1. OK, I made up the shimmering flash part.

```
class SomeApplication
  # ...

  def do_something
    doc = Document.load( 'resume.txt' )

    # Do something interesting with the document.

    doc.save
  end
end
```

We might, except that database interactions are not always successful, so we would probably want to sprinkle in some logging:

```
class SomeApplication

  def initialize( logger )
    @logger = logger
  end

  def do_something
    @logger.debug( 'Starting Document load' )
    doc = Document.load( 'resume.txt' )
    @logger.debug( 'Completed Document load' )

    # Do something interesting with the document.

    @logger.debug( 'Starting Document save' )
    doc.save
    @logger.debug( 'Completed Document save' )
  end
end
```

Even better is an explicit log message informing us of disaster:

```
class SomeApplication

  # Rest of the class omitted...
```

```
    def do something
      begin
        @logger.debug( 'Starting Document load' )
        @doc = Document.load( 'resume.txt' )
        @logger.debug( 'Completed Document load' )
      rescue
        @logger.error( 'Load failed!!' )
        raise
      end

      # Do something with the document...

      begin
        @logger.debug( 'Starting Document save' )
        @doc.save
        @logger.debug( 'Completed Document save' )
      rescue
        @logger.error( 'Save failed!!' )
        raise
      end
    end
  end
```

This last bit of code is great. It gives us a full account of the document's adventures as it gets loaded and saved, and even shouts for help if something goes wrong. The only problem with this code is that it's horrible! We have managed to take a couple of simple operations—one lonely line of code to load a document and a similar line to save it—and turned them into a nightmare that goes on for half a page. And it only gets worse from there. Between the load and the save we will probably do something with the document, something that will likely rate its own logging. We might even (gasp!) need to deal with more than one document at a time.

Not only is all this logging code tedious to write, it is also hard to read, which means that we have managed to violate both ends of our "clear and concise code" goal. How can we do better? Perhaps we could write special load and save methods, methods that do the logging for us:

```
class SomeApplication

  # Rest of the class omitted...
```

```ruby
def do_something
  @doc = load_with_logging( 'resume.txt'  )

  # Do something with the document...

  save_with_logging( @doc  )
end

def load_with_logging( doc  )
  begin
    @logger.debug( 'Starting Document load' )
    doc = Document.load( doc )
    @logger.debug( 'Completed Document load' )
  rescue
    @logger.error( 'Load failed!!' )
    raise
  end
  doc
end

def save_with_logging( doc )
  begin
    @logger.debug( 'Starting Document save' )
    doc.save
    @logger.debug( 'Completed Document save' )
  rescue
    @logger.error( 'Save failed!!' )
    raise
  end
end
end
```

The trouble with this approach is that we will need one of these special "with_logging" methods for everything we do. On top of that, each one of our "with_logging" methods will keep endlessly repeating the same logging code.

Fortunately, there is a way out. Delivering code where it is needed is exactly what code blocks do so well. We can hide all of the logging nonsense—complete with its associated exception handling—in a method that takes a code block:

```
class SomeApplication

  def do_something
    with_logging('load') { @doc = Document.load( 'resume.txt' ) }

    # Do something with the document...

    with_logging('save') { @doc.save }
  end

  # Rest of the class omitted...

  def with_logging(description)
    begin
      @logger.debug( "Starting #{description}" )
      yield
      @logger.debug( "Completed #{description}" )
    rescue
      @logger.error( "#{description} failed!!")
      raise
    end
  end
end
```

Take a look at the do_something method in this last example—it's almost back to
its original brevity, but *with logging*. Even better, it's obvious what is going on: We are
loading and saving the document, *with logging*. Best of all, since we can pass an arbitrary block into with_logging, with_logging is completely general; we can do *anything* with logging:

```
class SomeApplication
  def do_something_silly
    with_logging( 'Compute miles in a light year' ) do
      186000 * 60 * 60 * 24 * 365
    end
  end
end
```

When It Absolutely Must Happen

This simple "bury the details in a method that takes a block" technique goes by the name of **execute around**. Use execute around when you have something—like the logging in the previous example—that needs to happen before or after some operation, or when the operation fails with a exception. Instead of laboriously sprinkling intention-obscuring code far and wide, you build a method that takes a code block. Inside the method you do whatever preparation needs doing; in our example it was logging the initial message. Then you call the block, followed by any clean-up work, which in the example was the second log message. You can (and probably should) also catch any exceptions that come roaring out of the block[2] and do the right thing with them.

Now, although the name "execute around" comes from the full-blown idea of a method that does something before and after the block gets executed, there is no rule saying you can't build a slightly degenerate execute around method that omits the after bit:

```ruby
def log_before( description )
  @logger.debug( "Starting #{description}" )
  yield
end
```

Or the before part:

```ruby
def log_after( description )
  yield
  @logger.debug( "Done #{description}" )
end
```

Even if you do leave one or the other parts out, the idea is the same: Execute around uses a code block to interleave some standard bit of processing with whatever it is that the block does.

---

2. Of course, unexpected exceptions never appear in any of my code, but I understand other people do occasionally experience them.

Setting Up Objects with an Initialization Block

Execute around can also help you get your objects initialized. You can, for example, change the Document initialize method to take a block, one that it calls with the new Document instance:

```
class Document
  attr_accessor :title, :author, :content

  def initialize(title, author, content = '')
    @title = title
    @author = author
    @content = content
    yield( self ) if block_given?
  end

  # Rest of the class omitted...
end
```

Doing this allows an application that creates a new document to isolate the code that initializes the new document in the block:

```
new_doc = Document.new( 'US Constitution', 'Madison', '' ) do |d|
  d.content << 'We the people'
  d.content << 'In order to form a more perfect union'
  d.content << 'provide for the common defense'
end
```

Using execute around for initialization is generally less about making sure that things happen in a certain sequence and more about making the code readable: *Here*, it says, *is the code that sets up the new object.*

Dragging Your Scope along with the Block

A key part of doing a successful execute around method is paying attention to what goes into and what comes out of the code block. Let's start with the input side of the equation. Programmers who are still getting used to code blocks will sometimes have the urge to pass lots of arguments from their application code, through the execute around method and down into the code block. For example, you might see something like this:

```ruby
class SomeApplication

  # Rest of the class omitted...

  def do_something
    with_logging('load', nil) { @doc = Document.load( 'book' ) }

    # Do something with the document...

    with_logging('save', @doc) { |the_object| the_object.save }
  end


  def with_logging(description, the_object)
    begin
      @logger.debug( "Starting #{description}" )
      yield( the_object )
      @logger.debug( "Completed #{description}" )
    rescue
      @logger.error( "#{description} failed!!")
      raise
    end
  end
end
```

This code is more complex than it needs to be because it misses a key point about code blocks: All of the variables that are visible just before the opening do or { are still visible inside the code block. Code blocks drag along the scope in which they were created wherever they go. In the last example, this means that @doc object is automatically visible inside the code block—no need to pass it down as an argument.[3]

This doesn't mean that respectable execute around methods don't take any arguments. A good rule of thumb is that the only arguments you should pass from the

---

3. The technical term for objects with this scope dragging property is *closure*, and some Ruby programmers will use the terms *closure* and *block* interchangeably.

application into an execute around method are those that the execute around method itself, not the block, will use. We can see this in our `with_logging` method. We passed in strings like `'Document load'` and `'Document save'` to the `with_logging` method, strings used by the method itself.

Similarly, there is nothing wrong with the execute around method passing arguments that originate in the method itself into the block; in fact, many execute around methods do exactly that. For example, imagine that you need a method that opens a database connection, does something with it, and then ensures that the connection gets closed. You might come up with something like this:

```ruby
def with_database_connection( connection_info )
  connection = Database.new( connection_info )
  begin
    yield( connection )
  ensure
    connection.close
  end
end
```

Note that the `with_database_connection` method creates the new database connection and then passes it into the block.

Carrying the Answers Back

Another thing you need to consider with execute around methods is that the application might want to return something from the block. It would be reasonable, for example, to expect that our light-year computing method would actually return a very large number:

```ruby
def do_something_silly
  with_logging( 'Compute miles in a light year' ) do
    186000 * 60 * 60 * 24 * 365
  end
end
```

It might be reasonable, but right now it won't happen. The rub is that, up to now, all of our `with_logging` methods have simply tossed out the return value from the block. To make the example above work, we need to do something like:

```ruby
def with_logging(description)
  begin
    @logger.debug( "Starting #{description}" )
    return_value = yield
    @logger.debug( "Completed #{description}" )
    return_value
  rescue
    @logger.error( "#{description} failed!!")
    raise
  end
end
```

This new and improved with_logging method captures the return value from the block and returns it as its own return value.

Staying Out of Trouble

Aside from making sure you know what arguments are going into your execute around method and making sure you deliver any return value out of it, the main way to go wrong with execute around is to forget about exceptions. In fact, exception handling is even more important with execute around than it is with iterators, because execute around is all about guarantees. The whole idea of execute around is that the caller is guaranteed that *this* will happen before the code block fires and *that* will happen after. Don't let some stray exception sully the reputation of your method for absolutely, positively getting the job done.

With execute around you also need to consider the human factor: A critical difference between just using execute around and really applying it elegantly lies in the name you pick for your method. A good name should make sense in the context of the application code, the code that is calling the method. Don't think of it so much as naming a new method as naming a new feature that you are adding to the Ruby language.

To see what I mean, imagine that we had been a little less careful in naming our logging execute around method:

```ruby
execute_between_logging_statements( "update" ) do
  employee.load
  employee.status = :retired
  employee.save
end
```

Somehow the code above just doesn't sing to you the way this does:

```
with_logging( "update" ) do
  employee.load
  employee.status = :retired
  employee.save
end
```

Sure, we all know that no matter what the name is, it is just a method call. But if you blur your vision a little you can imagine that `with_logging` is an actual bit of Ruby syntax, like `while` or `if`. In fact, your imagination would not be that far off: After defining the `with_logging` method, you now have a language that not only will let you conditionally execute code with an `if` statement and repeatedly execute some code in a `while` loop, but also will let you execute some code wrapped in logging with `with_logging`.

In the Wild

If the `open_database` example of a few pages ago seems strangely familiar, it should—I modeled it on the very familiar `File.open` method that comes with Ruby:

```
# No open file here.

File.open('/etc/passwd') do |f|
  # File open here!
  # Begin cracking the passwords on Russ' computer...
end

# The password file is guaranteed to be closed here.
```

It's also easy to find execute around used to initialize objects. Part of building a Ruby gem, for example, is creating a `Gem::Specification` instance, which describes your new gem in excruciating detail. Here's Rake in the process of filling in its specification:

```
SPEC = Gem::Specification.new do |s|

  #### Basic information.
```

```
s.name = 'rake'
s.version = $package_version
s.summary = "Ruby based make-like utility."
s.description = <<-EOF
  Rake is a Make-like program implemented in Ruby. Tasks
  and dependencies are specified in standard Ruby syntax.
EOF

# Lots and lots omitted!
end
```

By letting you put all the initialization code in the block, the Gem::Specification initialize method is helping you make your code a bit easier to read. This is code block as a literary device!

You can find another real-world example of execute around in the ActiveRecord say_with_time method. Here is say_with_time along with its buddy, say:

```
class Migration
  # Most of the class omitted...

  def say(message, subitem=false)
    write "#{subitem ? "   ->" : "--"} #{message}"
  end

  def say_with_time(message)
    say(message)
    result = nil
    time = Benchmark.measure { result = yield }
    say "%.4fs" % time.real, :subitem
    say("#{result} rows", :subitem) if result.is_a?(Integer)
    result
  end
end
```

As you can see, the say_with_time method takes a string argument as well as a block. When you call say_with_time it executes the block and then prints your message along with the amount of time that it took to execute the block.

Finally, since we have spent so much time in this chapter talking about using execute around to add logging to your code, we should probably also give equal time to the ActiveRecord silence method, which turns logging off[4] for the duration of a code block.

Wrapping Up

In this chapter we have looked at the execute around technique. Execute around can help you cope with those times when you have code that frequently needs to come before or after some other code, or both. Execute around suggests that you build a method that takes a block; inside of that method you execute whatever code needs executing before and after you call the block. Creating an execute around method is simple, but, like any method that you build, you do need to pay attention to get the maximum mileage. Name your execute around method carefully—keeping in mind how the method will be used—and pay particular attention to the arguments, both those that go into the method and those that pass between the method and the block.

---

4. Technically, silence turns the logging level up (or is it down?) to ERROR.

CHAPTER 19

Save Blocks to Execute Later

It's hard to believe, but we are not done with code blocks yet. There is still one more bit of software goodness that we can squeeze out of the programming construct that keeps on giving. Two chapters ago we called on code blocks as iterators to sequence through collections. In the last chapter we looked to the block as a mechanism for delivering the right code to the right context. The topic of this chapter is similar to the last: using blocks as a device for delivering your code where it is needed. The difference is that, while the execute around technique was all about getting your code to the right place, this chapter will focus on using blocks to transport your code through time. In the pages that follow, we are going to learn how you can grab hold of the code block that is passed into your method and simply hang on to it until you need it.

Explicit Blocks

So far in our adventures with code blocks we have used `block_given?` to determine whether someone has passed in a code block to a method and `yield` to fire off the block. As we have seen, `block_given?` and `yield` rely on the fact that Ruby treats a code block appended to the end of a method call as a sort of implicit parameter to the call, a parameter that only `yield` and `block_given?` know how to get at.

However, implicitly is not the only way to pass blocks to your methods. If you add a parameter prefixed with an ampersand to the end of your parameter list,[1] Ruby will turn any block passed into the method into a garden-variety parameter. After you have captured a block with an explicit parameter, you can run it by calling its `call` method. Here, for example, is a very simple method with an explicit code block parameter:

```
def run_that_block( &that_block )
  puts "About to run the block"
  that_block.call
  puts "Done running the block"
end
```

It's also trivially easy to figure out whether the caller actually did pass in a block: Just check to see if the value of the block parameter is `nil`:

```
that_block.call if that_block
```

Explicit code blocks are easy and clear enough that some Ruby programmers (including me!) habitually use them rather than the implicit variety. Explicit block parameters make it easy to determine at a glance which methods expect a code block. Methods with an explicit code block parameter can also treat the block as an ordinary object instead of some freakish special case. Stylistic considerations aside, explicit code block parameters allow you to do something that is impossible with the implicit variety: When you use explicit block parameters, you can hold onto the block and store a reference to it like any other object. And that means you can execute the block later, perhaps much later, possibly long after the method that caught the block has returned.

The Call Back Problem

To see the utility of being able to hold on to code blocks, let's imagine that some of your colleagues are writing CopyEdit, a word-processing program built around your Document object. The CopyEdit folks are thrilled with the Zenlike simplicity of your Document class, but they have requested an enhancement. They need a call back to go

---

1. The phrase "end of your parameter list" really does mean the end. The &block parameter goes after all the other stuff in your parameter list, including those starred catch-all parameters.

off when the document is read from a file, and another that will fire when the document is saved.

The traditional way to solve this problem is to build separate listener objects, something like this:

```ruby
class DocumentSaveListener
  def on_save( doc, path)
    puts "Hey, I've been saved!"
  end
end

class DocumentLoadListener
  def on_load( doc, path)
    puts "Hey I've been loaded!"
  end
end
```

You then give your documents references to the listeners and call the methods at the right time:

```ruby
class Document

  attr_accessor :load_listener
  attr_accessor :save_listener

  # Most of the class omitted...

  def load( path )
    @content = File.read( path )
    load_listener.on_load( self, path ) if load_listener
  end

  def save( path )
    File.open( path, 'w') { |f| f.print( @contents ) }
    save_listener.on_save( self, path ) if save_listener
  end
end
```

Armed with all this, you can hook up your listener to a document and find out when the document gets loaded and saved:

```
doc = Document.new( 'Example', 'Russ', 'It was a dark...' )
doc.load_listener = DocumentLoadListener.new
doc.save_listener = DocumentSaveListener.new

doc.load( 'example.txt' )
doc.save( 'example.txt' )
```

Run the code above and you will see:

```
Hey I've been loaded!
Hey, I've been saved!
```

This listener class approach has some real advantages. The listening code is separate from the inner workings of the Document class, and you can swap different listeners in and out whenever you like. The trouble with separate listener classes is that, well, they are a lot of trouble. To make the traditional listener object approach work you need to create those listener classes, instantiate them, and manage their relationships with your documents.

Banking Blocks

A different, and really elegant, way to solve the call back problem is to use explicit code block parameters. Think about it: When you capture a code block in an explicit parameter, you end up with an object that has a single method (the call method) containing some code. Isn't this exactly what we laboriously built when we created the DocumentSaveListener and DocumentLoadListener classes?

Here's our Document class rewritten to use code blocks as call backs:

```
class Document

  # Most of the class omitted...

  def on_save( &block )
    @save_listener = block
  end
```

```ruby
  def on_load( &block )
    @load_listener = block
  end

  def load( path )
    @content = File.read( path )
    @load_listener.call( self, path ) if @load_listener
  end

  def save( path )
    File.open( path, 'w' ) { |f| f.print( @contents ) }
    @save_listener.call( self, path ) if @save_listener
  end
end
```

Listening for the comings and goings of documents is now much simpler; no need for those extra listener objects:

```ruby
my_doc = Document.new( 'Block Based Example', 'russ', '' )

my_doc.on_load do |doc|
  puts "Hey, I've been loaded!"
end

my_doc.on_save do |doc|
  puts "Hey, I've been saved!"
end
```

Not only is the block-based version shorter, using the on_load and on_save methods has a nice declarative feel to it—concise and clear.

Saving Code Blocks for Lazy Initialization

Being able to capture a code block for later use opens ups other possibilities: For example, you can use saved code blocks for lazy initialization. To see how this works, let's return to the problem of creating lazy documents. This time, imagine that we need to deal with a large number of archival documents. Mostly we just need the title and author of the document so that we can display them to the user, but occasionally we

need the actual content. It would be nice if we could avoid reading the content until
we absolutely need it. To this end, we might do something like this:

```ruby
class ArchivalDocument
  attr_reader :title, :author

  def initialize(title, author,  path)
    @title = title
    @author = author
    @path = path
  end

  def content
    @content ||= File.read( @path )
  end
end
```

At first glance the solution shown here seems fine, but it does have one real draw-
back. The problem is that the ArchivalDocument class knows all about where the document content comes from: a file. Contrast this with the original Document class, which
neither knew nor cared where its contents originated. With ArchivalDocument, if you
suddenly decide you want to get your document text via HTTP or FTP, well, you are
kind of stuck.

Fortunately, we can fix this problem with a simple wave of our saved-code-block
wand. Instead of passing in a path when we make a new ArchivalDocument instance,
we pass in a block, one that returns the document contents when it is called:

```ruby
class BlockBasedArchivalDocument
  attr_reader :title, :author

  def initialize(title, author, &block)
    @title = title
    @author = author
    @initializer_block = block
  end

  def content
    if @initializer_block
      @content = @initializer_block.call
      @initializer_block = nil
```

```
      end
    @content
  end
end
```

This latest implementation means we can still get our document contents from a file, like this:

```
file_doc = BlockBasedArchivalDocument.new( 'file', 'russ' ) do
  File.read( 'some_text.txt' )
end
```

But we can also get them via HTTP:

```
google_doc = BlockBasedArchivalDocument.new('http', 'russ') do
  Net::HTTP.get_response('www.google.com', '/index.html').body
end
```

Or just make something up:

```
boring_doc = BlockBasedArchivalDocument.new('silly', 'russ') do
  'Ya' * 100
end
```

The examples above look a lot like the initialization block examples we saw in the last chapter, but there is a critical difference. In those earlier examples, the `initialize` method called the code block immediately as the object was being constructed. In contrast, the `BlockBasedArchivalDocument` class waits until someone actually calls the `content` method before firing off the block. In fact, if you never call `content`, then the block will never get called. By using a code block, we get the best of both worlds. We can conjure up the document contents in any way we want, and the conjuring is delayed until we actually need it.

Instant Block Objects

Sometimes it's handy to produce a code block object right here, right now. You want to get hold of the object version of a block, which is actually an instance of the `Proc` class, without creating a method to catch it. You might, for example, want to create a block object that you can use as the default value for your document listeners. Fortunately, Ruby supplies you with a method for just such an occasion: `lambda`. Here is our earlier document example, the one with the listeners, rewritten to use `lambda` to create a default `Proc` object.

```ruby
class Document
  DEFAULT_LOAD_LISTENER = lambda do |doc, path|
    puts "Loaded: #{path}"
  end

  DEFAULT_SAVE_LISTENER = lambda do |doc, path|
    puts "Saved: #{path}"
  end

  attr_accessor :title, :author, :content

  def initialize( title, author, content='' )
    @title = title
    @author = author
    @content = content
    @save_listener = DEFAULT_SAVE_LISTENER
    @load_listener = DEFAULT_LOAD_LISTENER
  end

  # Rest of the class omitted...
end
```

The idea behind the `lambda` method is that you pass it a code block and the method will pass the corresponding `Proc` object right back at you.

Staying Out of Trouble

When it comes to creating `Proc` objects, beware of false friends. Although calling `Proc.new` is nearly synonymous with `lambda`:

```ruby
from_proc_new = Proc.new { puts "hello from a block" }
```

It's not quite synonymous enough. The object you get back from `Proc.new` differs from what you would get back from `lambda` in two key ways. One relatively innocuous difference is that a `Proc.new` object is very forgiving of the number of arguments passed to its `call` method. Pass too few and it will set the excess block parameters to `nil`; pass too many and it will quietly ignore the extra arguments. In contrast, the `call` method on an object returned by `lambda` acts more like a regular method and will throw an exception if you mess up the argument count.

The second difference is much more critical. Objects from `Proc.new` feature all of the interesting `return`, `break`, and `next` behavior that we touched on in the last couple of chapters. For example, if a `Proc.new` block executes an explicit `return`, Ruby will try to return not just from the block but from the *method that created the block*. This behavior is great for iterators, but it can be a disaster for applications that hang onto code blocks long after the method that created them has returned. In contrast, the `Proc` object returned from `lambda` acts more like a portable method—a return from a `lambda` wrapped block will simply return *from the block* and no further.

Although the issues are deep, the lessons are simple. Lesson one is that if you are calling a method that takes a block, pause for a second before you put a `return`, `next`, or `break` in that block. Does it make sense here? Lesson two is that if you want a block object that behaves like the ones that Ruby generates when you pass a couple of braces into a method, use `Proc.new`. If you want something that will behave more like a regular object with a single method, use `lambda`.[2]

You can also get into trouble with the closure nature of code blocks. The fact that code blocks drag along the variables from the code that defines them is mostly a convenience, but it can also have unexpected and unpleasant consequences. Mostly this has to do with variables staying in scope, and therefore in existence, for longer than you might expect. For example, suppose you write a method that needs to create a large array, one that it will use for a short while. No problem: Just keep the array in a local variable in the method and the array will go out of scope when the method returns:

```ruby
def some_method( doc )
  big_array = Array.new( 10000000 )

  # Do something with big_array...

end
```

---

2. Just to make things even more exciting, Ruby supports a third way to create `Proc` instances, the `proc` method. The interesting bit is that in 1.8, `proc` was synonymous with `lambda`. In 1.9 it is more like `Proc.new`. Some days I wonder why I get of bed.

So far, so good. But what if you happen to create one of those long-lasting blocks while that large array is still in scope?

```
def some_method( doc )
  big_array = Array.new( 10000000 )

  # Do something with big_array...

  doc.on_load do |d|
    puts "Hey, I've been loaded!"
  end
end
```

What happens is this: Because the big array was in scope when you created the block and the block drags along the local environment with it, the block holds onto a reference to the array—even if it never uses it. This means that the array, with all ten million elements, is going to stay around for as long as the block does, in this case as long as the document is around. Once you are aware of what is going on, a very simple solution offers itself:

```
def some_method(doc)
  big_array = Array.new(10000000)

  # Do something with big_array...

  # And now get rid of it!

  big_array = nil

  doc.on_load do |d|
    puts "Hey, I've been loaded!"
  end
end
```

The lesson here is not that holding onto block references is dangerous, but that you should keep in mind the stuff that you might be unconsciously dragging along with your blocks.

In the Wild

We caught a glimpse of saved code blocks way back in Chapter 9 when we looked at RSpec. If you look at a spec:

```
it "should know how many words it contains" do
  doc = Document.new('example', 'russ', 'hello world')
  doc.word_count.should == 2
end
```

You will see an example of a code block that gets saved for use later. In this case, later comes when RSpec runs all the tests.

You can also find lots of saved code blocks in Rails. There are, for example, the filters you can set up in your controller:

```
class DocumentController < ActionController::Base
  before_filter do | controller |
    # Do something before each action...
  end

  # Rest of the controller...
end
```

As well as the life-cycle hooks in ActiveRecord:

```
class DocumentVersion < ActiveRecord::Base
  after_destroy do | doc_version |
    # My Document is gone!
  end
end
```

Both Rails methods say, "Here's a code block, hang onto it and run it when the time is right."

Both Rake and Capistrano also make extensive use of saved code blocks. Both tools are built around the idea of a task—some defined bit of work that occasionally needs doing, the difference being that while Rake focuses on doing things here on your local machine, Capistrano seeks to rule, or at least configure, machines scattered across the network.

Rake and Capistrano capture what needs to be done in blocks, which they salt away until the time is right. Here is a very simple Capistrano task that knows how to list the /home directory on the production machines:

```
desc "List the home directories"
task :list_home, :role => 'production' do
  run "ls -l /home"
end
```

If you pull the covers off of Capistrano, you will find some familiar-looking code. Here, for example, is the Capistrano task method:[3]

```
def task(name, options={}, &block)
  name = name.to_sym
  raise ArgumentError, "expected a block" unless block_given?

  # Some code deleted...

  tasks[name] = TaskDefinition.new( name, self,
    {:desc => next_description(:reset)}.merge(options), &block)

  # Some more code deleted...
end
```

For our purposes the key bit of the task method is right there at the end. Notice how the code passes &block into the TaskDefinition constructor. The TaskDefinition class holds onto the block, ready to fire it off should Capistrano decide that this is the task that needs to be done.

Wrapping Up

In this chapter we finished our look at code blocks by seeing them as long-lived containers for Ruby code. We saw how, by using explicit block parameters, you can delay running the code inside of a block until you need it. We looked at a couple of practical applications of this including using code blocks as call backs, whereby your object

---

3. Edited, as they say on television, to fit your screen.

grabs a code block and executes it when some event occurs. We also saw how you can use code blocks to effect lazy initialization. Since there are rarely silver linings without dark clouds, we also looked at how the code block habit of vacuuming up all the variables in scope when you create the block can turn on you if you are not careful.

Although this chapter completes our hard look at code blocks, we're not really done with them. Code blocks are such an important part of Ruby programming that they will continue to pop right up until the end of this book. For now we are going to turn our attention to Ruby's system of programming hooks, a mechanism devoted to keeping you informed about what's happening as your application runs. It turns out that one way of doing this is to let you supply a code block and . . . . Well, perhaps we should leave that for the next chapter.

PART III

Metaprogramming

CHAPTER 20

Use Hooks to Keep Your Program Informed

Metaprogramming is one of those words that seems to exist purely to scare people. Are we talking about programming beyond programming? Programming turned up to 11? Programming in the next dimension? In fact, metaprogramming—at least as it is practiced in the Ruby world—is a very workman set of coding techniques that allow you to get the results you need with less code. Ruby support for metaprogramming starts by allowing your code to stay amazingly well informed about what's going on around it. With a tiny bit of effort, you can write Ruby programs that know when a new class is created, when a method gets called, and even when the application is about to exit. Of course, all this knowledge would be so much trivia if your program couldn't do anything about it. Fortunately, Ruby programs can do all sorts of things: They can decide that there are still just a few details to take care of before the application exits. They can decide that this error is not really an error but a reasonable request. And they can even reprogram themselves.

In this chapter we will begin our exploration of metaprogramming with the "staying informed" side of the equation by looking at hooks. A Ruby hook is some way—sometimes by supplying a block and sometimes by just overriding a method—to specify the code to be executed when something specific happens. We are going to see how you can use hooks to find out that a class has gained a new subclass, or that a module has been included, or that your program is getting ready to terminate. As usual, we will spend time talking about how you would use these features, and also about how you might stay away from the pointy end of the hook.

Waking Up to a New Subclass

As I say, a **hook** is code that gets called to tell you that something is about to happen or has already happened. A great example of a hook is the one that tells you when a class gains a subclass. To stay informed of the appearance of new subclasses, you define a class-level method called `inherited`. To see how this might work, let's define a very simple base class that does indeed define `inherited`:

```
class SimpleBaseClass
  def self.inherited( new_subclass )
    puts "Hey #{new_subclass} is now a subclass of #{self}!"
  end
end
```

To see the `inherited` method in action, we just need to create a subclass:

```
class ChildClassOne < SimpleBaseClass
end
```

Define the `ChildClassOne` class and the `SimpleBaseClass` `inherited` hook will fire and print this:

```
Hey ChildClassOne is now a subclass of SimpleBaseClass!
```

The `inherited` hook is not a very complicated feature, but one question does immediately spring to mind: What the heck would we ever do with it? Well, you might manage a list of subclasses. To see how you could do that—and why it might be useful—imagine that you have documents stored in many different file formats. Some are stored in plain text files, some are in YAML files,[1] and some, sadly, might actually be stuck in XML files.

Since you do have a fair number of formats, it seems wise to separate the file-reading code from the `Document` class itself. That way you won't have a lot of file format conversion machinery cluttering up the `Document` class. Instead, you'll write a series of reader classes, where each reader class understands a single format and knows how to

---

1. YAML is a structured file format similar to, but more human friendly than, XML. If you have ever created a Rails database.yml file, you know what YAML looks like.

turn a file in that format into a Document instance. The simplest of the bunch is the one that reads plain text files:

```ruby
class PlainTextReader < DocumentReader
  def self.can_read?(path)
    /.*\.txt/ =~ path
  end

  def initialize(path)
    @path = path
  end

  def read(path)
    File.open(path) do |f|
      title = f.readline.chomp
      author = f.readline.chomp
      content = f.read.chomp
      Document.new( title, author, content )
    end
  end
end
```

Ignoring the DocumentReader superclass, which we will come to in a minute, the PlainTextReader class is about as straightforward as they come. It has an initialize method that picks up the path to the plain text file and a read method that actually turns the contents of that file into a Document instance. The one little twist is the can_read? method: This class method returns true if the PlainTextReader is able to read the file whose path is passed in as an argument. In real life, can_read? would probably peek at the first few bytes of the file to see whether it is in a recognizable format. But to keep the example simple, PlainTextReader actually just looks at the file extension: If the name of the file ends in .txt, then PlainTextReader assumes it is up to reading the file.

We can also define similar readers for YAML and XML:

```ruby
class YAMLReader < DocumentReader
  def self.can_read?(path)
    /.*\.yaml/ =~ path
  end
```

```
    def initialize(path)
      @path = path
    end

    def read(path)
      # Lots of simple YAML stuff omitted
    end
  end

  class XMLReader < DocumentReader
    def self.can_read?(path)
      /.*\.xml/ =~ path
    end

    def initialize(path)
      @path = path
    end

    def read(path)
      # Lots of complicated XML stuff omitted
    end
  end
```

You now have all the parts needed to read the different file formats, but the question is, how do you pull them together? Ideally you would have a list of all of the reader classes, a list that the code could search looking for a class that is able to read a given file. This is where the DocumentReader superclass comes in:

```
class DocumentReader

  class << self
    attr_reader :reader_classes
  end

  @reader_classes = [ ]

  def self.read(path)
    reader = reader_for(path)
    return nil unless reader
    reader.read(path)
  end
```

```
def self.reader_for(path)
  reader_class = DocumentReader.reader_classes.find do |klass|
    klass.can_read?(path)
  end
  return reader_class.new(path) if reader_class
  nil
end


# One critical bit omitted, but stay tuned...
end
```

DocumentReader sports the ultimate read method, a class method that takes a path,
calls the reader_for method to find a reader for the path, and then uses that reader
to read the file. The reader_for method looks through the @reader_classes array
trying to find a volunteer to read the file.

So here is the 64-gigabyte question: How do you populate the @reader_classes
array? Why, with the inherited hook:

```
# ... the vital missing piece

def self.inherited(subclass)
  DocumentReader.reader_classes << subclass
end
```

Every time you define a new DocumentReader subclass—in other words, a new
file reader—the DocumentReader inherited hook will go off and add the new class
to the running list of readers. That list of reader classes is exactly what the code needs
when it is time to find the correct reader for a file. The beauty of doing it this way is
that the programmer does not need to maintain the list by hand. You simply make
sure that all of the reader classes are subclasses of DocumentReader and things take care
of themselves.

Modules Want To Be Heard Too

The module analog of inherited is included. As the name suggests, included gets
called when a module gets included in a class. So, if we were interested in knowing
when our writing-quality module was included in a class, we might add an included
hook:

```
module WritingQuality
  def self.included(klass)
    puts "Hey, I've been included in #{klass}"
  end

  def number_of_cliches
    # Body of method omitted...
  end
end
```

A common use for the `included` hook is to add some class methods to the including class as your module gets included. Recall from Chapter 16 that when you include a module in your class, all of the module's instance methods suddenly show up as instance methods in the class. So, if you include the `WritingQuality` module in a class, instances of that class will suddenly start sporting the `WritingQuality` method `number_of_cliches`. We've also seen that if you pull a module into a class with `extend`, the module's methods become *class* methods of the class.

A sticky question is this: What should you do if you have a combination of class and instance methods that you want to mix into a class as a unit? You could simply create two modules, one for the instance methods and one for the class methods, and have your host classes do both an `include` and an `extend`, like this:

```
module UsefulInstanceMethods
  def an_instance_method
  end
end

module UsefulClassMethods
  def a_class_method
  end
end

class Host
  include UsefulInstanceMethods
  extend UsefulClassMethods
end
```

Making the class go through both an `include` and an `extend` isn't horrible, but it's not elegant either. It would be better if you could get all of the goodness of your modules mixed in, in one go. Fortunately you can. Remember that a module can find out when it is included in a class via the `included` hook. From there we just need a little bit of ingenuity to get the class methods mixed in:

```ruby
module UsefulMethods
  module ClassMethods
    def a_class_method
    end
  end

  def self.included( host_class )
    host_class.extend( ClassMethods )
  end

  def an_instance_method
  end

  # Rest of the module deleted...
end

class Host
  include UsefulMethods
end
```

Knocking off the extra step required to mix in the class methods may seem like a little thing, and it is. Good code is, however, built from just these tiny bits of courtesy.

Knowing When Your Time Is Up

The `at_exit` hook is the Ruby's equivalent of the Grim Reaper: It only drops in when you—or rather, your Ruby application—is on its way out. The `at_exit` hook gets called just before the Ruby interpreter exits, and this is your last chance to get a word in before it's all over. Using `at_exit` is a bit different from the other hooks we have seen. Instead of overriding something, with `at_exit` you just *call* `at_exit` with a block:

```
at_exit do
  puts "Have a nice day."
end
```

The Ruby interpreter will fire off the block just before it expires. An advantage of this code-block approach is that you can call at_exit several times, passing in different blocks each time. So along with the at_exit above, we might also do:

```
at_exit do
  puts "Goodbye"
end
```

If you do call at_exit more than once, then when your application is ready to exit each block will get called in "last in/first out" order. Thus, if we did the two at_exit calls in the order shown above, the final words of our program would be:

```
Goodbye
Have a nice day.
```

Such a polite program.

. . . And a Cast of Thousands

While inherited, included, and at_exit are among the most useful—and widely used—hooks that Ruby offers, they are by no means the only ones. The most notable of these remaining hooks is method_missing, which we will save for the next three chapters. A less famous, but occasionally useful hook is method_added that allows you to listen for new methods being added to a class. You can also listen for changes to global variables with trace_var.

The ultimate Ruby hook, however, has got to be set_trace_func. With this handy little method you can supply a block that will get called whenever a method gets called or returns, whenever a class definition is opened with the class keyword or closed with an end, whenever an exception get raised, and whenever—and here's the kicker—a line of code gets executed. This, for example, is one way to find out just how complicated date processing can be:

```
proc_object = proc do |event, file, line, id, binding, klass|
  puts "#{event} in #{file}/#{line} #{id} #{klass}"
end

set_trace_func(proc_object)

require 'date'
```

This code sets up a block to do tracing duty and then requires in date.rb from the Ruby standard library. Run the code and you will see something like this:

```
c-return in trace_func_demo.rb/5 set_trace_func Kernel
line in trace_func_demo.rb/7
c-call in trace_func_demo.rb/7 require Kernel
c-call in trace_func_demo.rb/7 set_encoding IO
c-return in trace_func_demo.rb/7 set_encoding IO
c-call in trace_func_demo.rb/7 set_encoding IO
c-return in trace_func_demo.rb/7 set_encoding IO
line in /home/russ/ruby1.9/lib/ruby/1.9.1/date.rb/196
...
```

In full, this output goes on for more than 2,000 lines—and that's just to read in date.rb. This loquaciousness underlines the main issue with set_trace_func: It's a little too much of a good thing. Turn on set_trace_func and prepare to be overwhelmed with data. Still, it's nice to know it's there if you need it.

Staying Out of Trouble

It may seem obvious, but the key to using Ruby hooks is knowing exactly when they will or will not get called. This can be more complicated than it seems. Take, for example, our DocumentReader that depends on the inherited hook. If all of our reader subclasses are in the same file with the DocumentReader file, then it is pretty obvious when the inherited method will go off—shortly after the Ruby interpreter reads the end statement of each subclass:

```
class DocumentReader
  # Stuff omitted...
end
```

```
class PlainTextReader < DocumentReader
  # Stuff omitted...
end


# inherited method for PlainTextReader goes off about now...


class YAMLReader < DocumentReader
  # Stuff omitted...
end


# inherited method for YAMLReader goes off about now...
```

Now consider what would happen if we break this code up into several files, with one reader class per file and we require them in:

```
require 'document_reader'


require 'plaintext_reader'   # inherited fires for PlainTextReader
require 'xml_reader'         # inherited fires for XMLReader
require 'yaml_reader'        # inherited fires for YAMLReader
```

The principal remains the same: The `inherited` method will get called just after each subclass is defined, but now it is obscured by the separate files and the `require` statements.

An even bigger surprise is in store if you happen to have a more complex document reader class hierarchy. What if you had some readers that were similar enough that it made sense to build a common subclass:

```
class AsianDocumentReader < DocumentReader
  # Lots of code for dealing with Asian languages...
end


class JapaneseDocumentReader <  AsianDocumentReader
  # Lots of stuff omitted...
end


class ChineseDocumentReader <  AsianDocumentReader
  # Lots of stuff omitted...
end
```

The problem is that this code is going to trigger a `DocumentReader.inherited` call *three* times, once each for the Japanese and Chinese readers and—perhaps unexpectedly—once for the `AsianDocumentReader`. After all, `AsianDocumentReader` is very much a subclass of `DocumentReader`. There are a number of ways to cope with this kind of situation, but in this case it's easiest to just make sure that the `AsianDocumentReader` class never volunteers to read anything:

```ruby
class AsianDocumentReader < DocumentReader
  def self.can_read?(path)
    false
  end

  # Lots of code for dealing with Asian languages...
end
```

The lesson here is that the `inherited` method fires for all of the subclasses, not just the ones you happened to be interested in.

Sometimes the problem is not with hooks getting called too often. Sometimes it's that they don't get called at all. For example, your helpful Ruby interpreter will try to ensure that the `at_exit` blocks do get called right before things shut down. Sometimes, such as during a program or system crash, your Ruby interpreter isn't able to make good on the `at_exit` promise. The bottom line is that to use hooks effectively you need to know exactly when they will be called.

In the Wild

Now let's clear up a mystery that has been with us since way back in Chapter 9. Recall that when we were talking about the `Test::Unit` framework we wondered how, if you had a test in a file, say `simple_test.rb`:

```ruby
require 'test/unit'

class SimpleTest < Test::Unit::TestCase
  def test_addition
    assert_equal 2, 1 + 1
  end
end
```

And you executed that file:

```
$ ruby simple_test.rb
```

The test would run:

```
Loaded suite simple_test
Started
.
Finished in 0.000247 seconds.

1 tests, 1 assertions, 0 failures, 0 errors
```

The question is, how did the test get run? After all, we didn't write a main program into simple_test.rb; we just wrote the test class and it seems to run itself.
You've probably already guessed the answer: Look inside Test::Unit and you will see
that it uses at_exit to trigger the test just before the Ruby interpreter exits. Here is
the actual code:

```
at_exit do
  unless $! || Test::Unit.run?
    exit Test::Unit::AutoRunner.run
  end
end
```

This actually is a fairly sophisticated bit of Ruby: The unless statement in the
at_exit block first looks at the $! variable[2] to see whether there has been an error and
does nothing if there has been. This check prevents Test::Unit from trying to run
the tests in the face of gross problems like syntax errors in the test code itself. If $! is
nil, the unless statement next checks to see whether the tests have already been run.
It is possible, using the Test::Unit API, to run the tests manually, and if that is the
case Test::Unit doesn't want to run them a second time. If neither of these conditions apply, then Test::Unit will happily—and automatically—run your tests for
you.

---

2. $! is a global variable that Ruby sets to the last exception raised.

Wrapping Up

In this chapter we looked at several of the Ruby hooks that allow you to get some code executed at key moments in the life of your Ruby application. We examined in some detail three of the most common hooks, starting with the `inherited` method that keeps you in the know when a subclass is added to some class. We also looked at module `included` method that lets you know when a module is included in some class, and finally at the `at_exit` hook that lets you get in a word before the Ruby interpreter exits. We saw how the `inherited` hook can be used to allow a class to keep track of its subclasses, how `included` can be used to modify a class as it includes a module, and how `at_exit` is used by `Test::Unit` to run tests automatically. We also saw that our list of three is by no means exhaustive. There are lots of other Ruby hooks, all of them dedicated to letting your code know what is going on.

CHAPTER 21

Use method_missing for Flexible Error Handling

My car worries too much. Well it's not the whole car, it's just the little embedded computer that lurks behind the door locks. That little processor seems to live in dread that I might someday accidentally leave my car unlocked. Thus, it devotes its whole being to making sure that no door stays unlocked for too long. I'm usually OK if I unlock the car and jump right in. But woe to me if I unlock the car and get a phone call. The time it takes to look at my cell phone to see who's calling is apparently too long by the exacting standards of Toyota, and the doors relock. They'll also lock in the time it takes to throw some groceries into the trunk. Or to kiss my wife goodbye. There have even been one or two occasions when the doors have locked on me a second time, in the interval it took for the initial rage to dissipate.

This kind of problem is not confined to cars. Whenever someone builds a system to handle an error condition there is always the chance that they will get it just a little wrong. You certainly see it in all kinds of software systems. People make mistakes often enough that it's useful to build software that helps deal with those mistakes. The problem is that sometimes the mitigating behavior is not quite right and you can't change it. Ideally, a good error-handing system will have some default behavior, but will also let you vary that behavior if you need to.

It's in that spirit that we're going to spend this chapter looking at `method_missing`, a feature of Ruby that allows you to handle a particular error condition: Someone has called a method that does not in fact exist. We will see how you can use `method_missing` to customize the way your code deals with this class of errors. We will also spend some time looking at `method_missing`'s close cousin, `const_missing`, and see how we can use it to increase the flexibility of our programs in some surprising ways.

Meeting Those Missing Methods

Imagine that the higher-ups in your company have decided to make the `Document` class the standard for manipulating text documents. Suddenly your little coding work of art goes from being used by a few departments to being the bytes behind the whole enterprise. For the most part the transition goes well, but you do get a series of bug reports from less-experienced engineers stating that the `Document` class "doesn't work" or that it is "utterly broken." Some of the reports say things like "I tried to get the text out of a `Document` instance and just got an exception." You think that the code does work,[1] so it seems likely that the cause of the trouble is pilot error, probably by doing something like this:

```
# Error: the method is content, not text!

doc = Document.new('Titanic', 'Cameron', 'Sail, crash, sink')
puts "The text is #{doc.text}"
```

You *think* this is what's going on, but how can you be sure?

One way to find out lies in the details of how Ruby calls a method, and, in particular, what it does when the method it is trying to call is not actually there. Take the previous example where the code tries to call a nonexistent `text` method on a `Document` instance. Initially, Ruby will look for the `text` method in the `Document` class and, failing to find it there, it will look in the superclass for `text`, and on up the line. If Ruby finds the method anywhere in the inheritance tree, then that's the method that gets called.

The real question is, what happens if, as with the phantom `text`, there just is no such method? The quick answer is that you get an exception. The not-so-quick answer is more interesting: When Ruby fails to find a method, it turns around and calls a second method. This second call, to a method with the somewhat odd name of `method_missing`, is what eventually generates the exception: It's the default imple-

---

1. Actually, given that you have tests, you *know* it works.

mentation of `method_missing`, found in the `Object` class[2] that raises the `NameError` exception.

The upshot of all of this is that you don't have to accept this default error-handing behavior. You are free to override `method_missing` in any of your classes and handle the case of the missing method yourself:

```
class RepeatBackToMe
  def method_missing( method_name, *args )
    puts "Hey, you just called the #{method_name} method"
    puts "With these arguments: #{args.join(' ')}"
    puts "But there ain't no such method"
  end
end
```

As you can see from this code, `method_missing` gets passed the name of the original method that was called along with the augments it was called with. If you make an instance of `RepeatBackToMe` and call some nonexistent methods on the instance, like this:

```
repeat = RepeatBackToMe.new
repeat.hello( 1, 2, 3 )
repeat.good_bye( "for", "now" )
```

Then `method_missing` will eventually fire and give you its cheerful summary of what just happened:

```
Hey, you just called the hello method
With these arguments: 1 2 3
But there ain't no such method
Hey, you just called the good_bye method
With these arguments: for now
But there ain't no such method
```

---

2. More specifically, the default `method_missing` actually lives in the `Kernel` module, which is included by `Object`.

Handling Document Errors

The method_missing method is tailor-made to help with the kind of problems you
are having with your new Document users. At the very least, you can give them a customized message if they call a bad method:

```
class Document
  # Most of the class omitted...

  def method_missing( method_name, *args )
    msg =  %Q{
      You tried to call the method #{method_name}
        on an instance of Document. There is no such method.
    }
    raise msg
  end
end
```

Alternatively, you could return the same old error message, but quietly log the
details of the mishap for later analysis:

```
class Document
  # Most of the class omitted...

  def method_missing( method_name, *args )
    File.open( 'document.error', 'a' ) do |f|
      f.puts( "Bad method called: #{method_name}" )
      f.puts( "with #{args.size} arguments" )
    end
    super
  end
end
```

You might even apply a little of that Ruby style programming customer service
and try to help your user figure out which method he or she really meant:

```
require 'text'  # From the text gem

class Document
  include Text
```

```
      # Most of the class omitted...

   def method_missing( missing, *args )
     candidates = methods_that_sound_like( missing.to_s )

     message = "You called an undefined method: #{missing}."

     unless candidates.empty?
       message += "\nDid you mean #{candidates.join(' or ')}?"
     end
     raise raise NoMethodError.new( message )
   end

   def methods_that_sound_like( name )
     missing_soundex = Soundex.soundex( name.to_s )
     public_methods.sort.find_all do |existing|
       existing_soundex = Soundex.soundex( existing.to_s )
       missing_soundex == existing_soundex
     end
   end
 end
```

This last method_missing implementation tries to figure out which method the user actually intended, based on the theory that the name of the method the user called is similar to the name of the method that the user meant to call. The code tries to guess the correct method by using the Soundex module (from the text gem) to compute a soundex code. The idea behind soundex is that similar-sounding words tend to generate the same soundex code. Thus, if you mistakenly call document.contnt you will get:

```
You called an undefined method: contnt.
Did you mean content or content=?
```

Coping with Constants

Methods are not, of course, the only things that can go missing in a Ruby program. Sometimes coders also misplace constants. In the same way that Ruby provides method_missing to cope with calls to nonexistent methods, it also gives you const_missing to deal with AWOL constants.

As you might guess, `const_missing` works a lot like `method_missing`: It gets called whenever Ruby detects a reference to an undefined constant. There are a couple of differences between the two `_missing` methods, one obvious and one more subtle. The obvious difference is that `const_missing` takes only a single argument, a symbol containing the name of the missing constant. References to constants, unlike method calls, do not have arguments.

The less obvious difference is that `const_missing` needs to be a class method:

```
class Document
    # Most of the class omitted...

  def self.const_missing( const_name )
    msg = %Q{
      You tried to reference the constant #{const_name}
      There is no such constant in the Document class.
    }
    raise msg
  end
end
```

Like our `method_missing` examples, this example presses `const_missing` into service to help somewhat shaky `Document` users.

In the Wild

The best example of applying `method_missing` to improve error handling is probably the Rails **whiny nil** facility. The idea behind whiny nils is to help journeyman Rails developers cope with the inevitable situation where they think they have an instance of some object, perhaps an array or an ActiveRecord model, but what they actually have is `nil`. For example, your Rails application might go looking for a certain `Author` record in the database:

```
book_author = Author.find( :first,
    :conditions => { :name => 'Bilbo Baggins' })
```

Unfortunately, Bilbo is a fictional *character*, not a real author, so `book_author` ends up being `nil`. Sadly, your code might not notice the `nil` and try to save the nonexistent author:

```
book_author.save
```

This, inevitably, is going to lead to something painful. The Rails whiny nil feature takes some of the sting out by catching the bad call with a `method_missing` implementation.[3] Like our `Document method_missing`, the Rails version of `method_missing` raises a `NoMethodError` with a customized message:

```
#<NoMethodError: You have a nil object when you didn't expect it!
```

Rails puts a cool spin on all of this by comparing the missing method name with the names of the methods supported by arrays and ActiveRecord model classes. If it finds a match, Rails will add a helpful suggestion to the exception it throws:

```
You might have expected an instance of ActiveRecord::Base.
The error occurred while evaluating nil.save.
```

Similarly, Rake uses `const_missing` to provide helpful warnings about deprecated names. It seems that earlier versions of Rake defined the core Rake classes at the top level, without any encapsulating modules. In those bygone days the class of a Rake task was simply `Task`, with no module. Somewhere along the way, however, the Rake classes were all enclosed in the `Rake` module, so `Task` morphed into `Rake::Task`. But what to do about all of those Rakefiles out there that still referred to plain old `Task`? You pull out `const_missing`, that's what:

```
def const_missing(const_name)
  case const_name
  when :Task
    Rake.application.const_warning(const_name)
    Rake::Task
  when :FileTask
    Rake.application.const_warning(const_name)
    Rake::FileTask
  when :FileCreationTask
    Rake.application.const_warning(const_name)
    Rake::FileCreationTask
```

---

3. We will deal with the question of how you add a new method to the existing `NilClass` in Chapter 24.

```
  when :RakeApp
    Rake.application.const_warning(const_name)
    Rake::Application
  else
    rake_original_const_missing(const_name)
  end
end
```

This clever bit of code catches the references to those old, naked class names and returns the correct class, printing out a helpful warning along the way.

Perhaps the most spectacular use of const_missing lies in the way that Rails uses it to load Ruby code as needed. Your ActiveRecord model classes are, for example, all loaded on an as-needed basis, driven by const_missing. The basic idea is to include a const_missing method that figures out what file to require from the name of the missing class, loads that file, and then returns the newly loaded class, something like this:

```
def self.const_missing( name )
  file_name = "#{name.to_s.downcase}"
  require file_name
  raise "Undefined: #{name}" unless const_defined?(name)
  const_get(name)
end
```

Once you have this const_missing method defined in your class (or some superclass of your class), any reference to the missing constant Wizard will trigger a require 'wizard'.[4]

Staying Out of Trouble

There are a few things to remember about method_missing- and const_missing-based error handling. First, you don't want to use it unless you really need it. The garden-variety Ruby error handling will suffice for about 99.9% of all of your misspelled

---

4. As an alternative, built into Ruby is the autoload method, which allows you to specify which file any given class is to be found. While the autoload method can be useful, it is nowhere near as flexible as the const_missing-based technique.

or misplaced methods, and there really is no reason to pepper your classes with
`method_missing` implementations unless, as in our little tale of "the Document class is
broken" woe, you really need to. Save the fancy `method_missing` for those cases where
you really do need to do something fancy with the error.

Second, keep in mind that the penalty for screwing up in `method_missing` and
`const_missing` can be pretty high. Think about it: Ruby executes `method_missing`
any time there is a method call that it can't locate. Be very, very careful that you don't
inadvertently call a nonexistent method inside your `method_missing` method. If you
do, Ruby will repeat the whole `method_missing` kerfuffle, eventually arriving back at
the `method_missing` method—which is likely to reach out again for the same nonexistent method, and off you are onto an all-expenses-paid trip to infinite recursion land.
If you value your programs, treat your `method_missing` and `const_missing` code like
anything else that you write. It ain't done until you've written the tests. Only more so.

Wrapping Up

In this chapter we looked at how Ruby deals with references to things that don't actually exist. We've seen that Ruby will call `method_missing` if you try to call a method
that doesn't actually exist and `const_missing` if you reference a constant that exists
only in your imagination. We saw how you can use `method_missing` and `const_
missing` to improve the error handling in your code and even how you can use
`const_missing` as a mechanism for auto-loading code.

Although error handling is the most obvious use for `method_missing`, it is certainly not the only use. In fact, error handling accounts for only a very small fraction
of `method_missing` use in the Ruby code base. The other, more common uses of
`method_missing` are where we now turn our attention.

CHAPTER 22

Use method_missing for Delegation

About ten years ago, for reasons that are still inexplicable to me, I gave up software development. I put down my keyboard and donned the coat if not the actual tie of a software development manager. I prepared schedules. I ran meetings. I did performance reviews. And I was miserable. The more time I spent with people, the more I loved my computer. I look back on those two or three years as the most difficult period of my professional life. Instead of rolling into work every morning, eager to do battle with the essential complexity of the universe, I dragged myself to the office to fight the pervasive stupidity of a Byzantine organization.

Still, my years in organizational purgatory were not completely wasted. During my stint as a manager I did learn some things, mainly things about people. The most important thing that I learned was that you just have to trust the folks who work for you. Make sure they know what they're doing. Make sure they know what you want them to do. Then get out of the way and let them do it. In short, I learned to delegate.

Delegation is important in object oriented programming too. In the programming world delegation is the idea that an object might secretly use another object to get part of the job done. Since getting out of the way is as important in the world of programs as it is in the real word, in this chapter we will look at doing delegation via method_missing. We will see that method_missing provides an almost painless mechanism for delegating calls from one object to another. We will also look at some of the dangers of delegating with method_missing and see whether we can find out how to balance those dangers with all the power that method_missing gives us.

The Promise and Pain of Delegation

Delegation—the coding edition—is a pretty basic concept: Sometimes you find your-self building an object that wants to do something and you happen to have another object that does exactly that something. You *could* copy all of the code from one class to the other, but that is probably a bad idea.[1] Instead, what you do is delegate: You supply the first object with a reference to the second, and every time you need to do that something you call the right method on the other object. Delegation is just another word for foisting the work on another object.

To make this more real, imagine that some secret spy agency has started using our Document class to store sensitive material. In fact, the material is so sensitive that *The Agency* would like to be able to create a special read-only version of any document, but a read-only version with a twist: Any program that gains access to one of these special documents is only allowed to see the document for five seconds. Any longer and the document should become unavailable. Oh, and the documents are liable to change anytime, so you can't just copy the original document. What's a coder to do?

Clearly, some sort of document wrapper is called for:

```ruby
class SuperSecretDocument
  def initialize(original_document, time_limit_seconds)
    @original_document = original_document
    @time_limit_seconds = time_limit_seconds
    @create_time = Time.now
  end

  def time_expired?
    Time.now - @create_time >= @time_limit_seconds
  end

  def check_for_expiration
    raise 'Document no longer available' if time_expired?
  end

  def content
    check_for_expiration
    return @original_document.content
  end
```

---

1. "Bad" in this context means abysmally horrible.

```
def title
  check_for_expiration
  return @original_document.title
end

def author
  check_for_expiration
  return @original_document.author
end

# and so on...
end
```

The `SuperSecretDocument` class holds onto a reference to the original `Document` instance and a time limit. As long as the time has not expired, the `SuperSecretDocument` will delegate any method calls off to the original document. Once the time is up, `SuperSecretDocument` stops cooperating and will only return an exception. Armed with the code above, we can now create some satisfyingly perishable documents:

```
original_instructions = get_instructions
instructions = SuperSecretDocument.new(original_instructions, 5)
```

Execute the preceding code and your instructions will self destruct in five seconds.[2]

The Trouble with Old-Fashioned Delegation

The trouble with this traditional style of delegation is that it is the programming equivalent of the manager who gives someone a job to do and then insists on supervising every detail.

To see the problem, imagine that our `Document` class was less of a toy and supported more of the features that you would find on a real document, features like page layout (landscape or portrait?), size (A4 or U.S. letter?), and so on. The trouble is that our `SuperSecretDocument` class needs to grow right along with the regular `Document` class:

---

2. With apologies to *Mission Impossible*—the old TV series, you understand, not those dreadful movies.

```ruby
class SuperSecretDocument
  def initialize(original_document, time_limit_seconds)
    @original_document = original_document
    @time_limit_seconds = time_limit_seconds
    @create_time = Time.now
  end

  def time_expired?
    Time.now - @create_time >= @time_limit_seconds
  end

  def check_for_expiration
    raise 'Document no longer available' if time_expired?
  end

  # content, title and author methods omitted
  # to keep from kill even more trees...

  # And some new methods....

  def page_layout
    check_for_expiration
    return @original_document.page_layout
  end

  def page_size
    check_for_expiration
    return @original_document.page_size
  end

  # And so on and so on and so on...
end
```

The problem with this lengthy stretch of delegating code is that your program isn't really getting all of the benefits of delegation. Yes, it's the Document instance that's really doing the work of getting the revision dates and paper sizes, but the SuperSecretDocument object is always there, looking over the document's shoulder with all of that dull, delegating code. In programming as in management, the key to delegation is getting out of the way.

The method_missing Method to the Rescue

The secret to getting out of the way lies in method_missing. Think about what would happen if we took all of those repetitive delegating methods out of the SuperSecretDocument class. Without the delegating methods, every time someone called a Document method on a SuperSecretDocument instance, they would be calling a method that wasn't there. Since the method is missing, Ruby would eventually call method_missing. Herein lies an opportunity: Instead of simply logging a message or raising an exception in method_missing, we can use a call to method_missing as an chance to delegate to the real Document:

```ruby
class SuperSecretDocument
  def initialize(original_document, time_limit_seconds)
    @original_document = original_document
    @time_limit_seconds = time_limit_seconds
    @create_time = Time.now
  end

  def time_expired?
    Time.now - @create_time >= @time_limit_seconds
  end

  def check_for_expiration
    raise 'Document no longer available' if time_expired?
  end

  def method_missing(name, *args)
    check_for_expiration
    @original_document.send(name, *args)
  end
end
```

This new, and much briefer, version of SuperSecretDocument uses method_missing to catch all of the calls that need to be delegated to the original document. When the SuperSecretDocument method_missing catches a method call it uses the send method to forward the call onto the original document:

```ruby
@original_document.send(name, *args)
```

Recall that we saw the send method back in Chapter 7, where we used it to get around the restrictions of private and protected methods. In the code above we are using send in its full glory as sort of the inverse of method_missing: While method_missing lets you catch arbitrary method calls from inside of a class, send lets you make arbitrary method calls on some other object. Best of all, the arguments for send, the name of the method (as a symbol) followed by the arguments to the method, line up exactly with the arguments to method_missing.

One obvious question with using this technique is, what happens when (inevitably) there is a real screwup, when someone accidentally calls instructions .continent instead of instructions.content? A little reflection will show that this is not really a problem. Since there is no continent method on the SuperSecretDocument instance, the call will get forwarded to the real Document instance. And since there is no continent there either, it will obligingly raise an exception.

The huge advantage of our new SuperSecretDocument implementation is that it is small—the whole class is under 20 lines—and doesn't need to grow as we add new methods to the Document class. The method_missing method will catch whatever methods you throw at SuperSecretDocument and will forward them, whatever they are, to the Document instance.

In fact, SuperSecretDocument is so generic that it isn't really Document specific at all. We could, for example, use SuperSecretDocument to wrap a String:

```
string = 'Good morning, Mr. Phelps'
secret_string = SuperSecretDocument.new( string, 5 )


puts secret_string.length           # Works fine
sleep 6
puts secret_string.length           # Raises an exception
```

The SuperSecretDocument class is effectively a perishable container for any object you might come up with.

More Discriminating Delegation

Although SuperSecretDocument will indiscriminately forward any method that comes its way, there is nothing to prevent us from doing a more selective job of delegation. We might, for instance, decide that we want `SuperSecretDocument` to deal only with a narrowly defined set of methods:

```ruby
class SuperSecretDocument
  # Lots of code omitted...

  DELEGATED_METHODS = [ :content, :words ]

  def method_missing(name, *args)
    check_for_expiration
    if DELEGATED_METHODS.include?( name )
      @original_document.send(name, *args)
    else
      super
    end
  end
end
```

This rendition of `SuperSecretDocument` has a list of the names of the methods it wants to delegate to `@original_document`. If a method call comes in for some other method, we just call `super`, which forwards the original method call (arguments and all!) up the class hierarchy where it will eventually meet its fate with a `NameError` exception.

Staying Out of Trouble

There is one nasty blemish on the otherwise smooth finish that is `method_missing`-based delegation: What if the method is not actually missing? To see what I mean, ask yourself what would happen if we had an instance of the original `SuperSecretDocument` class—the one that just delegates everything—and we called `to_s` on it:

```ruby
original_instructions = get_instructions
instructions = SuperSecretDocument.new(original_instructions, 5)
puts instructions.to_s
```

You might expect that this code would do one of two things: either call the `to_s` method on the `Document` instance or, if the time has expired, simply blow up. What actually happens instead is that you end up calling the SuperSecretDocument version of the to_s method, so that the output would be something like:

```
#<SuperSecretDocument:0x87273ac>
```

The trouble is that there actually *is* a to_s method on instances of SuperSecret-Document: They inherit it from the Object class. The same goes for all of the other methods your delegating object might have. If a delegating object actually has a method, the way our SuperSecretDocument instances all have a to_s method, then the method is not actually missing and method_missing is not going to go off for that method.

There is an easy way out of this conundrum, BasicObject. Recall from Chapter 7 that BasicObject was introduced in Ruby 1.9 and is the superclass of Object. As the name suggests, BasicObject is very stripped down: Instances of BasicObject inherit only a handful of methods. This means that BasicObject is an ideal candidate to start with when you are doing the kind of mass delegation we are looking for with SuperSecretDocument. Thus, if we redefined SuperSecretDocument to be a subclass of BasicObject:

```
class SuperSecretDocument < BasicObject
  # Most of the class omitted...
  def initialize(original_document, time_limit_seconds)
    @original_document = original_document
    @time_limit_seconds = time_limit_seconds
    @create_time = ::Time.now
  end

  def time_expired?
    ::Time.now - @create_time >= @time_limit_seconds
  end

  def check_for_expiration
    raise 'Document no longer available' if time_expired?
  end

  def method_missing(name, *args)
    check_for_expiration
```

```
        @original_document.send(name, *args)
      end
    end
```

Then the to_s method will time out just like title and content.[3]

In the Wild

The Ruby standard library comes with a very handy method_missing-based delegation utility in the delegate.rb file. This file contains a number of classes that take
what little sting there is in delegating with method_missing. The simplest one of the
bunch is probably the aptly named SimpleDelegator that you can use as a superclass
for your delegating class. All you need to do is call the SimpleDelegator constructor
with the object you are delegating to, and it will take care of the rest. Here, for example, is a SimpleDelegator based do-nothing wrapper for our Document class:

```
require 'delegate'

class DocumentWrapper < SimpleDelegator
  def initialize( real_doc )
    super( real_doc )
  end
end
```

That's pretty much it. With just seven lines of code, we have a fully functional
wrapper for any document:

```
text =  'The Hare was once boasting of his speed...'
real_doc = Document.new( 'Hare & Tortoise', 'Aesop', text )

wrapper_doc = DocumentWrapper.new( real_doc )
```

---

3. Sadly, it seems that in software engineering there is always at least a little catch. If you look carefully at the BasicObject version of SuperSecretDocument, you will see that we needed to
   explicitly specify the scope of the Time class with ::. We need to do this because of the discon-
   nected role of BasicObject as the sort of noble gas of Ruby classes.

Then any call to `wrapper_doc` will behave just like a call to the `real_doc`, so that running this:

```
puts wrapper_doc.title
puts wrapper_doc.author
puts wrapper_doc.content
```

Will print:

```
Hare & Tortoise
Aesop
The Hare was once boasting of his speed...
```

Aside from `delegate.rb`, the quintessential example of delegation by `method_missing` is probably the one you will find in ActiveRecord. Early versions of ActiveRecord used `method_missing`-based delegation to return the values of fields from a row in a table. For example, if you used ActiveRecord to find a row in a table, something like this:

```
the_employee = Employee.find( :first )
```

Then hidden inside of that record would be a hash containing the field values from the database, perhaps `{ :first_name => 'Bob', :last_name => 'Kiel' }`. You could then get at the fields as though they were ordinary methods:

```
puts the_employee.first_name
puts the_employee.last_name
```

This is slick enough, but more recent versions of ActiveRecord do something slicker still. In late-model ActiveRecord versions, the first time you access `the_employee.first_name`, the `method_missing` method will go off just like it did in the olden days. But instead of simply looking up the field value, the newer `method_missing` will also define the `first_name` and (for good measure) `last_name` methods on the class. It's these newly defined methods that get used on subsequent calls. Apparently, skipping the `method_missing` rigmarole improves performance enough to make the whole thing worthwhile. It is also impressive to watch.

Finally, if you happen to still be using a 1.8.X version of Ruby and need something like `BasicObject` for your delegating needs, don't despair. The blankslate gem provides, via the magic of Ruby metaprogramming, a more than adequate simulation of `BasicObject`.

Wrapping Up

In this chapter we explored the wonders of delegation via `method_missing`. We saw how you can put `method_missing` to work for something other than error handling. We also saw how easy it is to use `method_missing` to build a very painless delegation mechanism. Far from being a simple error-handling facility, `method_missing` provides the Ruby programmer with a very general-purpose way of catching and interpreting method calls. In the next chapter we will build on this idea to see how we can put `method_missing` to an even more exotic use: answering calls to methods that you may have never dreamed of.

CHAPTER 23

Use method_missing to Build Flexible APIs

Programmers in the business of producing systems for end users spend a lot of time thinking about interfaces. Should you do a plain Google-style search page or spiff things up with all kinds of AJAXy doo-dads? Should you let them pick the car model with a menu or a pull-down or a bunch of radio buttons? Should you support both drag and drop? When end users are involved it is critical that you think very carefully about interface issues. I'd like to think that much of this is simple professionalism: We work hard to build the best possible system because that's what we do. There is, however, the uncomfortable fact that end users tend to make their opinions pretty clear. Screw up an end user interface and you won't have to wait long or listen hard to experience their dissatisfaction, be it actual shouting or the ominous sound of feet going elsewhere.

The interfaces that programmers deal with—the APIs—have a lot more to do with method names and argument lists than they do with menus and radio buttons. But quality matters there too. Build a better API and you make the job of the coder trying to use that API easier. In this chapter we will explore how you can use `method_missing` to create extremely intuitive APIs, APIs where your users can, with some constraints, make up method names and just have them work. Who knows, you might save your users so much time that they will be able to build a better interface for *their* users.

Building Form Letters One Word at a Time

Imagine that your Document class is now being used in many different departments in your company, with whole teams of programmers building ever more interesting applications around it. One of these groups is involved in creating form letters, the kind we are all too familiar with, letters that proclaim YOU MAY ALREADY BE A WINNER or that Whiter Teeth Are Just a Phone Call Away!!

Since junk mail is a volume business, the programmers behind it are looking to you to create specialized code to make it easier to generate large numbers of letters. To that end, you come up with a Document subclass:

```
class FormLetter < Document
  def replace_word( old_word, new_word )
    @content.gsub!( old_word, "#{new_word}" )
  end
end
```

The only new feature of the FormLetter class is the replace_word method, which will run through the text of the letter, replacing one string with another. The idea is that you can start with a very generic template document containing place-holders like FIRSTNAME and LASTNAME and then swap in real first and last names with some simple code:

```
offer_letter = FormLetter.new( "Special Offer", "Acme Inc",
%q{
    Dear Mr. LASTNAME

    Are you troubled by the heartache of hangnails?
    ...

    FIRSTNAME, we look forward to hearing from you.
})

offer_letter.replace_word( 'FIRSTNAME', 'Russ' )
offer_letter.replace_word( 'LASTNAME', 'Olsen' )
```

Looking at the code, you realize that virtually all of the form letters will need to replace FIRSTNAME and LASTNAME. To make this common case easier, you add a couple of convenience methods:

```
class FormLetter < Document

  def replace_word( old_word, new_word )
    @content.gsub!( old_word, "#{new_word}" )
  end

  def replace_firstname( new_first_name )
    replace_word( 'FIRSTNAME', new_first_name )
  end

  def replace_lastname( new_last_name )
    replace_word( 'LASTNAME', new_last_name )
  end
end
```

You send your handiwork off to the form letter people and go back to your ordinary work. The next day the junk mail folks are back to tell you that (a) they love the FormLetter class, and (b) could you please just tweak it a bit?

It seems that the programmers using the FormLetter class would like a few more convenience methods along the lines of replace_firstname and replace_lastname. Specifically, they would like replace_gender, a method that would swap out GENDER for "sir" or "madam." Oh, and also replace_streetnumber, replace_streetname, replace_city, replace_state, replace_country, replace_zipcode, replace occupation, replace_age, and so on. For a simple little class, FormLetter seems like it's turning into a full-time job spent writing an inconveniently large number of convenience methods.

Magic Methods from method_missing

But do you actually have to write all of those methods? Not really: All you need is method_missing. Think about what method_missing does: It lets you know that someone is trying to call a method on your object, a method that does not actually exist. In the last couple of chapters we've seen how you can use method_missing to deal with programming errors and to help with delegation. Another thing you can do with method_missing is try to figure out what the user is asking you to do and actually *do it*. What if, whenever someone called a nonexistent method on one of your FormLetter objects, you looked at the method name to see whether you could make sense out of it? If you can, you do the right thing. If not, there is always NameException to raise.

Here is that idea in code:

```
class FormLetter < Document
  def replace_word( old_word, new_word )
    @content.gsub!( old_word, "#{new_word}" )
  end

  def method_missing( name, *args )
    string_name = name.to_s
    return super unless string_name =~ /^replace_\w+/
    old_word = extract_old_word(string_name)
    replace_word( old_word, args.first )
  end

  def extract_old_word( name )
    name_parts = name.split('_')
    name_parts[1].upcase
  end
end
```

This method_missing implementation deduces what it should do from the name of the method being called, If the method looks like replace_<<some word>>, then the method_missing above will extract the word from the name of the method, convert it to all uppercase, and call replace_word. So if you call replace_gender('Dude'), then the method_missing in the code above will end up calling replace_word('GENDER', 'Dude').

If, on the other hand, the method being called doesn't look anything like replace_<<some word>>, then you have a legitimate screwup. In that case, method_missing bails out by calling super, which will probably result in a NameException.

The best part of the new FormLetter class is no longer having to write any of the thousand or so convenience methods that the junk mail folks requested. In the same way that delegating method_missing in the last chapter enabled us to put a wrapper around any object—with any number of methods—the handful of method_missing lines in this latest version of FormLetter lets you create an infinite number of convenience methods, everything from replace_firstname to replace_lastcarmodelbought.

This variation on method_missing is sometimes called **magic methods**, since users of the class can make up method names and, as long as the names comply with the rules coded into method_missing, the methods will just magically work.

It's the Users That Count—All of Them

Now, a skeptic might observe that neither `replace_firstname` nor `replace_lastcarmodelbought` have added any particularly new capability to the `FormLetter` class.[1] These two methods, however they are implemented, simply expose an existing feature of the `FormLetter` class in a slightly different package. So why should we bother?

We bother because our users asked us to bother. If you reread my tale of intrigue and junk mail, you'll see that it was the coders who were using the `FormLetter` class that asked for the convenience methods. Those methods make the code generating the form letters cleaner and easier for the people who count—the programmers who need to deal with it. One of the key values of the Ruby programming culture is that the look of the code matters. It matters because the people who use the code, read the code, and maintain the code matter. Good software engineering is all about making everyone's job easier, not just because we want to go home on time but because we all want to turn out the best possible end product. So we add convenience methods, build `method_missing` methods, and go to enormous lengths to make our APIs easy to use because programmers with easy-to-use APIs tend to have the time to craft easy-to-use—and working—systems.

Staying Out of Trouble

One nice thing about using `method_missing` to build a flexible API, as opposed to using it for delegation, is that there is much less danger of a made-up method name colliding with a real method on the object. After all, you are making up the naming convention, so you can avoid any obvious name conflicts. You do have to be on your guard, however, because unfortunate naming collisions can still slip in. For example, in our `method_missing` powered `FormLetter` class, we cannot replace the word WORD in our document. If we try:

```
letter = FormLetter.new( 'Example', 'Acme', 'The word is WORD' )
letter.replace_word( 'Abracadabra' )
```

1. A real skeptic might observe that the whole `FormLetter` project is simply furthering the cause of junk mail and is therefore the work of the devil, but that's another issue.

We get a strange error:

```
#<ArgumentError: wrong number of arguments (1 for 2)>
```

The problem is that there is an actual `replace_word` method in the `FormLetter` class; it's the method that does the real work of changing the text. Since there is a real method there, it and not `method_missing` gets called and blows up. The real `replace_word` method takes two arguments, not one. The solution here is pretty easy: Simply rename the real method or devise a different naming convention for the magic methods. The deeper lesson is that you need to watch out for this sort of thing.

You also need to be aware of the likelihood that using `method_missing` will muck up the `respond_to?` method. Every `Object` instance includes a method called `respond_to?` which should return true if the object in question has a particular method. For example, if `doc` is an instance of `Document`, then `doc.respond_to?(:words)` will return true, while `doc.respond_to?(:abuse)` will return false, since there `Document` has a `words` method but no `abuse` method. The problem is that the default implementation of `respond_to?` only knows about the real methods; it has no way of knowing that you have slapped a `method_missing` on your class that will allow instances to cheerfully handle `doc.replace_gender`. Depending on how elaborate your `method_missing` implementation is, you may be able to fix `respond_to?`:

```ruby
def respond_to?(name)
  string_name = name.to_s
  return true if string_name =~ /^replace_\w+/
  super
end
```

As always, you need to balance the extra work involved with the likelihood that anyone is ever going to call `respond_to?` on this particular object.

In the Wild

You can find a very basic example of the magic method technique in the Ruby standard class `OpenStruct`. An `OpenStruct` instance is a cross between a simple data container object and a hash. Like a hash, you can use an `OpenStruct` to store whatever data you want, by whatever name you choose; the trick is that with `OpenStruct` you access your data with the `object.value` dot notation:

```
require 'ostruct'

author = OpenStruct.new
author.first_name = 'Stephen'
author.last_name = 'Hawking'

puts author.first_name
puts author.last_name
```

If you peek inside of the OpenStruct class you will find that it is built around a regular hash called @table and powered by method_missing. Here's the OpenStruct method_missing:

```
def method_missing(mid, *args) # :nodoc:
  mname = mid.id2name
  len = args.length

  if mname =~ /=$/
    # Some error handling deleted...
    mname.chop!
    self.new_ostruct_member(mname)
    @table[mname.intern] = args[0]
  elsif len == 0
    @table[mid]

  else
    raise NoMethodError,
      "undefined method `#{mname}' for #{self}", caller(1)
  end
end
```

The magic part of the OpenStruct method_missing is figuring out if the caller is trying to get an existing value from the hash or set a new value. To figure out which, the code looks at the name of the missing method: If the method name ends with an =, then the caller is trying to set a new value on the OpenStruct instance. If the method name doesn't end with an =, then this must be an attempt to access a value that has already been set. As magic goes, this is more of a card trick than making the Grand Canyon disappear, but it does illustrate the technique very nicely. ActiveRecord uses a much more serious bit of magic method conjuring: The ActiveRecord objects that represent database tables let you make up arbitrary finder methods. Imagine, for example, that you have an authors table in your database, a table that contains fname and lname fields. You also have an ActiveRecord class to go with your authors table:

```
class Author < ActiveRecord::Base
end
```

Given all this, ActiveRecord allows you to make up methods to find your records:

```
authors_named_henry = Author.find_by_fname(  'Henry'  )
james_family_authors = Author.find_by_lname( 'James' )
```

You can even combine the fields:

```
henry_james = Author.find_by_fname_and_lname( 'Henry', 'James' )
```

All of this courtesy of method_missing.

Wrapping Up

In this chapter we looked at using method_missing to create an infinite number of virtual methods, methods that don't actually exist as distinct blocks of source code but are there when you call them. To create these "there but not actually there" methods, we let method_missing catch the method call, parse the method name, and figure out what to do from there.

The method_missing-based technique of this and the last couple of chapters illustrates one of the basic ideas behind Ruby, that one of the main jobs of a programming language is to help the programmer get code executed when and where the programmer decides that code needs to be executed. This is what code blocks and modules do; they both allow you to package up code in one place and use it somewhere else. In this light, method_missing is just more of the same. It enables you to wedge some code in just where you need it.

CHAPTER 24

Update Existing Classes with Monkey Patching

I can remember the day I sat down and really understood object oriented programming. It was early in my career. At that point I had probably spent two or three years programming straight procedural code in languages ranging from assembly to the only slightly less primitive FORTRAN. I had heard about this new language called SMALLTALK, which featured things called objects that were somehow grouped together by other things called classes. I spent the better part of a weekend reading all about this new programming paradigm, and on Sunday afternoon I finally got it. I'd like to tell you that it changed my professional life. I'd like to tell you that, but I'm just not that big of a liar. If memory serves, and it usually does when it comes to remembering yourself being stupid, my conclusion was that all this object and class talk was a complete waste of time. It was only much later, after I had lived with object oriented programming for awhile, that I began to see its value.

I mention this because with this chapter we will begin an extended look at one of the most startling aspects of Ruby: open classes. Ruby's open classes means that you can change the behavior of any class at any time. You can add new methods. You can replace the code behind an existing method. You can even delete methods altogether. Of all the features in Ruby, open classes is the one most likely to provoke that "what a stupid idea!" reaction. So if you are already shaking your head, just stay with me. It turns out that open classes—and the monkey patching technique that goes with them—is actually a very practical solution to a number of programming problems.

Not only that, but looking into the mechanisms behind open classes will give us some deep insight into how the whole Ruby class model works.

This is a pretty big bill for one chapter, so let's jump right in.

Wide-Open Classes

The best way to think about Ruby's changeable classes is to start with variables. If we say this:

```
name = 'Issac'
```

We are doing one of two things: If `name` has not already been defined, then the code snippet above will define it and set it to the string `'Issac'`. Alternatively, if `name` is already defined, the line of code will set it to a new value, perhaps like this:

```
name = 'Asimov'
```

Ruby classes work in exactly the same way. The first time you define a new class, you are, well, defining a new class. You might start with a very minimal version of the `Document` class, one that consists of just the attributes and the `initialize` method:

```
class Document
  attr_accessor :title, :author, :content

  def initialize(title, author, content)
    @title = title
    @author = author
    @content = content
  end
end
```

There's nothing surprising there, but now for the interesting part. If you write another `class` statement for `Document`:

```
class Document
  def words
    @content.split
  end
```

```
     def word_count
       words.size
     end
   end
```

Then you are not defining a new class. Rather, you are *modifying* the existing Document class, the same one you defined in the first bit of code. The effect of this second chunk of code is to add the words and word_count methods to Document.

Even better, the changes you make to your classes will be felt instantly by all of the instances of the class. Thus, if we made a Document instance:

```
   cover_letter = Document.new( 'Letter', 'Russ', "Here's my resume" )
```

And then enhance our Document class with yet another method:

```
   class Document
     def average_word_length
       len = words.inject(0.0){ |total, word| word.size + total }
       len / words.size
     end
   end
```

Then the change will show up instantly in the existing instance:

```
   cover_letter.average_word_length
```

Fixing a Broken Class

Nor are you limited to simply adding new methods to an existing class. It is possible, and not that unusual, to redefine existing methods on Ruby classes. This works on the "last def wins" principal: If you reopen a class and define a method that already exists, the new definition overwrites the old. This sort of thing is handy when you need to fix a broken class. Consider that our average_word_length method features a really ugly bug, one that bites when you try to get the average word length of an empty document:

```
   empty_doc = Document.new( 'Empty!', 'Russ', '' )
   puts empty_doc.average_word_length
```

Run this code and you will see:

```
NaN
```

If you haven't had the pleasure, let me introduce you to NaN, which is short for "Not a Number." NaN is Ruby's way of telling you that you produced an invalid floating-point number. We managed it here by dividing 0.0 by 0.0.[1] Ideally, you would fix the average_word_length method right in the original Document code and re-release the whole thing. But what if you weren't the author of Document? What if you need a fix right now to make your application work? If you absolutely, positively must get it working, you can reopen the document class and fix the method directly:

```
require 'document'   # Pull in original, broken class

# And now fix the method.

class Document
  def average_word_length
    return 0.0 if word_count == 0
    total = words.inject(0.0){ |result, word| word.size + result}
    total / word_count
  end
end
```

This technique of modifying existing classes on the fly goes by the name of **monkey patching**.[2]

Improving Existing Classes

Once you become comfortable with monkey patching, many possibilities open up. This is especially true since there is no rule against monkey patching Ruby's built-in

---

1. In the world of integer arithmetic, division by zero will result in an exception. Things are not quite so clear cut in the fuzzier realm of floating-point numbers, where dividing by zero will either result in NaN or Infinity, depending on exactly what you divide.

2. Programming lore has it that the original name was guerrilla patching, which then morphed into gorilla patching (perhaps programmers simply can't spell?), which somehow evolved into monkey patching.

classes. If you are programming in Ruby and that thing is a class, you can change it. For example, we can finally fix a problem that has been nagging us since Chapter 11.[3] Recall that back then we tried to make the addition operator work between documents and strings. We had no trouble making document + string work, since doing the addition in that order called the + method from the Document class, and we had added the necessary smarts to the Document class. The trouble started when we tried to add in the reverse order: string + document. This expression resulted in a call to the + method on the string, and then we hit a brick wall. How could we possibly change the String class? Like this:

```ruby
class String
  def +( other )
    if other.kind_of? Document
      new_content = self + other.content
      return Document.new(other.title, other.author, new_content)
    end
    result = self.dup
    result << other.to_str
    result
  end
end
```

Let's run through this code step by step. The first thing we do is to say class String. This reopens the String class for our homegrown improvements. Next we define a new + method, one that becomes *the* String + method. In the new method we handle the new String + Document case along with the more mundane String + String case.

Renaming Methods with alias_method

One downside to our String modification is that we ended up reproducing the guts of the original String + method—the boring non-Document bit that creates a bigger string from the two smaller strings—when all we really wanted was to get the method to do the right thing with Document instances. We can avoid this with alias_method. Although the name suggests otherwise, alias_method actually copies a method

---

3. Well, it has been nagging me.

implementation, giving it a new name along the way. For example, our original Document class had a method called word_count. With alias_method, we can create a couple more methods that do exactly the same thing as word_count:

```ruby
class Document
  # Stuff omitted...

  def word_count
    words.size
  end

  alias_method :number_of_words, :word_count
  alias_method :size_in_words,   :word_count

  # Stuff omitted...
end
```

Run this code and you'll end up with a trio of methods on your Document instances that will all return the number of words in the document.

Aside from letting you easily give a method several different names, alias_method comes in handy when you are messing with the innards of an existing class. Here's a version of our String monkey patch that uses alias_method to avoid reproducing the logic of the original + method:

```ruby
class String
  alias_method :old_addition, :+

  def +( other )
    if other.kind_of? Document
      new_content = self + other.content
      return Document.new(other.title, other.author, new_content)
    end
    old_addition(other)
  end
end
```

Something quite subtle is going on in this code: The call to alias_method copies the implementation of the original + method, giving the fresh copy the name old_addition. Having done that, we proceed to override the + method, but—and here's the important part— old_addition continues to refer to the original unmodified implementation. When the new + method calls old_addition, we are actually invoking the original + method, which does all of the boring string addition work.

Do Anything to Any Class, Anytime

Our use of alias_method in the last section underscores another important aspect of open classes: When you reopen a class, you can do anything you could have done the first time. In the same way that we aliased an existing method, we can make a public method private:

```
class Document
  private :word_count
end
```

Or a private method public again:

```
class Document
  public :word_count
end
```

We can even get rid of it all together:

```
class Document
  remove_method :word_count
end
```

As I said earlier in this chapter, the Ruby classes are like variables. You can set them and leave them alone, or you can fiddle with them as much as you need.

In the Wild

Although this chapter has concentrated on the showier aspects of monkey patching, you can also use it to solve a very mundane problem. To see how, consider the Pathname class, which comes with your Ruby installation. Pathname tries to be the go-to class for all your file system programming needs. Because it does try to be all things to all paths, the `Pathname` class is long—it sports almost one hundred instance methods.

Since it is such a large class, the authors of `Pathname` have divided the class into chunks of related methods. There is, for example, an initial piece that defines the basics, things like the `initialize` method and various operators:

```
class Pathname

  # Bits deleted...

  def initialize(path)
    # Set up Pathname instance...
  end

  # ==, <=>, etc. methods deleted...
end
```

Then, there is a chunk containing code that will help you read and write the files your `Pathname` instance points at:

```
class Pathname    # * IO *
  def each_line(*args, &block) # :yield: line
    # Iterate through each line in the file...
  end

  def read(*args)
    # Read the contents of the file...
  end

  # ...
end
```

All told, `Pathname` is broken into nine separate bits and then put back together courtesy of monkey patching.

Another common motivation for monkey patching is to scratch an itch. Have you ever wished that there was just one extra method on the `String` class, a method that you seem to need all the time but is inexplicably missing? Apparently a lot of Ruby programmers have wished for exactly the same thing given that adding methods to the

String class is somewhat of a cottage industry. For example, the ActiveSupport gem, which provides miscellaneous helpful code to Rails, adds a number of methods to the String class. Among these is blank?, which returns true if the string is all white space:[4]

```
class String #:nodoc:
  def blank?
    self !~ /\S/
  end
end
```

Another ActiveSupport contribution to String has one of the best names in all of coding: squish!. The squish! method compresses all of the stretches of white space in a string down to a single space each. Thus, if you have ActiveSupport loaded, this:

```
s = ' Ruby        Rocks    '
s.squish!
```

Will leave s equal to 'Ruby Rocks'. Here is squish! in all of its evocative joy:

```
module ActiveSupport #:nodoc:
  module CoreExtensions #:nodoc:
    module String #:nodoc:
      module Filters

        # Some code deleted...

        def squish!
          strip!
          gsub!(/\s+/, ' ')
          self
        end

      end
    end
  end
end
```

---

4. Come to think of it, that's one I need a lot!

As you can see, squish! is not directly defined on the String class—it actually lives inside the ActiveSupport::CoreExtensions::String::Filters[5] module. The squish! method makes its way into String when its module is mixed into the String class, with another bit of monkey patching:

```
class String
  # Lots of stuff deleted...
  include ActiveSupport::CoreExtensions::String::Filters
end
```

Monkey patching the built-in classes is by no means limited to String. ActiveRecord adds a number of methods of the Array class, so that not only can you get the first item in an array by calling first, you can also get the second, third, fourth, and fifth items:

```
require 'active-support'

title =  'Hitch Hikers Guild To The Galaxy By Douglas Adams'
array = title.split(//)   # Make an array, one letter per entry

array.first         # 'H'
array.second        # 'i'
array.third         # 't'
array.fourth        # 'c'
array.fifth         # 'h'
```

The sequence stops at the fifth item, with one exception: You can ask for the forty-second element of the array:

```
array.forty_two     # 'a'
```

Ah, geek humor.

---

5. When you are tired of contemplating the metaphysics of monkey patching, you might consider whether this is an example of module nesting gone wild.

Staying Out of Trouble

The dangers of monkey patching really depend on what you are doing with it. For example, it's hard to see any real danger in the step-by-step assembly of a long class like `Pathname`.

A bit riskier is adding a brand new method to a class, along the lines of adding a `blank?` or `squish!` method on `String`. This is still a reasonably safe thing to do. After all, how much damage can a single additional method do? None, unless the class (or its superclass) already had a `blank?` or a `squish!` method, in which case you have just overwritten that original method. There is, of course, the chance that someone else might be patching in their own `squish!` method, overwriting your masterpiece in the process. Not much of a chance, but something to consider.

Next in our lineup of escalating danger is patching some application class, the way we did when we fixed the `average_word_length` method on `Document`. Here we're getting involved in the central mechanism of the class, although monkey patching a class isn't all that different from making a change to it the traditional way. What it comes down to is that safety lies in knowing what you are doing and in writing tests.

The biggest danger in monkey patching arises when you start messing with the primary mechanism of some critical class. We did exactly this kind of thing when we modified the `String +` method earlier in the chapter. It's hard to think of a class more critical than `String`, and by changing the + method we ran the risk of breaking a fundamental part of Ruby. The bad news is that there is a very high penalty for screwing up a basic class like `String`: All kinds of things are going to break. The good news is that even the most basic of tests are likely to uncover this kind of error very rapidly. You are writing tests, right?

Wrapping Up

In this chapter we took a very basic look at monkey patching classes. A monkey patch is an on-the-fly modification of an existing class. We saw how you can use monkey patching to add new methods to an existing class, to change methods that are already there, and even do things like aliasing or deleting a method. We saw how monkey patching enables you to fix a broken class, enhance a working one, and assemble large classes bit by bit.

Ironically, although simple monkey patching is the most visible aspect of open classes, it is by no means the only—or even the most important—programming technique to take advantage of this Ruby feature. In the next couple of chapters we will explore two other things we can do with classes that never make us say we're sorry.

CHAPTER 25

Create Self-Modifying Classes

In the last chapter we looked at how you can take advantage of Ruby's open classes to do monkey patching, to add to, modify, or even subtract from an existing class. We saw how you can get a lot of programming mileage out of this technique in the form of enhanced or repaired classes.

In this chapter we're going to continue our look at the dynamic nature of Ruby classes, and we'll start by asking a very fundamental question: How do Ruby classes get defined in the first place? Not only will the answer to this question illuminate how monkey patching works, but it will also enable us to build classes that can programmatically modify themselves. We will also learn how to cope with some of the common mistakes you can make when doing this kind of programming, and then we'll check out some examples from the Ruby code base.

Open Classes, Again

So far we've seen how you can change a Ruby class definition by simply repeating the class definition. If the `Widget` class is already defined and you come back a second time to say `class Widget`, then your widgets are going to change. Something we rather took for granted in that discussion was the question of how classes get defined in the first place. To see what I mean, take a look at this rather strange-looking class definition:

```
class MostlyEmpty
  puts "hello from inside the class"
end
```

Instead of methods and attributes and constants, the `MostlyEmpty` class lives up to its name by consisting of a single `puts` statement. Run the three lines above and you will see this output:

```
hello from inside the class
```

Along with the output—and the new, mostly empty class—we can pull something very important from this little demonstration—that Ruby class definitions are executable. That `puts` statement went off because when the Ruby interpreter hits a class declaration, it executes the code between the `class` and the `end`.[1]

We can use this little discovery to prove something you've been told but perhaps have never really seen before your eyes: the value of `self` inside a class definition is the class that you are defining. Run this:

```
class MostlyEmpty
  puts "The value of self is #{self}"
end
```

And there is your confirmation:

```
The value of self is #<Class:0x873698c>::MostlyEmpty
```

We can also use this trick to see *when* methods get defined. All we need is a class with an actual method along and some additional instrumentation:

```
class LessEmpty
  pp instance_methods(false)

  def do_something
    puts "I'm doing something!"
  end
```

---

1. Well, technically the interpreter reads in the whole class first and then executes the class body.

```
    pp instance_methods(false)
  end
```

Again, we have a class with some ordinary code to execute, this time two pp statements. Using the `instance_methods` method, those pp statements print the names of all the instance methods defined on the `LessEmpty` class.[2] Sandwiched between the pps is a method definition. The idea is to find out when the `do_something` method gets defined. When you run this code you will see the following:

```
[]
[:do_something]
```

This output is trying to tell us that the `do_something` method is not defined at the top of the class—before the `def do_something`—but it is defined at the bottom, after the method definition. We have just discovered that Ruby classes are defined piecemeal, one step—or method—at a time. When Ruby sees that initial `class LessEmpty`, it creates a new and completely empty class. It then executes the class body, the code between the `class` statement and the final end. Whatever is inside the class definition—be it an `if` or a `puts` or a method defining `def`—simply gets executed in turn.

Knowing all this gives us some interesting insight into how Ruby classes really operate. For example, given what we've learned so far, it's now no surprise that if you define the same method twice, like this:

```ruby
class TheSameMethodTwice

  def do_something
    puts "first version"
  end

  # In between method definitions

  def do_something
    puts "second version"
  end
end
```

---

2. Passing false to `instance_methods` says that we don't want to see any inherited methods, only the methods defined directly by `LessEmpty`.

```
twice = TheSameMethodTwice.new
twice.do_something
```

The first version of the method actually springs into existence, briefly, in the space between the two definitions, only to be snubbed out by the second definition. The second one wins, as you can see from the output:

```
second version
```

Now, given that you can reopen Ruby classes, the code above is only a shade different from:

```
class TheSameMethodTwice
  def do_something
    puts "first version"
  end
end

class TheSameMethodTwice
  def do_something
    puts "second version"
  end
end
```

This latest version is also a classic example of monkey patching. We started with the TheSameMethodTwice class with the first version of the method, and then we reopened the class and replaced it with the second rendition of the method.

Put Programming Logic in Your Classes

Beyond helping us understand how monkey patching works, all of this theory has some real, and useful, consequences. Being able to embed code in your classes means that your classes can make run-time decisions about what methods to define and the code that those methods will contain. For example, we might imagine that all the applications using the Document class want to be able to save their documents to a file, but only some of those applications need to encrypt the documents as they are saved. If there was a constant that turned the encryption off and on, then it's fairly easy to build a class that configures itself accordingly:

```
class Document

  # Lots of code omitted...

  def save( path )
    File.open( path, 'w' ) do |f|
      f.puts( encrypt( @title ))
      f.puts( encrypt( @author ) )
      f.puts( encrypt( @content ))
    end
  end

  if ENCRYPTION_ENABLED
    def encrypt( string )
      string.tr( 'a-zA-Z', 'm-za-lM-ZA-L')
    end
  else
    def encrypt( string )
      string
    end
  end
end
```

This code starts out with a mundane save method, which writes the data in the document out to a file, after running it through the encrypt method. The question is, which encrypt method? It's the class-level logic that makes the decision. If the ENCRYPTION_ENABLED constant is true, we end up with an encrypt method that does indeed shuffle the contents of the string. On the other hand, if ENCRYPTION_ENABLED isn't true, we get an encrypt method that does nothing. Critically, the ENCRYPTION_ENABLED logic runs exactly once, when the class is loaded.

Class Methods That Change Their Class

The code that executes inside a class definition has something in common with a class method: They both execute with self set to the class. This suggests that we can use class methods to make the same kind of structural changes that we have done so far with class-level logic, and so we can. Here is our encryption example again, this time wrapped in a class method:

```
ENCRYPTION_ENABLED = true

class Document

  # Most of the class left behind...

  def self.enable_encryption( enabled )
    if enabled
      def encrypt_string( string )
        string.tr( 'a-zA-Z', 'm-za-lM-ZA-L')
      end
    else
      def encrypt_string( string )
        string
      end
    end
  end

  enable_encryption( ENCRYPTION_ENABLED )
end
```

This code does the very recursive trick of defining a class method, enable_ encryption, which itself defines an instance method. Actually, it defines one of two versions of the encrypt_string method, depending on whether the enabled parameter is passed in as true or false. The last line of the class definition calls enable_ encryption, passing in true, thereby starting us off with encrypting turned on. A handy side effect of this latest implementation is that we can toggle encryption off and on by calling the class method from outside. Thus, if we wanted to be sure that we were going to write encryption-free documents we could run:

```
Document.enable_encryption( false )
```

And we would have the "do nothing" version of the encrypt_string method.

In the Wild

Executable class definitions are wonderfully useful when you need to write code that will work in different environments. Take the transition that the Ruby world is going through right now, from Ruby version 1.8.X to version 1.9. Progress is a great thing, but it can also be a pain in the neck. It's great that version 1.9 adds all sorts of new methods to the built-in classes, but what if you need to write code that will run in both Ruby versions?

For example, one of the differences between 1.8 and 1.9 lies in the String class. Take this string:

```
name = 'Robert Jordon'
```

In Ruby 1.9, name[2] will evaluate to a string containing one character, in this case 'b'. In Ruby 1.8, name[2] will give you 98, the number that lurks behind the letter b. Now think about the problems this will cause if we wanted to have a char_at method on our Document class, a method that always returns a one-character string. It's trivial in Ruby 1.9:

```
class Document
  # Ruby 1.9 version

  def char_at( index )
    @content[ index ]
  end
end
```

But in Ruby 1.8 we need to convert the integer back into a string with a call to the chr method:

```
class Document
  # Ruby 1.8 version

  def char_at( index )
    @content[ index ].chr
  end
end
```

The problem is, which version of char_at should we use at any given moment? One easy way to deal with this kind of problem is to simply put an if statement right at the class level, an if statement that will pick the right method:

```
class Document
  # Lots of stuff omitted...

  if RUBY_VERSION >= '1.9'
    def char_at( index )
      @content[ index ]
    end
  else
    def char_at( index )
      @content[ index ].chr
    end
  end
end
```

This code uses the built in RUBY_VERSION constant to figure out which Ruby version it's running on and works from there. The key thing to understand about the if statement in the code here is that it executes exactly once as the class is being defined.

You can find a spectacular example of on-the-fly class modification in the delightful habit that Rails has of picking up your code changes on the fly. One thing that makes using Rails such a delight is that once you have a basic project set up, you simply crank up the Rails server and start hacking. With a few exceptions, Rails will magically pick up your changes and incorporate them into the running application, without so much as a hiccup let alone a server restart. Clearly there is something interesting going on inside of Rails; the question is what?

To see whether we can glean the answer, let's modify Document to make it reloadable. What we need is a Document class method that will sync the code stored in the file with the code that is actually running. A naive approach is to have the reload method simply reread the Document source code in a recursive act of monkey patching:

```
class Document
  def self.reload
    load( __FILE__ )
  end

  # Rest of the class omitted...
end
```

There is a surprising amount happening in the one-line reload class method shown here. First, it uses the Ruby-supplied load method to reread its own source.

The `load` method is similar to the more familiar `require`. The difference between `load` and `require` is that `require` keeps track of which files are already loaded so that it doesn't load the same file twice. The `load` method just loads the file, no questions asked. Since loading the same file twice is exactly what we're after here, we'll use the dumber `load`. The `reload` method also uses `__FILE__`. `__FILE__` is also supplied via the magic of Ruby and is always set to the path of the source file of the current class, which is just what we need here.

The `reload` method above takes us a long way toward our goal of a Rails-like reloadable class. Calling `reload` in the example above will ensure that any new methods added to the source file will show up in the running system. It will also catch any changes to existing methods. This first version of `reload` falls short because it can't get rid of deleted methods. If you edit `document.rb` and remove a method and then reload the source file, the original method will stubbornly stay in place in the running Ruby interpreter. The solution is to remove all the methods from the class *before* reloading it:

```ruby
class Document
  def self.reload
    remove_instance_methods
    load( __FILE__ )
  end

  def self.remove_instance_methods
    instance_methods(false).each do |method|
      remove_method(method)
    end
  end

  # Rest of the class omitted...
end
```

The additional `remove_instance_methods` method in this last example prepares the Document class for reloading by systematically removing all of the instance methods from it, leaving behind an empty shell that is repopulated when the source file is reloaded.[3]

---

3. Not quite as empty a shell as we might like. It doesn't clear out any class methods, class variables, and class instance variables. One of the best things about writing books is that I get to leave something like that as an exercise for the reader.

Staying Out of Trouble

Let's face it: Where there is code, there will be bugs. Write enough of the kind of class-level logic discussed in this chapter and eventually you'll make all of the traditional bone-headed mistakes that have plagued engineers since the first `hello_world`. The difference is that the same old mistakes can have some interesting consequences when they occur in the middle of making structural changes to your classes. For example, take a look at this broken version of our encrypting document class:

```
ENCRYPTION_ENABLED = true

# Broken!!

class Document

  # Most of the class left behind...

  def self.enable_encryption( enabled )
    if enabled
      def encrypt_string( string )
        string.tr( 'a-zA-Z', 'm-za-lM-ZA-L' )
      end
    else
      def encrypt_string( string )
        string
      end
    end
  end
end
```

See the problem? We left out the call to `enable_encryption` at the bottom of the class, so this version of `Document` will start out with no `encrypt_string` method at all. This will give us an unpleasant shock when we try to save a document.

In the same vein, if you make a mistake in one branch of the class-level logic, it will not show up until you actually use the branch. Take a look at this unfortunate bit of code:

```
def self.enable_encryption( enabled )
  if enabled
```

```
      def encrypt_string( string )
        string.tr( 'a-zA-z', 'm-za-lM-ZA-L' )
      end
    else
      def incrypt_string( string )
        string
      end
    end
  end
end
```

With this code, trying to turn encryption off will only succeed in defining a second method with the very odd name of incrypt_string. The moral here is simple and is spelled R-S-P-E-C:

```
describe Document do
  before :each do
    @doc = Document.new( "test", "tester", "this is a test" )
  end

  it "should encrypt if encryption is enabled" do
    Document.enable_encryption( true )
    @doc.encrypt_string( 'abc' ).should_not == 'abc'
  end

  it "should not encrypt if encryption is disabled" do
    Document.enable_encryption( false )
    @doc.encrypt_string( 'abc' ).should == 'abc'
  end
end
```

While regular code needs unit tests, metaprogramming code absolutely cries out for them!

Wrapping Up

If this chapter did its job, you are walking away with two big ideas: The first is that Ruby classes are executable. During the process of defining a class, Ruby executes the code between the class and the end, modifying the class as it goes. The second is that since class definitions are executable, you can insert logic in your class definitions, logic that will determine exactly what the class will look like. And actually there is a third big idea, not a new idea but one that bears repeating: Programs—especially metaprograms—that lack automated tests are probably not going to work.

CHAPTER **26**

Create Classes That
Modify Their Subclasses

One of the fundamental principles of programming goes something like this: Never leave to a human that which can be done by a program. Or, to put it another way, some of the greatest leaps in software engineering have happened because some lazy sod simply got tired of repeating steps two through six over and over. So far in our adventures with Ruby's open classes we have seen how we can change classes with monkey patching, a more or less manual process of slapping some new code over the existing code. From there we moved to building classes that could change themselves, classes that say "Gee, I'm running in Ruby 1.8, so I had better define this method." In this chapter we'll make the final leap: We'll move that class-modifying code out of the class being modified and up into a superclass. We'll see that by doing this we can dramatically increase the amount of metaprogramming leverage that we can apply. With a bit of luck, this technique will allow you to finish your programs that much quicker and go back to your favorite pastime, being a lazy sod.

A Document of Paragraphs

Thus far we have kept our Document class conveniently, but unrealistically, simple. The sad fact is that you can't model the content of real-world documents with a simple string. Real documents have paragraphs and fonts, fonts that come in flavors like normal and bold and italics. A more realistic document class might actually start with a class for paragraphs:

```ruby
class Paragraph
  attr_accessor :font_name, :font_size, :font_emphasis
  attr_accessor :text

  def initialize( font_name, font_size, font_emphasis, text='')
    @font_name = font_name
    @font_size = font_size
    @font_emphasis = font_emphasis
    @text = text
  end

  def to_s
    @text
  end

  # Rest of the class omitted...
end
```

And only then turn to the document itself:

```ruby
class StructuredDocument
  attr_accessor :title, :author, :paragraphs

  def initialize( title, author )
    @title = title
    @author = author
    @paragraphs = []
    yield( self ) if block_given?
  end

  def <<( paragraph )
    @paragraphs << paragraph
  end

  def content
    @paragraphs.inject('') { |text, para| "#{text}\n#{para}" }
  end

  # ...
end
```

The new `StructuredDocument` class is mostly just a collection of paragraphs, where each paragraph consists of some text, a font name (i.e., `:arial`), a font size (perhaps 12 point), and an emphasis, something like `:bold` or `:italic`. Thus we might create a resume like this:[1]

```
russ_cv = StructuredDocument.new( 'Resume', 'RO' ) do |cv|
  cv << Paragraph.new( :nimbus, 14, :bold, 'Russ Olsen' )
  cv << Paragraph.new( :nimbus, 12, :italic, '1313 Mocking Bird Lane')
  cv << Paragraph.new( :nimbus, 12, :none, 'russ@russolsen.com')
  # .. and so on
end
```

Armed with the newfound power of the `StructuredDocument` class, we can build all sorts of specialized documents, everything from resumes to instructions for installing an LCD TV.

Subclassing Is (Sometimes) Hard to Do

The trouble is, all that building is going to be real work and, because most resumes and instruction manuals look more or less alike, fairly repetitious work at that. If our users are creating a lot of documents, we might want to help them along. Easy enough. We simply cook up a number of subclasses, each with some helpful methods. We might, for instance, create a subclass for resumes:

```
class Resume < StructuredDocument
  def name( text )
    paragraph = Paragraph.new( :nimbus, 14, :bold, text )
    self << paragraph
  end

  def address( text )
    paragraph = Paragraph.new( :nimbus, 12, :italic, text )
    self << paragraph
  end
```

---

1. Note the clever use of the initialize block!

```
  def email( text )
    paragraph = Paragraph.new( :nimbus, 12, :none, text )
    self << paragraph
  end


  # and so on
end
```

Using these methods, you can programmically build a resume with a minimum of fuss:

```
russ_cv = Resume.new( 'russ', 'resume') do |cv|
  cv.name( 'Russ Olsen' )
  cv.address( '1313 Mocking Bird Lane' )
  cv.email( 'russ@russolsen.com' )

  # Etc...
end
```

You might also do something similar with installation instructions:

```
class Instructions < StructuredDocument
  def introduction( text )
    paragraph = Paragraph.new( :mono, 14, :none, text )
    self << paragraph
  end

  def warning( text )
    paragraph = Paragraph.new( :arial, 22, :bold, text )
    self << paragraph
  end

  def step( text )
    paragraph = Paragraph.new( :nimbus, 14, :none, text )
    self << paragraph
  end

  # and so on
end
```

If we step back and look at our handiwork so far, we can see that it's a bit of a mixed bag. On the plus side, we have built a couple of friendly, user-oriented classes. If you need to build a resume or a set of instructions, we have a handy class that will help you out. The problem is that we still have a lot of repetitive code. Every one of our helper methods looks almost exactly like every other helper method. The method that adds an e-mail address to a resume is, plus or minus a font name and size, identical to the one that adds a warning to a set of instructions. Sadly, there seems to be no cure for this: If we want all those nice helper methods, we simply need to sit down and build them, right?

Class Methods That Build Instance Methods

Perhaps not. Armed with the knowledge that (a) you can change any Ruby class at any time, and (b) Ruby classes definitions are executed, we might just be able to avoid all of this redundant code. The effect we're looking for is to be able to say, "The `Instruction` class needs to have a method called `introduction` that will add a new paragraph rendered in the italic version of Arial at a glorious 18 points" and have Ruby create the method for you. Something like this:

```ruby
class Instructions < StructuredDocument
  paragraph_type( :introduction,
    :font_name => :arial,
    :font_size => 18,
    :font_emphasis => :italic )

  # And so on...
end
```

Let's try to make `paragraph_type` a reality, one step at a time. First, since we are calling it right inside the class definition, it's clear that `paragraph_type` needs to be a *class* method:

```ruby
class StructuredDocument
  def self.paragraph_type( paragraph_name, options )
    # What do we do in here?
  end

  # ...
end
```

The `paragraph_type` class method takes two arguments: the name of the new paragraph type (which is also going to be the name of the method we're going to add to the class) and a hash of options, one that will contain things like the font name and size. The real question is, what do we do inside of the `paragraph_type` class method? The answer is that we need to define a new instance method on the subclass of `StructuredDocument` that is calling the `paragraph_type` method. Your natural impulse is to write something like this:

```
class StructuredDocument

  def self.paragraph_type( paragraph_name, options )
    def <<the new method>>
        # Add a new paragraph
    end
  end

  # ...
end
```

Unfortunately that is not going to work. The trouble with the familiar `def` statement is that we have the name of the method we're trying to create in the `name` parameter but `def` requires an explicit "you type it right here" name for the method. In other words, we have the name of the new method as *data*, but `def` wants it as *code*.

The way around this roadblock is to make use of `class_eval`. Built into all Ruby classes, the `class_eval` method takes a string and evaluates it as if it were code that appeared in the class body. This is exactly what we need: We'll just build a string that contains the code for the new method definition and then `class_eval` the new method into reality:

```
class StructuredDocument
  def self.paragraph_type( paragraph_name, options )

    name = options[:font_name] || :arial
    size = options[:font_size] || 12
    emphasis = options[:font_emphasis] || :normal

    code = %Q{
      def #{paragraph_name}(text)
```

```
            p = Paragraph.new(:#{name}, #{size}, :#{emphasis}, text)
            self << p
          end
      }
      class_eval( code )
    end

    # ...
  end
end
```

To step through the code shown, imagine that we have this call to paragraph_type:

```
class Instructions < StructuredDocument
  paragraph_type( :introduction,
    :font_name => :arial,
    :font_size => 18,
    :font_emphasis => :italic )

  # And so on...
end
```

The paragraph_type method starts by pulling the font name, size, and emphasis out of the options hash, filling in defaults as needed. Now for the interesting part: The paragraph_type method creates a string that contains the code for the new introduction instance method, a string that will look something like this:

```
def introduction(text)
  p = Paragraph.new(:arial, 18, :italics, text)
  self << p
end
```

Finally, paragraph_type uses class_eval to execute the string, which creates the introduction method. Note that the new method ends up on the StructuredDocument subclass (i.e., Instructions) and not on the StructuredDocument class itself because the whole process started with a call from inside the Instructions class, which set self to Instructions.

Better Method Creation with define_method

Although creating new methods by `class_eval`'ing a string has a certain clarity to it—if nothing else, you can print out the string and actually see the method that you're defining—it is really not ideal. We generally like to avoid "evaluate some code on the fly"-type methods if there is a more normal API alternative. In the case of defining a new method, there definitely is an alternative, one with the very obvious name of `define_method`. To use `define_method`, you call it with the name of the new method and a block. You end up with a new method with the given name that will execute the block when called. Conveniently, the parameters of the block become the parameters of the new method. Thus, we can reformulate `paragraph_type` using `define_method` very easily:

```
class StructuredDocument
  def self.paragraph_type( paragraph_name, options )
    name = options[:font_name] || :arial
    size = options[:font_size] || 12
    emphasis = options[:font_emphasis] || :none

    define_method(paragraph_name) do |text|
      paragraph = Paragraph.new( name, size, emphasis, text )
      self << paragraph
    end
  end

  # ...
end
```

Either way you do it, you end up with a method in the superclass that can add methods to its subclasses. You also have a very powerful technique for creating custom subclasses with very little effort.

The Modification Sky Is the Limit

So far we have only been talking about writing classes that can hang new methods on their subclasses. Once you have the basic idea down, however, there is no limit to what you can do to a subclass from a superclass method. You might, for example, add a method that changes the visibility of the document methods in a subclass:

```
class StructuredDocument

  # Rest of the class omitted...

  def self.privatize
    private :content
  end
end
```

The thing to note about this code is that it doesn't change the accessibility of the content method on all `StructuredDocument` instances. But it does give its subclasses an easy way of declaring the content method private:

```
class BankStatement < StructuredDocument
  paragraph_type( :bad_news,
    :font_name => :arial,
    :font_size => 60,
    :font_emphasis => :bold )

  privatize
end
```

Now if you try to get at the contents of a `BankStatement`:

```
statement = BankStatement.new( 'Bank Statement', 'Russ')
statement.bad_news("You're broke!")
puts statement.content
```

You are in for a shock:

```
private method `content' called for #<BankStatement:0x8b8f544>
```

Nor are you limited to just messing with instance methods. You might, for example, want to mark any document that you privatize with a class method to announce that the document is confidential:

```
class StructuredDocument

  # Rest of the class omitted...
```

```
def self.disclaimer
  "This document is here for all to see"
end

def self.privatize
  private :content

  def self.disclaimer
    "This document is a deep, dark secret"
  end
end
end
```

This code starts by defining a default `disclaimer` method on the `Structured-Document` class, a method that proclaims the availability of the document. If you create a `StructuredDocument` subclass and don't call `privatize`, this is the method you will get. If, on the other hand, you do call `privatize` from your subclass:

```
class BankStatement < StructuredDocument
  paragraph_type( :bad_news,
    :font_name => :arial,
    :font_size => 60,
    :font_emphasis => :bold )

  privatize
end
```

Then `BankStatement` will end up with its own version of the disclaimer method, so that running:

```
puts BankStatement.disclaimer
```

Will give you this:

```
This document is a deep, dark secret
```

Remember, if you can do it to a class, you can do it from the superclass!

In the Wild

Once you know what to look for, it's hard to miss Ruby subclass-changing methods in real-world code. In fact, some are built into every Ruby class that you've ever written. These ubiquitous methods go by the name `attr_accessor`, `attr_reader`, and `attr_writer`. Think about what `attr_accessor` and friends do: They let you describe some methods that you want, so that if you say this:

```
class Printer
  attr_accessor :name
end
```

You really end up with a class that looks something like this:

```
class Printer
  def name
    @name
  end

  def name=(value)
    @name = value
  end
end
```

If you have read this far into this chapter, figuring out how `attr_accessor` and friends works is not hard. Here's a simple version of `attr_reader`[2] that uses `class_eval`:

```
class Object
  def self.simple_attr_reader(name)
    code = "def #{name}; @#{name}; end"
    class_eval( code )
  end
end
```

---

2. The real `attr_reader` method, along with its siblings, is defined in the Ruby C code (or Java if you are using JRuby). If you think that this makes the implementations of those methods inaccessible, then you need to read Chapter 30.

Similarly, here's a stripped-down version of `attr_writer`, this time using `define_method`:

```ruby
class Object
  def self.simple_attr_writer(name)
    method_name = "#{name}="
    define_method( method_name ) do |value|
      variable_name = "@#{name}"
      instance_variable_set( variable_name, value )
    end
  end
end
```

Aside from `attr_accessor` et al., the most well-known subclass changing methods are probably those that come with ActiveRecord. As every Rails programmer knows, doing this:

```ruby
class Automobile < ActiveRecord::Base
  has_one :manufacturer
end


my_car  = Automobile.find( :first )
```

Means that you can say `my_car.manufacturer` to get to the object that represents the company that made the car.

Finally, if you look in `forwardable.rb`, which is part of the Ruby standard library, you will find still more examples of class-modifying methods. The idea behind `forwardable.rb` is similar to `delegate.rb`, which we met when we were talking about using `method_missing` to delegate. Both of these library classes try to make delegation easy. The difference is that where `delegate.rb` takes the `method_missing` approach to delegation, catching calls to nonexistent methods and sending them off to the other object, `Forwardable` actually generates the delegating methods on the fly.

The interesting thing about `Forwardable` is that it's not a class at all. It's a module that you mix in at the class level with `extend`. Other than its slightly surprising packaging, `Forwardable` works exactly like the examples in this chapter. Here, for instance, is a simple class that looks like a document, but that actually just bounces all the method calls to `title`, `author`, and `content` off to a real `Document` instance:

```
class DocumentWrapper
  extend Forwardable

  def_delegators  :@real_doc, :title, :author, :content

  def initialize( real_doc )
    @real_doc = real_doc
  end
end
```

Like our earlier `delegate.rb`-based `DocumentWrapper`, this one lets you treat the wrapper just like the original:

```
real_doc = Document.new( 'Two Cities', 'Dickens', 'It was...' )
wrapped_doc = DocumentWrapper.new( real_doc )

puts wrapped_doc.title
puts wrapped_doc.author
puts wrapped_doc.content
```

Here is an edited version of the key method in `Forwardable`:

```
module Forwardable
  # Lots of code deleted...

  def def_instance_delegator(accessor, method, ali = method)
    str = %{
      def #{ali}(*args, &block)
        #{accessor}.__send__(:#{method}, *args, &block)
      end
    }
    module_eval(str, __FILE__, line_no)
  end
end
```

Aside from the fact that this code uses `module_eval`—which is synonymous with `class_eval`—this is exactly the string-based technique that we've been discussing.

Staying Out of Trouble

It's easy to get lost when you first try to do the sort of metaprogramming we looked at in this chapter. The problem is not that this is an extremely complex process; it's just that most programmers new to Ruby are not used to thinking in terms of modifying classes at all, let alone writing methods to do the modification for them, let alone moving those methods up to a superclass. If you feel like this technique has left you in a confusing maze of twisty passages,[3] here are some signposts that can help.

First, keep your goal firmly in mind. In our example, we wanted to make it easy to add paragraph-generating methods to StructuredDocument subclasses.

Second, know when things happen. For example, when you load the Structured-Document code, perhaps with this:

```
require 'structured_document'
```

You end up with the generic StructuredDocument class, which has the paragraph_type class method on it. A bit later (perhaps even on the very next line of code) you load the Instructions class:

```
require 'instructions'
```

As the Instructions class definition is getting executed, it will fire off calls to the paragraph_type method up in the StructuredDocument class. This will add methods with names like introduction, warning, and step to the Instructions class. Only when all of this defining is over do you make an instance of Instructions and call the generated methods.

The third thing to know is that the value of self is at every stage of this process. This starts out relatively straightforward but gets a little hairy as you go along. The straightforward bit is in the superclass:

```
class StructuredDocument

  # Self is StructuredDocument here

  def self.paragraph_type( paragraph_name, options )
    # ...
```

---

3. All of them alike.

```
      end

   end
```

When you say def self.paragraph_type, you are defining a new class method on the StructuredDocument class. But—and this is a key "but"—when you call the paragraph_type method from the subclass, self will be whatever class called the method. Thus, self inside paragraph_type will be Resume or Instructions (the subclass), not StructuredDocument. This is why the introduction method ends up on Instructions and not on StructuredDocument.

Finally, when you actually call the generated method on an instance of your subclass, maybe like this:

```
omlette_howto = Instructions.new( 'Russ', 'Omlettes' ) do |i|
   i.warning( "Careful of those sharp egg shells!")
end
```

The value of self inside the generated method will be the Instructions instance. As the philosophers say, "Know thyself"!

There is one other thing to beware of with the metaprogramming techniques we've covered in the past few chapters—the inclination of programmers to either avoid them completely or use them for everything in sight. So the question is: When should you pull out the metaprogramming and when should you stick to garden-variety code?

As usual, the extreme cases are the easiest. If you can solve your problem in a reasonable way with your traditional programming chops, do that. Do you need to share the same method between several different classes? You *could* add that method on the fly to both classes, but probably you are better off putting the method in a superclass or a mixin module. In the quest for software that is actually useful, simple solutions to straightforward problems have a plain eloquence all their own.

At the other extreme are the things you just cannot do without metaprogramming. If you need to build a generic method-agnostic proxy or a reloadable Document class, metaprogramming is the only solution.

The intermediate cases, problems like our "to encrypt or not to encrypt?" question and the Ruby 1.8/1.9 incompatibility handler are harder. If you can solve a problem with some traditional code or a touch of metaprogramming, how do you decide?

Again, it's all about striking a balance. Metaprogramming can dramatically reduce the volume and the complexity of your code. Hooks let you define code that will run at helpful times. Method missing and the techniques that rely on open classes can save you an enormous amount of coding toil. All of this, however, comes at a price. Those hooks might go off at unexpected times. Using method missing and open classes means that your application will be running code that has no obvious counterpart in your source tree.

The trick is to simply get back more programming goodness than you pay in meta-complexity. Take the Ruby 1.8/1.9 string example that we looked at in the last chapter. In real life, would I actually use class-level logic to deal with that one problem? Probably not. In real life I would probably code some ordinary run-time logic that asked itself about the Ruby version and did the right thing. If, however, I was doing this with scores of methods, or if the *this* or *that* logic was complex, I might well turn to metaprogramming. The bottom line is simple: Make that metaprogramming pay for itself.

Wrapping Up

The trouble with traditional programming languages is that they treat classes as if they were petrified. You make a class and there it is, eternal and unchanging. As we have seen in the last few chapters, the Ruby way of looking at things is that classes are objects just like any other. If you are somehow unhappy with the contents of your class, you can change them. Two chapters ago we saw how you can change Ruby classes manually, via monkey patching. In the last chapter we saw how you can write classes that reconfigure themselves. Finally, in this chapter we saw how you can share all of that class-changing logic by moving it into a superclass or a module.

One of the advantages of metaprogramming is the way you can use it to give your Ruby a customized "made just for this problem" feel. Page back and look at the examples in this chapter. One thing that stands out is how the `paragraph_type` and `privatize methods` feel less like methods and more like key words, specialized parts of a new Ruby-like language. Now there's an idea worth pursuing.

PART IV

Pulling It All Together

CHAPTER 27

Invent Internal DSLs

Rake. RSpec. ActiveRecord models. A build tool, a testing utility, and a database interface library. It seems unlikely that these three chunks of code could have anything in common, but they do. All three are examples of a particular style of programming, the internal Domain Specific Language, or DSL. More than any other technique, the internal DSL has come to represent the easy eloquence of Ruby; each is an illustration of how the language allows you to create tools that can solve whole classes of problems.

In this chapter we will look at building DSLs in Ruby. Actually, build is probably the wrong word: What we will really see is how you can *grow* a DSL, how you can start with an ordinary API and slowly transform it into something more, so that step by step it becomes its own little language. Along the way we will see how to pull together a number of the Ruby programming techniques covered in previous chapters into a really powerful combination. Finally, we will look at when an internal DSL is a good solution and when it is better to turn to something else.

Little Languages for Big Problems

Software engineering is all about trade-offs. There rarely is a "best" or "correct" solution to programming problems. We keep all the data in memory and the program runs faster—at the cost of all that memory. Or, we strike a different bargain and save the memory at the price of speed. We build plain-looking GUIs that work now or we create fancy ones that take a little longer. We drink the free but dubious coffee in the office or we go out and spend a few dollars for the real thing.

You see this kind of trade-off in the design of programming languages. The typical general-purpose programming language is good at solving a huge range of problems. C# is about as good at writing accounting systems as it is at building software that will predict earthquakes. You can use Java to build huge enterprise applications or tiny cell phone GUIs. Unfortunately, there is a price to be paid for being general purpose. A language that tries to do everything can't afford to be great at any one thing.

Domain specific languages, or **DSLs** for short, strike a different sort of bargain. Instead of being pretty good at a lot of things, a DSL tries to be really great at one narrowly defined class of problems. Imagine creating a programming language that pulls out all of the stops to make it easy to build earthquake prediction systems. But specialization has its own cost. The price is that a language that's great at earthquakes is probably going to be lousy at doing accounting. Still, if your problem is earthquakes, then a bit of inflexibility may be worth it.

If you do decide to go the DSL route, you have a choice to make. The traditional way to build a DSL is to get out your copy of "Parsers and Compilers for Beginners" and start coding a whole new language. Martin Fowler calls this traditional approach the **external DSL**, external in the sense that the new language is separate or external from the implementation language. The downside of the external DSL approach is right out in the open: You need to build a whole new programming language. Will you have `if` statements? Classes and methods? What will you use for a comment character? Building a brand-new programming language from scratch is not something to be undertaken lightly.

The alternative is to build your DSL atop an existing language. You add so much support for solving problems in your chosen domain into an existing language that it starts to feel like a specialized tool. The beauty of this second approach is that you don't need to recreate all of the plumbing of a programming language—it's already there for you. Fowler's term for this other kind of DSL is, logically enough, the **internal DSL**. Internal DSLs are internal in that the DSL is built right into the implementation language. The good news is that Ruby, with its "the programmer is always right" feature set and very flexible syntax, makes a great platform for building internal DSLs.

Dealing with XML

To turn all this theory into real code, let's put down our familiar and somewhat contrived Document class and look at a very real-world problem: XML. These days, XML is so common that it is a rare software engineer who manages to avoid it.[1] Imagine that we have a number of documents stored in XML files, files that look something like this:

```
<?xml version="1.0" encoding="UTF-8"?>
<document>

  <title>The Fellowship Of The Ring</title>
  <author>J. R. R. Tolken</author>
  <published>1954</published>

  <chapter>
    <title>A Long Expected Party</title>
    <content>When Mr. Bilbo Bagins of Bag End...</content>
  </chapter>

  <chapter>
    <title>A Shadow Of The Past</title>
    <content>The talk did not die down...</content>
  </chapter>

  <!-- ect -->
</document>
```

Now, the whole idea of an XML file is that the data is easily accessible and easy to manipulate. We go to the trouble of adding `<title>` and `<chapter>` tags to make it painless to extract data from the file. The XML world has defined XSLT, a language for doing this kind of thing, but XSLT is a complex technology in itself. For simple jobs a Ruby programmer will be happier with a little Ruby script. Fortunately, XML processing is also easy to do in Ruby. Here, for example, is a script that can read an XML file like the one above and tell you who the author is:

```
#!/usr/bin/env ruby

require "rexml/document"
```

---

1. Try as we might.

```
File.open( 'fellowship.xml' ) do |f|
  doc = REXML::Document.new(f)
  author = REXML::XPath.first(doc, '/document/author')
  puts author.text
end
```

This script relies on Ruby's very easy-to-use REXML XML parsing library, especially its XPath facility, which allows you to navigate through the XML hierarchy with convenient strings like '/document/author'. Given the author finding code above, it is just a tiny step to a script that finds all of the chapter titles:

```
#!/usr/bin/env ruby

require "rexml/document"

File.open( 'fellowship.xml' ) do |f|
  doc = REXML::Document.new(f)
  REXML::XPath.each(doc, '/document/chapter/title') do |title|
    puts title.text
  end
end
```

It's also easy to come up with a script to fix the misspelling of *Tolkien*'s name:

```
#!/usr/bin/env ruby

require "rexml/document"

File.open( 'fellowship.xml' ) do |f|
  doc = REXML::Document.new(f)
  REXML::XPath.each(doc, '/document/author') do |author|
    author.text = 'J.R.R. Tolkien'
  end
  puts doc
end
```

This last example is a little more complex than the first two, but not much. It reads the whole file, changes the text of the '/document/author' element, and then prints out the entire modified XML document.

As easy as REXML is to use, there is a lot of redundant code in those three little scripts. Each one needs to require in the REXML library, open the input file, and do some XPath-based searching. If we were going to do a lot of this sort of thing, we would want to factor out all of this repeated code into some kind of common utility, one that will help us rip through XML:

```
require "rexml/document"

class XmlRipper
  def initialize(&block)
    @before_action = proc {}
    @path_actions = {}
    @after_action = proc {}
    block.call( self ) if block
  end

  def on_path( path, &block )
    @path_actions[path] = block
  end

  def before( &block )
    before_action = block
  end

  def after( &block )
    @after_action = block
  end

  def run( xml_file_path )
    File.open( xml_file_path ) do |f|
      document = REXML::Document.new(f)
      @before_action.call( document )
      run_path_actions( document )
      @after_action.call( document )
    end
  end
```

```
    def run_path_actions( document )
      @path_actions.each do |path, block|
        REXML::XPath.each(document, path) do |element|
          block.call( element )
        end
      end
    end
  end
end
```

The `XmlRipper` class is built around the `@path_actions` hash, which maps strings containing XPaths to Ruby code blocks. The idea is that you fill out `@path_actions` hash by calling the on_path method repeatedly. When you are done you call the run method, passing in the name of an XML file. The run method will open the XML file, find the bits of XML that match the XPaths, and fire off the associated code block for each match.

The `XmlRipper` class dramatically reduces the drudgery of writing those XML processing scripts. Here's our author and chapter title examples all rolled into one, translated into `XmlRipper`:

```
ripper = XmlRipper.new do |r|
  r.on_path( '/document/author' ) { |a| puts a.text }
  r.on_path( '/document/chapter/title' ) { |t| puts t.text }
end

ripper.run( 'fellowship.xml' )
```

We can also fix the author's name with very little ceremony:

```
ripper = XmlRipper.new do |r|
  r.on_path( '/document/author' ) do |author|
    author.text = 'J.R.R. Tolkien'
  end
  r.after { |doc| puts doc }
end

ripper.run( 'fellowship.xml' )
```

This last example uses the XmlRipper after method to supply a block that gets run after all the other XPath-based processing is completed. The after method provides a convenient place to print out the whole XML document after we are done modifying it.[2]

Stepping Over the DSL Line

Although we didn't set out to create a new language, the XmlRipper scripts certainly have a very declarative, specialized language feel to them. This is the way that many Ruby internal DSLs are born: You set out to build a helpful class with a good API, and gradually that API gets so good that it forgets that it's just an API. This is also where many Ruby APIs finish, which is fine since there is nothing wrong with a really good, natural-feeling, almost DSL-style API. Sometimes, however, you want to go further. You might want to take the next step if you need to write a lot of scripts, if there are a lot of programmers who will need to use your utility, or if the folks using XmlRipper are less technical. So how do you push XmlRipper along?

One way that you can make the XmlRipper scripts more DSL-like is to get rid of the need to constantly refer to the new XmlRipper instance (the r parameter) inside of the block. You can simplify the code inside of the block by turning to a method common to every Ruby object, instance_eval. Pass instance_eval a block and, just like call, it will execute the block. The difference is that instance_eval changes the value of self as it executes the block: Say some_object.instance_eval(block) and the value of self will be some_object as the block executes. Thus, if you rewrite the XmlRipper initialize method to use instance_eval:

```
class XmlRipper

  def initialize(&block)
    @before_action = proc {}
    @path_actions = {}
    @after_action = proc {}
    instance_eval( &block ) if block
  end
```

---

2. If you look carefully at the XmlRipper class you will see that there is also a before method, which operates as the mirror image of after. Although I'm generally against adding features that aren't used simply because they "make sense," this one makes so much sense that I'll make an exception. For more on this kind of thing, see Chapter 31.

```
# Rest of the class omitted...

end
```

Then `self` will be equal to the new `XmlRipper` instance as the block evaluates.[3] Since the `on_path` and `before` methods are defined on the `XmlRipper` instance, you can drop the initialization block argument and simply call `on_path` and `after` directly:

```
ripper = XmlRipper.new do
  on_path( '/document/author' ) do |author|
    author.text = 'J.R.R. Tolkien'
  end
  after { |doc| puts doc }
end

ripper.run( 'fellowship.xml' )
```

Getting rid of all those pesky r parameters is a step forward in making the `XmlRipper` scripts more language-like, but it's not the only thing you can do. Notice how each `XmlRipper` script always starts with the `XmlRipper.new` line and ends with the `ripper.run` call. In an ideal world you would get rid of all that boilerplate code, cutting down the code that the user has to write to the chewy center:

```
on_path( '/document/author' ) do |author|
  author.text = 'J.R.R. Tolkien'
end
after { |doc| puts doc }
```

Once again, `instance_eval` comes to your rescue. If, instead of passing a block to `instance_eval` you feed it a string, `instance_eval` will evaluate the string as Ruby code. Here's a new, slightly rewritten version of the `XmlRipper` class that can read the script from a file:

---

3. If this seems confusing, consider that `instance_eval( &block )` is equivalent to `self.instance_eval( &block )` and `self` is the newly created `XmlRipper` instance.

```
class XmlRipper

  def initialize_from_file( path )
    instance_eval( File.read( path ) )
  end

  # Rest of the class omitted...

end
```

Now you can write a short script that will read and execute a file full of befores, on_paths, and afters:

```
ripper = XmlRipper.new
ripper.initialize_from_file( 'fix_author.ripper' )
ripper.run( 'fellowship.xml')
```

More realistically, you would probably want to pass in command-line arguments so that you could pass in the name of the file containing your XML-manipulating script first, followed by the XML file itself:

```
r = XmlRipper.new
r.initialize_from_file( ARGV[0] )
r.run( ARGV[1] )
```

Congratulations! You have just witnessed the birth of a new Ruby internal DSL: Ripper. Based very firmly in Ruby and yet with a declarative, XML-processing feel all its own, Ripper tries to get the best of both worlds. By building atop Ruby, you managed to avoid all the work of creating a complicated parser for a brand new language. Since Ripper sits atop Ruby, you don't have to worry about implementing if statements and comments and the thousand other things that a useful programming language has. Ruby supplies them all for free:

```
# Correct a common mistake

on_path( '/document/author' ) do |author|
  author.text = 'J.R.R. Tolkien' if author.text =~ /Tolken/
end
```

```
# Print out the whole document when done

after { |doc| puts doc }
```

Free is always a good price.

Pulling Out All the Stops

Be aware that Ruby internal DSLs are more a state of mind than a single technology. By building a DSL, you're going all out to make it easy for your user to do whatever the DSL does. Any programming technique that makes the job easier, that makes the code clearer, is fair game. Think about the possibilities of the metaprogramming techniques of the last few chapters: You might, for example decide that it would be helpful if Ripper users could specify very simple XPaths as part of the method name, like this:

```
on_document_author { |author| puts author.text }
```

Definitely a job for method_missing:

```
class XmlRipper

  # Rest of the class omitted...

  def method_missing( name, *args, &block )
    return super unless name.to_s =~ /on_.*/
    parts = name.to_s.split( "_" )
    parts.shift
    xpath = parts.join( '/' )
    on_path( xpath, &block )
  end
end
```

The method_missing implementation here catches any method call that starts with on_, turns the rest of the method name into a simple XPath like 'document/author', and works from there. This is exactly the magic method technique that we explored in Chapter 23.

In the Wild

Once you get the hang of the internal DSL techniques, the inner workings of a lot of seemingly magic Ruby utilities becomes obvious. Take a typical RSpec file:

```
describe "Array#each" do
  it "yields each element to the block" do
    a = []
    x = [1, 2, 3]
    x.each { |item| a << item }.should equal(x)
    a.should == [1, 2, 3]
  end

  # Lots of stuff omitted
end
```

This is either a structured description of the behavior of arrays or it is a call to a method named `describe`, a call that passes in a string and a block. Inside the block there is a call to a method called `it`, a method that also takes a string and a block. It's all very pedestrian when you know what is going on.

Another superb example of a Ruby DSL is Rake. Here's a simple Rakefile:

```
task :default => [ :install_program , :install_data ]

task :install_data => :installation_dir do
  cp 'fonts.dat', 'installation'
end

task :install_program => [ :installation_dir ] do
  cp 'document.rb', 'installation'
end

task :installation_dir do
  mkdir_p 'installation'
end
```

Again, we either have four task definitions or four calls to the `task` method. One very elegant thing about Rakefiles is the use of the hash literal syntax to specify dependency relationships. This:

```
task :default => [ :install_program , :install_data ]
```

Is just a brilliant way of saying that the `:default` task depends on both the `:install_program` and `:install_data` tasks.

As slick as RSpec and Rake are in all their "push Ruby to the limit" glory, many real-world Ruby programs are satisfied with less-ambitious DSL-like APIs. We've already looked at the ActiveRecord model API with its superclass-generated table relationships:

```
class Book < ActiveRecord::Base
  has_many :authors
  belongs_to :publisher
end
```

Even more basic, but no less effective are ActiveRecord migrations.

```
class AddBooks < ActiveRecord::Migration
  def self.up
    create_table :books do |t|
      t.string  :title
      t.integer :publisher_id
    end
  end

  def self.down
    drop_table :books
  end
end
```

It's just a class that defines a couple of class methods, up and down, but it's also a description of how to build—and tear down—a database table.

Staying Out of Trouble

As useful and easy as internal DSLs can be, they do have their downsides. The first is that internal DSLs tend to produce really bad error messages. Think about what would happen if we made a mistake in a Ripper script, perhaps like this:

```
# Error: Note the missing do on the first line...

on_path( '/document/author' ) |author|
  author.text = 'Tolkien'
end


after { |doc| puts doc }
```

Clearly, we forgot the do in the call to on_path. Unfortunately, as Ripper stands right now, this is the less-than-illuminating error message that our little screwup will produce:

```
ripper.rb:6:in `instance_eval': (eval):5:
  syntax error, unexpected keyword_end,
    expecting $end (SyntaxError)
  from ripper.rb:6:in `initialize_from_file'
  from ripper_main.rb:4:in `<main>'
```

The problem is that we messed up the Ripper program, but the error messages are coming back to us in Ruby terms. We can improve on this by using yet another bit of instance_eval magic. The instance_eval method has an optional second parameter, one that will tell instance_eval where the code it is evaluating came from. Pass in the name of the Ripper file as this second parameter:

```
class XmlRipper

  def initialize_from_file( path )
    instance_eval( File.read( path ), path )
  end

  # Rest of the class omitted...

end
```

And at least the error will point the user to the right file:

```
ripper.rb:6:in `instance_eval': broken.ripper:5:
  syntax error, unexpected keyword_end,
    expecting $end (SyntaxError)
  from ripper.rb:6:in `initialize_from_file'
  from ripper_main.rb:4:in `<main>'
```

You should also keep in mind that however helpful your DSL, you may still want to use your classes as an ordinary API. This is fairly easy if you keep the language-oriented bits of your DSL separate from the business end of the code, the part that actually does things. This way you can use your code via the DSL, or you can use it as part of an ordinary Ruby program.

Finally, it's worth noting that the biggest danger with internal DSLs is not really a computing problem but a psychological one. It goes by the name *programmer over enthusiasm*. Creating an internal DSL can help you squeeze a lot of power and flexibility out of very little code. The trick is to keep squarely focused on solving your real problem and avoid getting carried away with building a really cool syntax. Could we, for example, take the whole "XPath as Ruby code" idea to its logical conclusion? Perhaps, instead of the simple method_missing based on_chapter_title thing that we did in our last XmlRipper example, we could map the entire XPath syntax onto some Ruby code. So instead of saying this:

```
on_path( '/document/author' ) { |author| puts author.text }
```

We could say something like:

```
on_path /document/author { |author| puts author.text }
```

We might do this with a clever combination of operator overloading (think about the possibilities of the division operator!) and method_missing. Could it be done? I doubt it. Consider that while the XPaths that we used in this chapter are extremely simple, you can say some XPath things guaranteed to make Ruby gag. Any attempt to map document/*/title or @* into some DSL-like Ruby expression is destined to end in tears.

The real question is whether this kind of thing is even worth trying. Whatever goodness you bestow on your users by eliminating the quotes around '/document/author' is going to be more than canceled out by the Rabbinical complexity of the internal DSL code you'll need to write to make it all work. You can only push the Ruby parser so far; if you need to go beyond that point, roll up your sleeves and start thinking about writing your own parser.

Wrapping Up

Internal DSLs are one of the hallmarks of Ruby done right. You take advantage of the flexibility of the language to create support for solving a whole class of problems. You can package that support as either a friendly API or you can keep pushing it to the point where it really is a new, specialized little language.

As useful as internal DSLs are, they are not the whole story. Sometimes you need a DSL but you simply cannot fit the syntax of your DSL into the strictures of Ruby. In those circumstances you will need to build an external DSL, which is where this book goes next.

CHAPTER 28

Build External DSLs for Flexible Syntax

My older brother turned out to be a pretty great guy. He works hard. He's dedicated to his family. If you have a problem, he's willing to help. Since he did turn out so well, I guess I can forgive him for being really, really popular in high school. Back then my days seemed to be filled with a continuous stream of pretty girls asking me if I was *really* Charlie Olsen's brother.[1] The thing is, even in my teens I was witty, I was intelligent, and I had the mesmerizing Olsen blue eyes. There's no doubt that my high school career would have been a bigger social success if only I could have stepped out of my brother's shadow for five minutes.[2]

Given this, I can sympathize with every external DSL ever written in Ruby. Ruby is a really great language for building external DSLs, those DSLs that (unlike the internal flavor) use their own parser instead of the Ruby parser. The trouble is that as useful as Ruby-based external DSLs are, they are overshadowed by the really stellar things that people have done with internal DSLs. To remedy this injustice, and because they are a real part of the Ruby style of programming, this chapter is going to explore building Ruby-based external DSLs. We will start by looking at why you might go to all the trouble of building a parser instead of just using the one that comes with Ruby. We will then examine some of the Ruby tools that you can use to create an external

---

1. My standard answer: "No." Long pause. "He's my brother."

2. I'm over it now. Really.

DSL. Finally, we will look at some of the external DSLs that exist in the Ruby world and some of the dangers inherent in building an external DSL.

The Trouble with the Ripper

To see why you might build an external DSL instead of taking advantage of all of the wonders of the internal variety, consider what might happen if our Ripper DSL from the last chapter found its way to a wider audience. Perhaps from its modest start as a handy little utility used only by you, Ripper has been picked up by your immediate and very technical colleagues. Then it spread to the equally capable system administrators, and finally to some decidedly nontechnical support staff. This last group, although they like the features of Ripper, do have some complaints. For starters, they don't understand why the Ripper syntax is so complex. Take this typical Ripper example:

```
on_path( '/document/author' ) { |author| puts author.text }
```

What's the deal, they want to know, with all the quotes and braces and vertical pipe characters? Could you please, your less-technical users ask, make some minor modifications to Ripper so that they could say this instead:

```
print /document/author
```

In the same way they would like simpler `delete` and `replace` commands:

```
delete /document/published
replace /document/author Tolkien
```

As we saw at the end of the last chapter, the quick answer is that no, it is not possible. This:

```
replace /document/author Tolkien
```

Is just not a valid Ruby expression. Since the whole idea of internal DSLs is that the DSL code is Ruby, you cannot build an internal DSL able to cope with this input.

Internal Is Not the Only DSL

While an internal DSL is out, an external DSL is entirely possible. Recall that an external DSL is the more traditional language-building approach: You think up a syntax and you build a parser for it, a parser that sucks in the domain-specific program and does the right thing with it. Since you build the parser, you are not encumbered by the rules of Ruby grammar. Despite all the hoopla around Ruby internal DSLs, the fact is that Ruby, with its powerful strings and built-in regular expressions, is a pretty good language for building the external flavor of DSLs too.

Let's see if we can't put together a parser for our new, simplified XML processing language:

```ruby
class EzRipper
  def initialize( program_path )
    @ripper = XmlRipper.new
    parse_program(program_path)
  end

  def run( xml_file )
    @ripper.run( xml_file )
  end

  def parse_program( program_path )
    File.open(program_path) do |f|
      until f.eof?
        parse_statement( f.readline )
      end
    end
  end

  def parse_statement( statement )
    tokens = statement.strip.split
    return if tokens.empty?

    case tokens.first
    when 'print'
      @ripper.on_path( tokens[1] ) do |el|
        puts el.text
      end
```

```
    when 'delete'
      @ripper.on_path( tokens[1] ) { |el| el.remove }

    when 'replace'
      @ripper.on_path( tokens[1] ) { |el| el.text = tokens[2] }

    when 'print_document'
      @ripper.after do |doc|
        puts doc
      end

    else
      raise "Unknown keyword: #{tokens.first}"
    end
  end
end
```

This class will parse the simplified XML processing commands that our users are requesting. For example, if we wanted to change the author's name and delete the publication date from an XML file, we might create a file called `edit.ezr` containing:

```
delete /document/published
replace /document/author Tolkien
print_document
```

The last command, `print_document`, will tell `EzRipper` to output the modified XML. To run our little program we simply feed it and the name of the XML file into `EzRipper`:

```
EzRipper.new( 'edit.ezr' ).run('fellowship.xml' )
```

The `EzRipper` class really just provides a fancy front end for the original `XmlRipper` class. All of the real XML processing work is still done by `XmlRipper`. The parser reads in a line at a time—we are assuming that each statement fits on a single line—and breaks up the statement into space-separated tokens using the handy `String` `split` method. To keep things simple, we also assume there are no embedded spaces in the arguments in a statement.[3] Once it has broken the line up into tokens,

---

3. Keep reading though, because we will fix the "no space" limitation in a bit.

the EzRipper parser looks at the first token, which should be something like replace or delete, and works from there.

Compared with an internal DSL, you have a lot of fine control over the behavior of an external DSL. Given, for example, that EzRipper is aimed at less-technical users, we might want to provide more extensive error messages:

```ruby
def parse_statement( statement )
  tokens = statement.strip.split
  return if tokens.empty?

  case tokens.first
  when 'print'
    raise "Expected print <xpath>" unless tokens.size == 2
    @ripper.on_path( tokens[1] ) do |el|
      puts el.text
    end

  when 'delete'
    raise "Expected delete <xpath>" unless tokens.size == 2
    @ripper.on_path( tokens[1] ) { |el| el.remove }

  when 'replace'
    unless tokens.size == 3
      raise "Expected replace <xpath> <value>"
    end
    @ripper.on_path( tokens[1] ) {|el| el.text = tokens[2]}

  when 'print_document'
    raise "Expected print_document" unless tokens.size == 1
    @ripper.after do |doc|
      puts doc
    end

  else
    raise "Unknown keyword: #{tokens.first}"
  end
end
```

Within limits, it is also fairly easy to add new features to `EzRipper`. We might, for example, add an `uppercase` command that converts the text of an element to all uppercase:

```
when 'uppercase'
  raise "Expected uppercase <xpath>" unless tokens.size == 2
  @ripper.on_path( tokens[1] ) { |el| el.text = el.text.upcase }
```

We might also add comments, delimited by #:[4]

```
def parse_statement( statement )
  statement = statement.sub( /#.*/, '' )
  tokens = statement.strip.split
  return if tokens.empty?
```

This last version of `parse_statement` deals with comments by stripping them out with a carefully aimed `gsub` call.

Regular Expressions for Heavier Parsing

As I say, our current implementation of `EzRipper` does have one potentially serious limitation: It can't handle spaces in the command arguments. By ignoring the possibility of embedded white space, we were able to devise a little language that we can parse very easily. But what if we really needed to deal with embedded spaces? We could change the syntax so that all of the command arguments are surrounded by quotes, which would allow for spaces while enabling us to keep the individual arguments straight:[5]

```
replace '/document/author' 'Russ Olsen'
```

---

4. In the interest of keeping the example simple, the comment addition ignores the very real possibility that the statement itself might contain a # character.

5. And no, the addition of the quotes does not make this valid Ruby susceptible to an internal DSL solution. Think about it. Since there is no comma between the two strings, Ruby would concatenate the two strings together, leaving us with the impossible job of trying to figure out where the XPath ends and the argument begins.

There is just no way we'll be able to use a simple call to split to break up the command. This situation calls for some regular expressions. Here's a new **parse_statement** method, one that uses regular expressions to cope with the more complex syntax:

```ruby
def parse_statement( statement )

  statement = statement.sub( /#.*/, '' )

  case statement.strip
  when ''
    # Skip blank lines

  when /print\s+'(.*?)'/
    @ripper.on_path( $1 ) do |el|
      puts el.text
    end

  when /delete\s+'(.*?)'/
    @ripper.on_path( $1 ) { |el| el.remove }

  when /replace\s+'(.*?)'\s+'(.*?)'$/
    @ripper.on_path( $1 ) { |el| el.text = $2 }

  when /uppercase\s+'(.*?)'/
    @ripper.on_path( $1 ) { |el| el.text = el.text.upcase }

  when /print_document/
    @ripper.after do |doc|
      puts doc
    end

  else
    raise "Don't know what to do with: #{statement}"
  end
end
```

The key to this code is the gaggle of somewhat intimidating-looking regular expressions. Although they may look formidable, these regular expressions are really not that complex. Take the one that deals with the replace statement:

```ruby
/replace\s+'(.*?)'\s+'(.*?)'$/
```

This expression starts with the obvious: A `replace` command needs to start with the word `replace`. Next we have the real key to the regular expression, a couple of instances of this:

```
\s+'(.*?)'
```

This bit of regular expression magic is designed to match one quoted argument, something like `'/document/chapter/title'` or `'Russ Olsen'`. Again, the way to understand it is to disassemble it into its constituent parts. The expression starts with `\s+`, which will match one or more characters of white space. Next we have a quote, followed by anything at all [that's the `(.*?)` part] followed by another quote. We use `*?` instead of a plain `*` because we want to match the smallest bit of text surrounded by quotes: The addition of the question mark prevents the expression for the first argument from matching the initial quote all the way to the quote at the end of the whole statement. By putting parentheses around the "anything" part of the regular expressions, we get Ruby to capture exactly what the anythings are and store them in the `$1`, `$2`, and `$3` variables, where the rest of the code can get at them.

There is no doubt that the regular expression-based parser is more complicated than our original "just pull things apart with split" approach. It's the price you pay for a more complex syntax.

Treetop for Really Big Jobs

Sometimes the price of regular expressions can get too high. The problem is that regular expressions don't really scale that well. While they are great for medium-sized jobs like our last version of the `EzRipper` syntax, it is easy to invent a grammar that will induce regular expression madness in most coders. Think, for example, about the regular expressions that you would need to handle escaped quotes within the arguments. Or multiline statements. Or variables. Or all of the above in various combinations. As your external DSL gets more and more complex, at some point it's going to overwhelm your ability to write and, more importantly, *read*, the regular expressions required to handle the grammar. If you do get to that stage, the thing to do is to turn to a real parser-building tool.

One of the more interesting of these tools is Treetop.[6] Treetop describes itself as "a language for describing languages."[7] Another way to say this is: Treetop is a DSL for building parsers.

To use Treetop you need to build a treetop file that describes your grammar. Here's the Treetop file for our improved `EzRipper` grammar:

```
grammar EzRipperStatement

  rule statement
    comment/delete_statement/replace_statement/print_statement
  end

  rule comment
    "#" .*
  end

  rule delete_statement
    "delete" sp quoted_argument sp
  end

  rule replace_statement
    "replace" sp quoted_argument sp quoted_argument sp
  end

  rule print_statement
    "filter" sp quoted_argument sp
  end

  rule quoted_argument
    "'" argument "'"
  end
```

---

6. Treetop is by no means the only Ruby-based tool for building sophisticated parsers. There is, for example, RACC, which is the Ruby rendition of the venerable Unix program YACC. Like Treetop, RACC reads in a file that describes the syntax of your language and produces Ruby code that can parse the language.

7. You can learn all about Treetop at www.treetop.rubyforge.org.

```
rule argument
  (!"'" . )*
end

rule sp
  [ \t\n]*
end

end
```

As you can see from this example, Treetop allows you to build a reasonably clear description of your grammar, one that is not completely obscured by the nuts and bolts of parsing. To use Treetop, you store your language description in a file with a name like `ez_ripper_statement.tt` and then run it through the treetop compiler:

```
tt ez_ripper_statement.tt
```

When you run this command, Treetop will create a file called `ez_ripper_statement.rb` and fill it with a class called `EzRipperStatementParser`, which, logically enough, will know how to parse our `EzRipper` statements. From there it's all just ordinary Ruby:

```
require 'treetop'
require 'ez_ripper_statement'

statement = "replace '/document/author' 'Russ Olsen'"
parser = EzRipperStatementParser.new
parse_tree = parser.parse( statement )
```

Run this code and you will end up with your statement parsed out into a tree structure that you can programmatically descend and interpret.

Staying Out of Trouble

To no one's great surprise, the advantages and disadvantages of external DSLs are a mirror image of those of internal DSLs. With an internal DSL, you get all of Ruby, complete with comments, loops, `if` statements, and variables more or less for free. With an external DSL, you need to work for—or at least parse—every feature. You can see this in the implementation of HAML. HAML is a very terse language for doing HTML templating. HAML lets you write this:

```
%html
  %body
    #main
      Today is
      = Time.new
```

And get this:

```
<html>
  <body>
    <div id='main'>
      Today is
      2010-09-19 15:10:01 -0400
    </div>
  </body>
</html>
```

All of this convenient terseness does come at a price. Like our intermediate EzRipper example, HAML relies on a combination of regular expressions and some clever hand-built code for parsing. Here is a bit of the HAML parse_line method, which corresponds to the parse_statement method in EzRipper:

```
def process_line(text, index)
  @index = index + 1

  case text[0]
   when DIV_CLASS; render_div(text)
  when DIV_ID
    return push_plain(text) if text[1] == ?{
    render_div(text)
  when ELEMENT; render_tag(text)
  when COMMENT; render_comment(text[1..-1].strip)
  when SANITIZE
    return push_plain(text[3..-1].strip,
            :escape_html => true) if text[1..2] == "=="
```

```
      return push_script(text[2..-1].strip,
            :escape_html => true) if text[1] == SCRIPT
      return push_flat_script(text[2..-1].strip,
            :escape_html => true) if text[1] == FLAT_SCRIPT
      return push_plain(text[1..-1].strip,
            :escape_html => true) if text[1] == ?\s
      push_plain text

    # and on and on and on...
  end
end
```

Wow. Clearly, writing the HAML parser took some real effort, which seems worth it when the result is HAML. The key question you need to ask before embarking on an external DSL is: Will *my* language be worth it?

Another thing we can glean from HAML is that the line between internal and external DSLs is not really all that sharp. Right in the middle of the HAML example above, we specified some plain old Ruby code (in the form of a call to `Time.new`) for HAML to execute. We can do the same kind of thing with `EzRipper`, perhaps adding a new command that lets us execute arbitrary Ruby code for each path, something like this:

```
execute '/document/author' 'puts "the author is #{el.text}"'
```

Implementing `execute` involves adding just a couple of lines to the `EzRipper` `parse_statement` method. Here's the regular expression version:

```
when /execute\s+'(.*?)'\s+'(.*?)'$/
  @ripper.on_path( $1 ) { |el| eval( $2 ) }
```

The `execute` statement gives us a magic portal from our external DSL back into the world of internal Ruby-based code.

In the Wild

For a language known for its internal DSLs, there are a surprising number of Ruby-based external DSLs around. For example, before HAML came along, almost all Rails applications used ERB for templating. With ERB, you write something like this:

```
    Today is <%= Time.new %>
```

And end up with something like this:[8]

```
    Today is 2009-10-18 00:25:35 -0400
```

Where the text inside the `<%= %>` brackets gets evaluated as Ruby code. ERB actually uses a variant of the `String` `split` technique that we used in our first version of EzRipper. ERB takes advantage of the fact that the `split` method itself can take a regular expression as an argument. If you do feed a regular expression into it, `split` will treat the text that matches the regular expression as delimiters, the cleavage points on which the text gets split. Thus, ERB defines this regular expression:

```
    SplitRegexp = /(<%%)|(%%>)|(<%=)|(<%#)|(<%)|(%>)|(\n)/
```

Which it then uses to break up its input.

Even more interesting is the testing tool Cucumber. Cucumber presents us with the fascinating spectacle of an external DSL used in combination with an internal DSL. The idea behind Cucumber is that you build acceptance tests in a sort of structured natural language, like this:

```
    Feature: Count words in a document
        In order to be sure that documents hold on to their content
        Start with an empty document and add some text to it
        and check to see that the text is actually there

        Scenario:
          Given that we have a document with 1000 words
          When I count the words
          Then the count should be 1000
```

You can take this friendly feature description to a nontechnical customer and talk it over: Is this what we really need to be testing? Is there anything missing? Obviously, the feature description syntax is not Ruby; this is a very external DSL requiring a separate parser.[9] Cucumber is particularly useful because you can turn the more or less

---

8. Like mileage, your time and date will vary.

9. A parser that just happens to be built with Treetop.

natural language description into real executable tests. To do this you create "step descriptions," expressed in an internal DSL:

```
Given /^that we have a document with (\d+) words$/ do |n|
  @document = Document.new( 'russ', 'a test' )
  @document.content = 'crypozoology ' * n.to_i
end

When /^I count the words$/ do
  @count = @document.word_count
end

Then /^the count should be (\d+)$/ do |n|
  @count.should == n.to_i
end
```

Cucumber weaves the step descriptions into the feature using the regular expressions you supply with the step descriptions. In the end you get a test that reads like a natural language specification but that's also executable.

Finally, a very handy example of an external DSL with a really sophisticated parser is Treetop itself. Obviously, Treetop comes with a parser that understands the Treetop grammar files. And what, you might ask, is the parser for that grammar file written in? Why, Treetop itself, of course![10] Here is the Treetop rule for Treetop rules:

```
rule parsing_rule
    'rule' space nonterminal space ('do' space)?
          parsing_expression space 'end' <ParsingRule>
end
```

You have to love this kind of recursion.

Wrapping Up

In this chapter we explored some of the possibilities of Ruby-based external DSLs. We have seen that an external DSL can be anything from a program that uses a few string

---

10. We can deduce that at sometime in the past there must have been a non-Treetop parser for Treetop grammar files to kick things off.

methods to break up its input to code that uses regular expressions, all the way to using a parser-generating tool like Treetop. Simple or complex, external DSLs free you from the constraints of Ruby syntax. But external DSLs also relieve you of that free Ruby parser. If you need to build a DSL, the choice is up to you: Do you take the ease and relative low cost of an internal DSL or go for the higher cost—and freedom—of an external DSL?

CHAPTER 29

Package Your Programs as Gems

Once you get past the occasional pet project or the odd bit of experimental programming, there are really only two kinds of software projects: those that ship and those that no one cares about. Shipping software, whether to paying customers or to a grateful open source community, is the ultimate goal of virtually every programmer.

In this chapter we will look at Ruby gems, the Ruby solution to packaging up your masterpiece so that it not only goes out the door, but also arrives on your user's system with all the fragile bits intact. We'll start with a brief look at how gems work from the point of view of a user. From there we will dive right into the details of building your own gem. We will also look at some of the things you can do to ensure that your gem actually does arrive intact. Finally, we'll look at some recursively useful gems whose purpose in life is to help you package up your own code as a gem.

Consuming Gems

If you've been programming in Ruby for any length of time then chances are that you are already familiar with being a gem consumer. Not that there is much to it; I am, for example, a very happy user of the ruby-mp3info gem, a wonderful chunk of code that lets you read and write the informational tags hidden inside MP3 files:

```
require 'mp3info'

Mp3Info.open( 'money.mp3' ) do |info|
  puts "title: #{info.tag.title}"
  puts "artist: #{info.tag.artist}"
  puts "album: #{info.tag.album}"
end
```

As a gem, ruby-mp3info is fairly typical. To use it, first you need to install it:

```
gem install ruby-mp3info
```

Depending on your operating system and exactly how your Ruby is installed, you may need special permissions to do the install. On various Unix and Linux systems as well as on OS X, you can do this by running gem with sudo:

```
$sudo gem install ruby-mp3info
```

Once you get the gem installed, you can use the code it supplies just like any other bit of Ruby.[1]

Gem Versions

A really useful feature of the gem system is its complete versioning support. Every gem is tagged with a version number and, since coders are forever fixing bugs and adding features, most gems exist in multiple versions. You can see what versions are available for any given gem with the gem list command, so that if you run:[2]

```
gem list -a --remote ruby-mp3info
```

---

1. Note that using gems in pre-1.9 versions of Ruby was a bit more complicated. Before 1.9, the Ruby Gems infrastructure was not completely integrated into Ruby. Because of this, you needed to be sure that you ran require 'rubygems' somewhere in your program or added the equivalent –rubygems argument to your Ruby command line.

2. The -a parameter asks the gem command to print out all of the versions of the gem, instead of just the latest. The --remote parameter means that the command should list the gems stored in the default remote repository, not just on your local machine.

You will discover that there have been lots of versions of the ruby-mp3info gem:

```
ruby-mp3info (0.6.13, 0.6.12, 0.6.11, 0.6.10, 0.6.9,
0.6.8, 0.6.7, 0.6.6, 0.6.5, 0.6.4, 0.6.3, 0.6.2, 0.6.1,
0.6, 0.5.1, 0.5, 0.4)
```

When you install a gem, you will get the latest version unless you ask for something earlier. Thus, if for some reason you needed the very first version of ruby-mp3info, you can ask for it with the --version option:

```
gem install --version 0.4 ruby-mp3info
```

Keep in mind that RubyGems is perfectly happy having multiple versions of the same gem installed on your system. There is, for example, no problem with pulling down several more versions of ruby-mp3info:

```
gem install --version 0.5 ruby-mp3info
gem install --version 0.5.1 ruby-mp3info
gem install --version 0.6 ruby-mp3info
```

If you do have more than one version of a gem installed, the default when you ask for the gem in your code is the latest version. Thus, since 0.6.13 is the latest version of ruby-mp3info I have on my machine, this is the version I'll get with a simple `require 'mp3info'`. If your code depends on a specific gem version, you can ask for it with the gem method:

```
gem 'ruby-mp3info', '=0.5'
require 'mp3info'
```

The version number argument on the gem method even supports more general expressions like `'>0.4'` or `'<=0.5'` so that you don't have to be quite so explicit with your version numbers.

The Nuts and Bolts of Gems

The technology behind RubyGems is pretty simple: The gem developer (the folks behind ruby-mp3info, for example) package up their work into a single file, a standardized archive containing not only the code but also lots of useful metadata, like the gem version number and the other gems on which this gem depends. Once the code is packed tidily into its **gem file**, the developer uploads it to a well-known repository, which is where gem install will find it.

Considering the immense amount of good it does by making code widely available and preventing most cases of VCIS,[3] the gem file is actually a simple and familiar thing. Well, familiar if you happen to be a Unix user. It turns out that the gem file is just a TAR file.[4] Open a gem file with your favorite archive tool—virtually all of them can handle TAR files—and you will discover that inside each gem is two more TAR files![5] Presumably this Russian doll, TARs within a TAR, organization makes it easier for the gem software to do its thing.

Inside the first inner TAR file is where you will finally find the real contents of the gem, including the README file, all of the Ruby source files, as well as any executables—the stuff that really makes the gem go. Inside the second inner TAR file is the metadata—all of that version, authorship, and dependency information that makes a gem more than just a pile of random software.

When you install a gem, Ruby will unpack it to a well-known directory, and from then on Ruby will ensure that the directory containing the code for that gem is searched when you do a require or a load. Although there are endless details (What if I have more than one version of the gem? What if the gem has more than one directory full of code?), that is the simple story behind gems.

Building a Gem

For any Ruby developer worthy of the name, knowing how to use gems is only half of the story. You also need to be able to create them. Happily, there are only two key things you need to do to create a gem. The first is to organize your project directories to match the standard gem layout. So, if you wanted to release the Document class as a gem,[6] you would need to create a directory structure like that shown in Figure 29-1.

---

3. That's Version Conflict Induced Insanity. VCIS is also known as DLL Hell or JAR file Hell, depending on your programming background.

4. TAR files are the Unix answer to ZIP files, a simple archive file format that allows a single file to hold a whole tree full of files and directories.

5. Actually, the two inner TAR files are themselves compressed—and thus have an additional .gz suffix.

6. And why not? We've worked on it long enough!

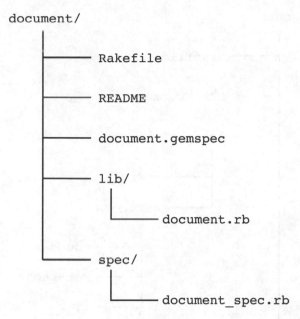

Figure 29-1 Simple Gem Directory structure

As you can see from the figure, convention calls for a top-level directory whose name matches the name of the gem, in this case document. Under that you have a README file, a directory for unit tests, and, most important of all, the lib directory that will hold the Ruby code.[7] Since the document gem is very simple, there is only a single Ruby file in the lib directory, document.rb. It's no accident that the name of the Ruby file matches the name of the gem—this is yet another convention, one that allows users of your gem to easily deduce that if they want to get at the good stuff in the document gem, they only need to code:

```
require 'document'
```

Naming your main Ruby file after gem is polite, but not absolutely required. The ruby-mp3info gem, for example, more or less honors the convention by calling its main Ruby file mp3info.rb.

---

7. By default, this is the directory that gets included in the Ruby load path when your gem is installed.

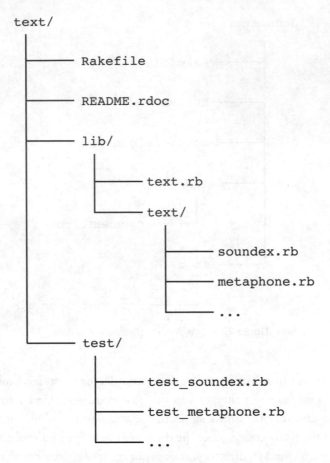

Figure 29-2 Text Gem Directory structure

If your gem is more complicated and carries around multiple source files, don't simply drop them in the `lib` directory. Instead, create a directory under the `lib` directory, whose name matches the name of the gem, and put your code there. For example, the text gem, which we used a few chapters back, carries around a fair number of files. As you can see in Figure 29-2, most of those Ruby files do indeed live one directory down from the `lib` directory.

Notice there is still a `text.rb` file in the `lib` directory. The convention is that this top-level Ruby file requires the files buried a directory down. So, if we peek into `text.rb`, we see:

```
require 'text/util'
require 'text/double_metaphone'
require 'text/levenshtein'
require 'text/metaphone'
require 'text/porter_stemming'
require 'text/soundex'
require 'text/version'
```

The nice effect of doing things this way is that the gem user doesn't have to care how complicated your gem is. Whether your gem is simple or Byzantine, your user simply says require 'text' and they get what they need.

The second thing we need for our document gem is the metadata. We need to tell RubyGems the name of our gem, its version and the like. We do this by creating a gemspec file. A gemspec file is nothing more than a file full of Ruby code that creates an instance of the Gem::Specification class.[8] Here's the gemspec for the document gem:

```
Gem::Specification.new do |s|
    s.name = "document"
    s.version = "1.0.1"
    s.authors = ["Russ Olsen"]
    s.date = %q{2010-01-01}
    s.description = 'Document - Simple document class'
    s.summary = s.description
    s.email = 'russ@russolsen.com'
    s.files = ['README', 'lib/document.rb','spec/document_spec.rb']
    s.homepage = 'http://www.russolsen.com'
    s.has_rdoc = true
    s.rubyforge_project = 'simple_document'
end
```

If your gem depends on having other gems installed in order to work, you can say that in the gemspec file too. Perhaps the document gem depends on the text gem. If so, you would add:

```
    s.add_dependency('text')
```

---

8. If the gemspec file seems like a simple internal DSL, that's because it is.

You can even depend on a specific version or range of versions:

```
s.add_dependency('text', '= 0.1.13' )
```

If your gem includes executable scripts—snippets of Ruby code that users can run from the command line, like the `rake` command from the Rake gem or `spec` from RSpec—you can specify that too. Here's how we might specify that our document gem has a spell-checking command:

```
s.bindir = "bin"              # Specify the directory
s.executables = ["spellcheck"]  # Then the file in the dir
```

Once you have all of your Ruby files in place under `lib`, your README file written, and your `gemspec` file built, creating the actual gem file is easy: Just run the `gem build` command and call out the `gemspec` file:

```
gem build document.gem
```

This command will create a file called `document-1.0.1.gem`, a tidy little package of document goodness. You can install your new gem on your system by simply specifying the gem file:

```
gem install document-1.0.1.gem
```

Uploading Your Gem to a Repository

If you are creating gems for your own—or perhaps your company's—private consumption, then you are done. Your newly minted gem file rolls up your code into an easily transportable unit that you can install into any Ruby environment. If, however, you are working on an open source project, something that will be available to the general public, then there is one more step. You need to put your gem where other people can get at it. In fact, you will probably want to put it in the place where the `gem` command will look by default when someone uses the `gem install` command.

Under the covers, the gem command turns to `http://gems.rubyforge.org` when it goes looking for gems to install. Behind this URL is the open source project,

Gemcutter,[9] which is devoted to being the place to get gems. Getting your gem into the Gemcutter repository could not be easier. You only need to go to http:// gemcutter.org and set up a free account. You will also need to install the gemcutter gem:

```
gem install gemcutter
```

Now you are ready to push your gem up to the Gemcutter repository:

```
gem push document-1.0.0.gem
```

The push command will ask for your Gemcutter account information and then upload your gem to the repository. It really is that simple. A few minutes after running the push command your gem will be available to anyone who wants to use it.

Automating Gem Creation

The trouble with building and uploading your gem by hand is that someone, probably you, needs to supply the hand. It's much better to automate the whole process, and the best way is to build a Rakefile that takes care of all the details:

```
require 'spec/rake/spectask'
require 'rake/gempackagetask'

task :default => [ :spec, :gem ]

Spec::Rake::SpecTask.new do |t|
  t.spec_files = FileList['spec/**/*_spec.rb']
end

gem_spec = Gem::Specification.new do |s|
  s.name = "document"
  s.version = "1.0.1"
```

---

9. Historically, most gems where hosted by RubyForge, the Ruby community's one-stop super store for all your open source Ruby project needs. RubyForge provides a source repository, a bug-tracking system and a host of other nifty features for the Ruby community. As of early 2010, the main gem repository duties have been taken up by the Gemcutter folks.

```
    s.authors = ["Russ Olsen"]
    s.date = %q{2010-05-23}
    s.description = 'Document - Simple document class'
    s.summary = s.description
    s.email = 'russ@russolsen.com'
    s.files = ['README','lib/document.rb', 'spec/document_spec.rb']
    s.homepage = 'http://www.russolsen.com'
    s.has_rdoc = true
    s.rubyforge_project = 'simple_document'
  end


  Rake::GemPackageTask.new( gem_spec ) do |t|
    t.need_zip = true
  end
```

This Rakefile takes advantage of the built-in tasks that will build a gem for you. All you need to do is specify the gemspec information in the `Rakefile`.

Rake doesn't have a built-in task to push the final gem file up to Gemcutter,[10] but it's easy enough to create one ourselves:

```
task :push => :gem do |t|
  sh "gem push pkg/#{gem_spec.name}-#{gem_spec.version}.gem"
end
```

Add this task to the bottom of your `Rakefile` and you are ready to release your masterpiece with a simple `rake push`.

In the Wild

In the real world we automate everything that can be automated, including things like making directories and writing `Rakefiles`. Fortunately there are a number of gems available whose purpose is to make it easy for you to build your gem.

Among the most popular is hoe.[11] Hoe tries to automate everything that could possibly be automated when building a gem. For example, if you are starting from

---

10. Yet.

11. Hoe was developed by Ryan Davis; the web site can be found at http://seattlerb.rubyforge.org/hoe.

scratch with a new gem, you can have hoe generate the whole gem directory structure for you.[12] To do this you run the `sow` command, which comes with hoe:

```
sow document
```

The `sow` command will generate the gem directory structure, including the `lib` and `test` directories, a skeletal `README.txt` file and a `Rakefile`. It will even tell you what to do next:

```
$ sow Document
...

... done, now go fix all occurrences of 'FIX':

  document/README.txt:3:* FIX (url)
  document/README.txt:7:FIX (describe your package)
  document/README.txt:11:* FIX (list of features or problems)
  document/README.txt:15:  FIX (code sample of usage)
  document/README.txt:19:* FIX (list of requirements)
  document/README.txt:23:* FIX (sudo gem install, anything else)
  document/README.txt:29:Copyright (c) 2010 FIX
  document/Rakefile:9:  # p.developer('FIX', 'FIX@example.com')
```

The only thing left for you to do is to fill in the appropriate blanks in `README.text` and the `Rakefile` and supply the actual code for your gem.

When you are done you can build your gem:

```
rake gem
```

Hoe also supports plug-ins that will help you upload your gem to Gemcutter.

Staying Out of Trouble

A key danger in using gems is the possibility of name collisions which, unfortunately, come in two nasty flavors. The first is the classic "my class has the same name as your class" problem: If your application already includes a class called `Document`, you are

---

12. Of course, you will have to install hoe with the usual `gem install hoe` first.

going to have a problem trying to use the `Document` class from the document gem. To lessen the chance of this sort of thing, the wise gem builder will reread Chapter 15 and wrap his or her work in a module:

```
module WordProcessor
  class Font
  end

  class Printer
  end

  class Document
    # ...
  end
end
```

Using modules reduces, but doesn't completely eliminate, the chance of a name collision; after all, there is always the chance of running into two `WordProcessor` modules.[13]

The second collision risk is the possibility of filename collisions. What happens if I'm using the document gem, with its `document.rb` file, and I also happen to have another `document.rb` file somewhere in my application? The short answer is nothing good. The longer answer is that whenever your program tries to load `document.rb`, it will end up loading the gem version of the file.

Fortunately, all is not lost. You can usually work your way around a filename collision by specifying the full path for the local file. If you happen to have a local file called `document.rb` and also want to load a local file called `document.rb`, you can load it with the full path:

```
dir = File.expand_path( File.dirname(__FILE__) )
require File.join( dir, 'document' )
```

Unsurprisingly, there are also some ways to screw up gem creation. Fortunately, the vast majority of gem construction errors are of the easily avoided variety. For example, make sure that you include all the other gems on which your gem depends in the

---

13. Or a `WordProcessor` class and a `WordProcessor` module, which comes down to the same thing.

dependency list. Missing a dependency is easier than it seems. Remember, if you happen to have that required but unlisted gem installed on your system, then everything will work fine for you. It will be a different story when your masterpiece arrives on some computer that happens to be missing that critical gem. It's always a good idea to test your newly minted or modified gem by trying it out on a clean install of Ruby.

The flip side of this is that your gem should avoid claiming that it uses some gem that it does not. This kind of thing usually happens when you stop using a gem but forget to remove it from the list of dependencies. The best defense against this kind of thing is to do two things: (1) stop, and (2) think. Pause every now and then to consider whether you still really need that ActsAsSnafu gem.

Finally, you need to keep your gems location independent. One of the best things about the gem system is that once a gem is installed, any application that wants to use the gem doesn't have to worry about where the gem lives—the gem system simply handles that part. So, if you install the widget gem, your application can say require 'widget' without having to know where the widget.rb file is to be found. Your job, as the author of a gem, is to avoid screwing up this location independence.

Unfortunately, it is fairly easy to build a very location-dependent gem. To see how easy, imagine that your gem depends on some supporting, non-Ruby files. The document package, for example, might need a font file. You might naively march ahead and read in the font:

```
class Document
  # Most of the class omitted...

  def read_default_font_file
    File.read( 'times_roman_12.font')
  end
end
```

Sadly, this is one of those situations where the simple thing does not actually work, or at least does not work very often. The problem with this code is that it is looking for the font file in the current directory. That font file might well be in your current directory when you are developing the document gem, but the users of your gem, working out of their own directories, are not going to be so lucky. Once you know there is a problem, the solution is not hard to find. As we have seen, you can always get the full path to your Ruby file with __FILE__:

```
def read_default_font_file
  File.read( "#{File.dirname(__FILE__)}/times_roman_12.font")
end
```

The message here is that you should always test your gems in as realistic a setting as possible. Fixing this kind of location independence problem is cheap; knowing that you have the problem in the first place is priceless.

Wrapping Up

There is an almost infinite number of ways that software can go wrong. It can simply be broken, or just buggy. It can be too slow. It can be completely incomprehensible to the people it is supposed to help. Any of these things is enough to bring a tear to the coder's eye. There is, however, something especially heartbreaking about code that might be great, might run like the wind, might speak to its users like poetry—but *will not install*. In this chapter we looked at the Ruby gem system, software that will help you avoid having your code come to a dismal "I just couldn't install it" end. We've seen that the gem system lets you package up your code into a bundle, along with its documentation and a list of other gems on which it depends. We've also seen how, by uploading your gem to a public repository like GemCutter, you can make it widely available. Finally, we've looked at hoe, a gem that eases some of the pain of building your own gem.

Now that we have seen how to package up your code, in the next chapter we will turn to getting to know the Ruby implementation that will run your code.

CHAPTER 30

Know Your Ruby Implementation

Back in the days when I programmed in C, every development team seemed to contain one engineer who knew something about assembly language. Since I did little or no coding in assembly language, this appeared to me to be a fairly useless skill—except that those assembly language-enabled engineers always seemed to have a unique perspective on how everything worked. Eventually I figured out that these two things were related: Having a basic understanding of the lower levels of your programming language helps you be a better programmer, even if you never actually work in those lower levels.

So, in this chapter we are going to look at the gears and pulleys of the major Ruby implementations. As we go along we will see there is something in this chapter for Rubyists who know something about C and for those who are bilingual in Java. Even if you are one of those people who think the word *Java* actually translates to "Run away! Run away!" or that the C programming language looks like a unfortunate editor incident, keep reading. You will be surprised at the insight you'll gain from even a naive inspection of a Ruby implementation. After all, there is no substitute for knowing your tool.

A Fistful of Rubies

Of course, to really know your tool you need to know *which* tool you are talking about. As I write this the Ruby community is going through a version transition: While much of our code still runs on Ruby 1.8, version 1.9 is out and stable, and there is a general upgrade movement in progress. To make things even more interesting, there are also three widely used implementations of Ruby, and not all of them support all versions of the language:

- First, there is the original Ruby implementation written by Yukihiro Matsumoto, the beloved father of Ruby and widely known as Matz. Rubyists call this founding implementation Matz's Ruby Interpreter, or MRI. MRI is written in C and supports Ruby 1.8.7.

- Next we have an implementation known as Yet Another Ruby VM, or YARV, which runs version 1.9.X of the language. YARV is slated to take over as the Ruby implementation once the 1.8 to 1.9 transition is complete. Like MRI, YARV is written in C.

- Finally, there is JRuby, an implementation of Ruby for the Java VM. JRuby supports version 1.8 and is rapidly closing in on complete support for Ruby 1.9.

Along with the "big three" implementations, there are a number of less well-known or less complete Ruby implementations. These include:

- Rubinius, which aspires to be a self-hosting implementation of Ruby. In simple English, the folks behind Rubinius hope to produce an implementation of Ruby that is completely written in Ruby.

- IronRuby, an implementation of Ruby for the .Net platform. IronRuby is to Microsoft's CLR what JRuby is to the Java virtual machine.

- Cardinal, a Ruby implementation that runs on Parrot, a VM that aspires to host a number of dynamic languages.

In this chapter I will focus primarily on the more popular Ruby implementations, MRI, YARV, and JRuby, although we will take one quick detour into the land of Rubinius.

MRI: An Enlightening Experience for the C Programmer

It all started with a man, a dream, and lots of C code. The man was, of course, Matz. The dream was of a simple, flexible, powerful programming language. The code was

MRI, the original Ruby implementation. You can get the MRI source code from www.ruby-lang.org. Unpack the archive into some suitable directory and you can see how it all began.

What you will see is a top-level directory containing about 55 C source files and headers, along with a bunch of subdirectories. Remarkably, the subdirectories are just the supporting code, things like the SSL library and the TK GUI interface. Those 55 top-level source files are the heart of the Matz Ruby interpreter.

If you can speak any C at all, looking through the Ruby 1.8 implementation can be an enlightening experience. As language interpreters go, MRI has a kind of plain-spoken eloquence. Obviously, the main job of any Ruby implementation is to turn your code into a living, breathing program. The first step of that process is to take the program text, break it up into the individual words and numbers and other assorted bits, and then reassemble those bits into a tree structure, the **abstract syntax tree**, or **AST**.

For example, if you fed MRI this trivial bit of Ruby code:

```
if denominator != 0
  quotient = numerator / denominator
end
```

You would end up with an AST that looks something like Figure 30-1.[1] The task of turning your Ruby code into the AST falls mainly on the code in `lex.c` and `parse.y`.[2]

Once MRI has the AST it executes it, and therefore your program, using the simplest technique imaginable. Starting at the root of the abstract syntax tree, MRI works its way down, recursively doing what the tree tells it to do. So in the previous example, MRI would start at the top of the tree, see that it had an `if` statement, know that it needed to evaluate the condition, realize that it needed to evaluate the variable `denominator`—and the constant 0—and . . . well, you get the picture. You can find the bulk of the code to do the evaluation in the aptly named `eval.c` file.

All of this basic parsing and executing code only occupies a handful of the core MRI source files.[3] Most of the rest of the 50 or so top-level files follow a very consistent

---

1. To keep things simple, Figure 30-1 is very schematic. For various practical reasons, an actual MRI AST tree is a bit more complex than I'm showing here—a bit, but not much.

2. The funny `.y` name comes from the fact that `parse.y` is actually the half-code/half-grammar input to a parser-generating tool called YACC.

3. To be fair, each of those files is pretty lengthy and full of some fairly sophisticated C.

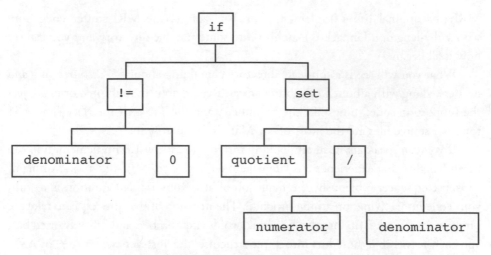

Figure 30-1 AST for a simple Ruby `if` statement

pattern: Each implements one or a few closely related Ruby classes. At the bottom of
each file is an initialization function, with a name like `Init_Array` or `Init_Object`
that defines each Ruby class and associates the class with its methods. So, if you ever
wondered how the `Object` class gets defined, you can satisfy your curiosity by peek-
ing into `object.c`. Toward the bottom of the file you will find `Init_Object`, and in
there you will find the following three lines:

```
rb_cObject = boot_defclass("Object", 0);
rb_cModule = boot_defclass("Module", rb_cObject);
rb_cClass =  boot_defclass("Class",  rb_cModule);
```

This is the ruby interpreter creating the `Object`, `Module`, and `Class` classes. The
second parameter of `boot_defclass` method is the superclass of the new class; thus,
we can see that the superclass of `Class` is `Module` and the superclass of `Module` is
`Object`, and that `Object` doesn't have a superclass—at least not in version 1.8. We
already knew this, but it's good to see it in black and white.

The `object.c` file is just full of other fascinating stuff. Here, for example, is the
default implementation of the `==` method:

```
static VALUE
rb_obj_equal(obj1, obj2)
    VALUE obj1, obj2;
```

```
    {
        if (obj1 == obj2) return Qtrue;
        return Qfalse;
    }
```

Read the code carefully and you will discover a whole range of interesting tidbits about MRI. Notice how the two parameters of `rb_obj_equal` are both declared in the C code to be of type VALUE: Inside of MRI, when you have a reference to an object, you have a VALUE. It's also easy to deduce that Qtrue and Qfalse are the C versions of the Ruby true and false objects.

Looking a little further, you can find the code behind the `Array map!` method (also known as `collect!`), code that replaces the contents of an array with the values returned from invoking a block on each original array element:

```
static VALUE
rb_ary_collect_bang(ary)
    VALUE ary;
{
    long i;

    rb_ary_modify(ary);
    for (i = 0; i < RARRAY(ary)->len; i++) {
        rb_ary_store(ary, i, rb_yield(RARRAY(ary)->ptr[i]));
    }

    return ary;
}
```

Again, even without being a C hacker it is easy enough to follow the flow: Run through the array with a `for` loop, calling the code block (with `rb_yield`) with the value of each element and replacing each element (via `rb_ary_store`) with the result of the code block as you go.

YARV: MRI with a Byte Code Turbocharger

If you pull down and unpack YARV,[4] you will discover that YARV is the next generation of MRI. If you did take the time to look at MRI, you will also have no problem

---

4. Also to be found at www.ruby-lang.org.

finding your way around the YARV source code. For example, here is the YARV implementation of the `map!`/`collect!` method:

```
static VALUE
rb_ary_collect_bang(VALUE ary)
{
    long i;

    RETURN_ENUMERATOR(ary, 0, 0);
    rb_ary_modify(ary);
    for (i = 0; i < RARRAY_LEN(ary); i++) {
        rb_ary_store(ary, i, rb_yield(RARRAY_PTR(ary)[i]));
    }
    return ary;
}
```

The family relationship between this code and the MRI version we saw earlier is very striking.

Still, YARV is a real advance over MRI. One big difference is that MRI supports Ruby 1.8 while YARV has moved on to version 1.9. So if you look at the YARV code that creates the `Object` class, you find that it now has a Ruby 1.9-style `BasicObject` as a superclass:

```
rb_cBasicObject = boot_defclass("BasicObject", 0);
rb_cObject = boot_defclass("Object", rb_cBasicObject);
rb_cModule = boot_defclass("Module", rb_cObject);
rb_cClass =  boot_defclass("Class",  rb_cModule);
```

A more subtle difference between the two Ruby implementations is that when running Ruby code, YARV adds an extra step between the parse tree and execution. After parsing the Ruby source, YARV turns the resulting tree into a more or less flat list of byte codes. It is these byte codes that YARV actually executes. Thus, in YARV, our little Ruby fragment:

```
if denominator != 0
  quotient = numerator / denominator
end
```

Turns into a list of byte codes that looks something like this:

```
0014 trace            1    (    4)
0016 getdynamic       denominator, 0
0019 putobject        0
0021 opt_neq          <ic>, <ic>
0024 branchunless     41
0026 trace            1    (    5)
0028 getdynamic       numerator, 0
0031 getdynamic       denominator, 0
0034 opt_div
0035 dup
0036 setdynamic       quotient, 0
0039 leave            (    4)
0040 pop
0041 putnil           (    5)
```

Although the difference between executing byte codes and the original tree may seem esoteric, the effect is there for all the world to see: YARV and its byte codes are dramatically faster than MRI.

JRuby: Bending the "J" in the JVM

Unlike YARV, which comes with its own homegrown virtual machine, the challenge that faced the authors of JRuby was to adopt Ruby to the existing Java virtual machine, the JVM. Their answer was a Ruby that is completely implemented in, and integrated with, Java. Since running in the Java world presents different challenges from building a C application, the JRuby source code is something of a departure from MRI and YARV—a departure, but still recognizable.

For example, if you download the JRuby source archive[5] and unpack it, you will find what looks like a very conventional Java development project. Under the top-level directory, there is an ant `build.xml`[6] file and bin and lib and src directories. Go looking for the JRuby equivalent of `array.c` and you will find it in the most obvious (at least to a Java programmer) place: `src/org/jruby/RubyArray.java`. And in `RubyArray.java`

---

5. You can find it at http://jruby.org. The code here is from Jruby 1.4 RC1.

6. Ant is the traditional Java build tool, along the lines of rake.

you will find the JRuby implementation of the `map!/collect!` method, complete
with a helpful comment pointing us back to the original C function:

```
/** rb_ary_collect_bang
 *
 */
public RubyArray collectBang(
    ThreadContext context, Block block) {

    if (!block.isGiven())
        throw context.getRuntime().
            newLocalJumpErrorNoBlock();

    modify();
    for (int i = 0, len = realLength; i < len; i++) {
        store(i, block.yield(context, values[begin + i]));
    }
    return this;
}
```

In C or Java,[7] `collect!` is pretty much the same: Run through the array, replacing values as you go.

Rubinius

If your head is swimming from all of this C and Java in a Ruby book but you are still
interested in Ruby implementations, let me invite you to have a look at Rubinius.
Rubinius (http://rubini.us) is a Ruby implementation whose ambition is to be self-
hosting: The goal of Rubinius is to implement Ruby *in Ruby*. Although Rubinius is
not really finished, it is a very informative source of Ruby implementation knowledge.
Here, for example, is the Rubinius version of our favorite array rewriting method, this
time called `map!`:

```
# Replaces each element in self with the return value
# of passing that element to the supplied block.
def map!
  Ruby.check_frozen
```

---

7. I did edit the code a bit to make it fit on the page.

```
      return to_enum(:map!) unless block_given?

      i = -1
      each { |x| self[i+=1] = yield(x) }

      self
    end
```

Life is a bit easier if you get to use Ruby as your implementation language.

In the Wild

One of the best ways to gain some insight into how your Ruby implementation works is to look into how to extend it. Every Ruby implementation allows you to add features to the native implementation. Since you need some understanding of the implementation in order to extend it, the "how to extend Ruby" documentation is a great source of insight into how that Ruby works. Both the MRI and YARV source code come with a README.EXT file[8] that does a good job of explaining the basics.

The JRuby project has an entire section of its website devoted to explaining how JRuby works. As I write this the URL for this documentation is www.kenai.com/projects/jruby/pages/Internals. It is well worth a look.

Staying Out of Trouble

There is really only one danger with knowing your language implementation, and it's a very easily avoidable risk. The problem arises when you think too hard about what's going on under the covers: "Gee, an awful lot of C . . . or Java . . . or whatever gets fired for every Ruby class I write and every method I call. That has got to be slow. Maybe I should start writing fewer classes or longer methods or. . . ."

Don't go there. A half century of software engineering says that you should write the code first and worry about making it faster only if it is too slow. Donald Knuth is right: Premature optimization is the root of all evil. Don't let a little bit of insight into your Ruby implementation blind you to this fundamental truth. Your Ruby was fast enough yesterday, before you started poking around in its innards. It is still fast enough.

---

8. Yes, that suffix is .EXT, as in "extension," not .TXT.

Wrapping Up

In this chapter we took a very rapid "If it's Tuesday this must be YARV"-style tour of Ruby implementations. We saw how MRI was the original, C-based implementation, now being eclipsed by YARV. We also saw that JRuby is bringing Ruby to the JVM. We even visited briefly with Rubinius. Mostly, though, we spent our time trying to get a feel for how these implementations actually work, how MRI and YARV turn C into Ruby while JRuby performs the same miracle for Java.

The ironic thing about this chapter is that many, perhaps most, of us got into Ruby so we would never have to write C or Java ever again. And yet here we are, back again. Ironic or not, the simple fact is that the better you understand Ruby, the less it seems like magic, and the better Ruby programmer you will be.

CHAPTER 31

Keep an Open Mind to Go with Those Open Classes

Throughout the writing of this book I have been haunted by a feeling of irony. On page after page I have been talking up the technical flexibility of Ruby. I've gone on and on about how wonderful it is to program without the straitjacket of static typing, about how being able to change your classes on the fly makes for the magic of meta-programming, and about how the flexible syntax enables us to build really nice DSLs.

But on these same pages I have also been laying down the law: Indent your code this way, be careful with `method_missing`, and avoid those class variables. Do what I tell you to do or you will put an eye out.

Stand back a little and the irony goes away: Ruby is a very, very sharp programming tool, and it pays to know what you are doing before you pick it up. If you are a relative newcomer to the language you will do well to build on the work of those who have come before you. So we have books like this one, full of rules and guidelines. But the rules and guidelines are only a means to an end. Really mastering a tool is not simply about knowing the rules and always following them. Real mastery comes when you know the rules and follow them—except in those rare moments when it's time to throw the rule book away.

In that spirit, I'd like to leave you with one last bit of advice. It's from George Orwell, who closed an essay on writing good English prose with this:

Break any of these rules sooner than say anything outright barbarous.[1]

---

1. Orwell, G. *A Collection of Essays.* San Diego, CA: Mariner Books, 1970.

If you ever find yourself in a situation that makes you want to throw this rule book away, visit www.eloquentruby.com or write to me at russ@russolsen.com. I'd love to hear about it.

Appendix

Going Further

Life was a lot easier a few years ago when I was writing *Design Patterns in Ruby*. Back then there were only a handful of Ruby books available, so making suggestions about where to go next was not much of a problem. These days there are so many good books about Ruby around that it's hard to know where to start. Still, some classics never go out of style. So if your command of Ruby is not what it should be, try:

Thomas, D., Fowler, C., and Hunt, A. *Programming Ruby 1.9: The Pragmatic Programmers' Guide.* Raleigh, NC: Pragmatic Bookshelf, 2008.

Programming Ruby is a very thorough but free-flowing exploration of the Ruby programming language. If you like your information more systematic and less stream-of-consciousness, you might want to go back to the source:

Flanagan, D. and Matsumoto, Y. *The Ruby Programming Language.* Cambridge, MA: O'Reilly, 2008.

Two other excellent references are:

Cooper, P. *Beginning Ruby: From Novice to Professional, Second Edition.* New York, NY: Apress, 2009.

And

Black, D. *The Well-Grounded Rubyist.* Greenwich, CT: Manning Publications, 2009.

If you are interested in the larger issues around building software with Ruby, you might also want to have a look at my own:

Olsen, R. *Design Patterns in Ruby.* Boston, MA: Addison-Wesley, 2008.

There are also a number of other how-to style books. Here again, there is a classic:

Foulton, H. *The Ruby Way, Second Edition: Solutions and Techniques in Ruby Programming, Second Edition.* Boston, MA: Addison-Wesley, 2006.

And a relative newcomer:

Carlson, L. and Richardson, L. *Ruby Cookbook.* Cambridge, MA: O'Reilly, 2006.

Another excellent choice, very much in the spirit of this book is:

Brown, G. *Ruby Best Practices.* Cambridge, MA: O'Reilly, 2009.

Regular expressions are a key part of any Rubyist's toolkit. Two excellent references are:

Friedl, J. E. F. *Mastering Regular Expressions.* Cambridge, MA: O'Reilly, 2006.

And

Goyvaerts, J. and Levithan, S. *Regular Expressions Cookbook.* Cambridge, MA: O'Reilly, 2009.

There are two other sources of invaluable design knowledge out there. One is the source code for the various Ruby projects. Find an open source project that interests you and dig into the code. Or dig into your Ruby implementation. A good workman knows his tools.

A good workman also learns from the past. All too often when a new technology comes along—Ruby, for example—we tend to toss out the hard-won lessons of experience along with the old code. Take the time to learn from the smart people who came before you.

You might start with Paul Graham's 1993 book, *On LISP.* The entire text of this book is available at www.paulgraham.com/onlisp.html. It is worth reading even if you never type a single parenthesis of LISP.

In many ways this book, especially the chapter on object equality, was inspired by:

Bloch, J. *Effective Java, Second Edition.* Boston, MA: Addison-Wesley, 2008.

Other books of this sort that are well worth a look are:

Beck, K. *Smalltalk Best Practice Patterns*. Upper Saddle River, NJ: Prentice Hall, 1996.

Kernighan, B. and Plauger, P. J. *The Elements of Programming Style*. New York, NY: McGraw-Hill, 1974.

Brodie, L. *Thinking Forth*. Los Angeles, CA: Punchy Publishing, 2004.

Thinking Forth is available as a free download at http://thinking-forth.sourceforge.net.

The George Orwell quote mentioned in Chapter 31 comes from an essay called *Politics and the English Language*, which is widely available on the Internet and is also included in:

Orwell, G. *A Collection of Essays*. San Diego, CA: Mariner Books, 1970.

Finally, there is the granddaddy of them all. I'm convinced that if Strunk had been a software engineer and White a coder, my personal AI assistant would be typing the last lines of this book:

Strunk, W. and White, E. B. *The Elements of Style, Fourth Edition*. White Plains, NY: Longman, 1999.

Index

Symbols

" (double quotes), use with string literals, 44–45

' (single quotes), use with string literals, 44–45

- (subtraction) operator
  as binary or unary operator, 132
  overloading, 131

. (period)
  for matching any single character, 54
  in module syntax, 185
  using asterisk (*) in conjunction with, 58

/ (division) operator, 131

/ (forward slashes), in regular expression syntax, 58–59

: (colon), in symbol syntax, 66–67

:: (double-colon), in module syntax, 185

; (semicolon), for separating statements in Ruby code, 10–11

\ (backslash)
  escaping special meanings of punctuation characters in regular expressions, 54
  escaping strings, 44–45

| (or) operator, 131

| (vertical bar), in syntax of alternatives in regular expressions, 56–57

||= operator, in expression-based initialization, 26–27

+ (addition) operator
  as binary or unary operator, 132
  non-commutative nature of, 137

overloading, 131
when to use, 136–137

=~ operator, testing if regular expression matches a string, 59–60

== (double-equals) operator
  broadening the scope of, 145–146
  numeric classes accepting Float as equals, 154–156
  overview of, 143–144
  RSpec and, 138
  symmetry principal and, 146–147
  transitive property of, 147–149

=== (triple equals) operator, for case statements, 23, 149–150

=> (hash rocket), 30

! method names ending with, 48

! unary operator, 131–132

#, in comment syntax, 6

$, as string delimiter, 45

% (formatting operator), strings, 137–138

% (modulo) operator, 131, 152

%q, for arbitrarily quoted strings, 45–46

& (and) operator, 131

( ) (parentheses)
  readability and, 12
  Ruby conventions for calling defining/ methods, 9–10

* (asterisk)
  in method definition with extra arguments, 31–32
  in regular expressions, 57–58

* (multiplication) operator, 131
? (question mark), using with regular
        expressions, 62–63
?: (ternary operator), in expression-based
        decision making, 26
@@, in class variable syntax, 169
[ ] (square brackets)
  adding to indexing-related class, 135
  operator-like syntax and, 133
  as string delimiter, 45
  using with regular expressions, 55
[ ]=
  adding to indexing-related class, 135
  operator-like syntax and, 133
^ (exclusive or) operator, 131
{} (braces), in code block syntax, 11
<< (left shift operator), 131, 135
<=> operator
  Float and Fixnum classes and, 154–156
  sort method and, 214

A

accessor methods, using with class variables, 170
ActiveRecord
  callbacks and, 177
  composed method approach and, 127–128
  as database interface library, 335
  DataMapper compared with. see DataMapper
  example of delegation, 282–283
  example of execute around, 230
  example of saved code blocks, 243
  examples of internal DSLs, 346
  find method, 66–67
  magic methods, 291–292
  silence method, 231
add_unique_word method, 120
addition (+) operator. see + (addition) operator
alias_method, for renaming methods, 297–299
alternatives, in regular expressions, 55–57
ancestors method, for viewing inheritance
        ancestry, 199
and (&) operator, 131
APIs
  avoiding trouble when using method_missing
        for, 289–290

building form letters one word at a time,
        286–288
building with method_missing, 292
examples of use of method_missing for,
        290–292
review of applying method_missing to, 292
supported by strings, 47–49
transition from API to DSL, 341–344
user focus in creating easy-to-use APIs, 289
when to use instead of internal DSLs, 348
archives, gems and, 370
arguments
  code blocks taking, 208
  execute around methods taking, 226–227
  methods taking fixed or variable numbers of,
        30–31
  naming conventions, 8
  singleton methods accepting, 159
arrays
  APIs for, 35
  caution when iterating over, 40–41
  each method, 34, 217
  improper use of, 41
  method-passing with, 30–32
  monkey patching for adding methods to, 302
  order of, 38
  overview of, 29
  public methods for array instances, 36
  reverse method, 36–37
  shortcuts for accessing, 30
  sort method, 37
assert method, Test::Unit, 98
assert_equal method, Test::Unit, 98
assert_match method, Test::Unit, 101
assert_nil method, Test::Unit, 101
assert_not_equal method, Test::Unit, 101
assert_not_nil method, Test::Unit, 101
assertions, in Test::Unit, 101
asterisk (*)
  in method definition with extra arguments,
        31–32
  in regular expressions, 57–58
asymmetrical equality relationships, 147
at_exit hook
  informing when time is up, 255–256
  in Test::Unit, 259–260

attr_accessor
    accessing class instance variables, 176
    in default set of methods in Object class, 82
    as subclass-changing method, 327–328
attr_reader, as subclass-changing method, 327
attr_writer, as subclass-changing method,
        327–328
attributes, at class level, 176–177
automating
    gem creation, 375–377
    testing gems, 94

B

backslash (\)
    escaping special meanings of punctuation
        characters, 54
    escaping strings, 44–45
BasicObject, use in delegation with
        method_missing, 280–281
Bignum class, 154–156
binary operators
    operating across classes, 134–135
    overview of, 131–132
bitwise operators, 131
blank? method, adding to String class, 301
block_given? passing code blocks in methods,
        208, 233
blocks. see code blocks
boolean logic
    false and true values in Ruby, 23–25
    mapping boolean operators to union and
        intersection operations, 135
braces ({}), in code block syntax, 11
break, in code blocks, 216
bugs, 94. see also tests
bytes, strings as collections of, 49–50

C

C language, 382
C# language, 336
call backs
    ActiveRecord objects and, 177
    creating listeners for, 234–236
    using explicit code blocks for, 236–237

call method
    calling code blocks explicitly, 234
    Proc.new and, 241
camel case, class naming conventions, 8
Capistrano, 243–244
Cardinal, 382
case sensitivity, working with strings, 47
case statements
    example of use of, 21–23
    triple equals operator (===) for, 149–150
characters
    matching any one of a bunch of characters, 55
    matching one character at a time, 54–55
    strings as collections of, 49
chomp method, working with strings, 47
chop method, working with strings, 47
clarity
    of code, 94
    qualities of good code, 4
class definitions, executable. see classes, self
        modifying
class instance variables
    avoiding trouble when using, 179
    examples of use of, 177–179
    for holding onto classwide values, 174–175
    review of, 179
    singleton class used to add convenience to,
        176–177
    subclasses and, 175–176
class methods. see also singleton methods
    adding convenience to class instance variables,
        176–177
    avoiding trouble when using, 165–166
    for building instance methods, 321–323
    defining, 163–164
    extending modules and, 197–198
    handling missing constants. see const_missing
    included hook used with, 254–255
    making structural changes to classes, 309–310
    overview of, 162
    uses of, 164–165
class variables
    avoiding trouble when using, 179
    example of use of, 170
    problems associated with global nature of,
        171–174

class variables (*continued*)
  review of, 179
  storing class level data with, 169
  tendency to wander from class to class, 171
  URI class and, 177–178
`class_eval`, for creating methods, 322–323,
    329
classes
  accessing in modules, 182–183
  adding iterator methods to, 210–211
  avoiding name collisions, 377–378
  benefits of dynamic typing, 85, 89
  binary operators used across, 134–135
  as both factory and container, 182
  changing class definition, 305–308
  class/instance approximation in defining
      methods, 157
  composed method for building, 122–123
  as container for methods, 74
  defining, 294
  do anything to any class, anytime, 297–299
  as factory for creating instances, 74–75
  fixing broken, 295–296
  flexibility resulting from decoupling, 90–91
  holding onto classwide values, 174–175
  hook for informing when a class gains a
      subclass, 250–253, 257–259
  hook for informing when a module gets
      included in a class, 253–255
  mixins for sharing code between unrelated
      classes, 195–197
  modifying, 295–297
  modules for grouping related, 182
  modules for organizing into hierarchies, 181
  modules for swapping groups of related classes
      at runtime, 186–187
  naming conventions, 8
  open nature in Ruby. *see* open classes
  preference for bare collections over specialized
      classes, 38–40
  renaming methods using `alias_method`,
      297–299
  storing class level data, 169
  superclasses, 75–76
  when to use modules vs. naked classes, 189
  writing methods for. *see* methods, writing

classes, self modifying
  adding programming logic to classes, 308–309
  avoiding trouble when using, 314–315
  class methods that change class, 309–310
  defining classes and, 305–308
  examples of use of, 310–313
  overview of, 305
  review of, 315–316
classes, that modify subclasses
  avoiding trouble when using, 330–332
  class methods that build instance methods,
      321–323
  `define_method` for creating methods, 324
  difficulty of subclassing and, 319–321
  example of paragraph subclass of document
      class, 317–319
  examples of use of, 327–329
  no limits on modifying subclasses from
      superclass methods, 324–326
  overview of, 317
  review of, 332
closure (scope)
  avoiding trouble when using, 241–242
  code blocks drag scope along to wherever they
      are applied, 225–227
code
  clarity and conciseness of, 94
  concise vs. cryptic, 94
  dynamic typing increasing compactness of,
      85–89
  embedding in classes, 308
  format of. *see* code format
  less code, less likelihood of error, 84
  qualities of good code, 4
  readability of, 12–13
  sharing between unrelated classes, 195
code blocks
  `at_exit` hook, 255–256
  multiline vs. single line, 12
  Ruby conventions, 11
code blocks, as iterators
  adding multiple iterators, 210–211
  adding single iterator, 209–210
  avoiding trouble when using, 215–216
  creating by tacking on to the end of method
      calls, 207–208

`Enumerable` module and, 213–215
  overview of, 207
  returning values, 208–209
  review of, 218
  spectrum of iterator types, 217–218
  taking arguments, 208
  writing iterators for collections that do not yet
    exist, 211–213
code blocks, saving for later use
  applying to call backs, 234–237
  applying to lazy initialization, 237–239
  avoiding trouble when using, 240–242
  examples of use of, 243–244
  explicit vs. implicit approaches to passing
    blocks, 233–234
  overview of, 233
  producing instant block objects, 239–240
  review of, 244–245
code blocks, using execute around
  applying to logging, 222–224
  applying to object initialization, 225, 229–230
  avoiding trouble when using, 228–229
  delivering code where needed, 219
  dragging scope along to wherever they are
    applied, 225–227, 241–242
  for functions that must happen before or after
    operations, 224
  returning something from, 227–228
  `silence` method for turning logging off, 231
code format
  breaking rules and, 14–15
  code blocks, 11
  indentation, 5–6
  naming conventions, 8–9
  "one statement per line" convention, 10–11
  parentheses in calling/defining methods, 9–10
  qualities of good code, 4
  readability and, 12–13
  review of conventions, 15
collections
  adding left shift operator to collection class, 135
  caution when iterating over, 40–41
  collection-related methods in `Enumerable`
    class, 213
  improper use of arrays and hashes, 41–42
  iterating through, 33–36

knowing which methods change and which
    leave as is, 36–38
  method calls for accessing, 30–33
  order of hashes, 38
  overview of, 29
  preference for bare collections over specialized
    classes, 38–40
  review of, 42
  shortcuts for accessing, 29–30
colon (:), in symbol syntax, 66–67
comments
  dynamic typing and, 93
  example in `set.rb` class, 13–14
  when and how often to use, 6–8
comparison operator, 23
complexity, simplicity as solution to, 92
composed method
  `ActiveRecord::Base` class example, 127–128
  applying to `TextCompressor` class, 121
  for building classes, 122–123
  characteristics of, 121–122
compression algorithm, 117–118
conciseness, of code, 4, 94
conditions, syntax in control statements, 10
consistency, of Ruby object system, 76–77
`const_missing`
  avoiding trouble when using, 270–271
  examples of use of, 269–270
  handling missing constants, 267–268
  review of, 271
constants
  accessing in modules, 183
  handling missing. *see* const_missing
  modules for organizing into hierarchies,
    181–182
  modules for swapping groups of related
    constants at runtime, 186–187
  naming conventions, 8–9
  stashing in mixins, 204–205
containers
  modules as, 181–182
  treating modules as object rather than static
    containers, 186
control structures
  ||– in expression-based initialization, 26–27
  boolean logic and, 23–25

control structures (*continued*)
  case statement, 21–23
  code capturing values of while or if
      statements, 25
  each method preferred over for loops, 20–21
  if, unless, while, and until statements,
      17–19
  modifier forms, 19–20
  overview of, 17
  review of, 27
  syntax for conditions in, 10
  ternary operator (?:) in decision making, 26
Cucumber testing tool, 363–364

D

data
  storing class level, 169, 174
  using strings for processing, 66–67
data types
  built-in, 58–60
  disadvantages of adding type checking code, 91
  dynamic. *see* dynamic typing
  static. *see* static typing
  type documentation, 92
DataMapper
  example of use of modules in, 190–191
  mixins used by, 202–203
debugging, logging for, 219
decomposing classes
  into small methods, 123
  troubles arising from, 126–127
decoupling, with dynamic typing, 89–92
def
  class methods that build instance methods, 322
  last def principle, 295
define_method, for creating methods, 324, 328
defined? boolean logic and, 24
delegate.rb file, 281–282
delegation
  avoiding trouble when using, 279–281
  example of use by ActiveRecord, 282–283
  method_missing applied to, 277–278
  overview of, 273
  problems with traditional style of, 275
  pros/cons of, 274–275

  review of, 283
  selective approach to, 278–279
  SimpleDelegator class, 281–282
delete method, for arrays, 37
Dir class, 217
directories
  generating directory structure of gems, 377
  organizing for gems packaging, 370–372
division (/) operator, 131
DLL Hell, 370
do keyword, in code block syntax, 11
documentation
  compensating for lost documentation due to
      required type declarations, 92–93
  Ruby implementations, 389
DocumentIdentifier class, 142
documents
  compressing specification documents, 117–118
  creating identifier, 142
  handling document errors, 266–267
  lazy documents, 86–89
  paragraph subclass of document class, 317–319
  Ruby coding conventions illustrated in
      Document class, 5
Domain Specific Languages, external. *see* DSLs
    (Domain Specific Languages), external
Domain Specific Languages, internal. *see* DSLs
    (Domain Specific Languages), internal
double quotes ("), use with string literals, 44–45
double-colon (::), in module syntax, 185
double-equals (==) operator. *see* == (double-
    equals) operator
downcase method, working with strings, 47
DSLs (Domain Specific Languages), external
  avoiding trouble when using, 360–362
  building parser for XML processing language,
    353–356
  examples of use of, 362–364
  overview of, 336, 351–352
  regular expressions for parsing, 356–358
  review of, 364–365
  Treetop parsing tool, 358–360
  when to use as alternative to internal DSL, 352
DSLs (Domain Specific Languages), internal
  avoiding trouble when using, 347–349
  based on Ruby code, 352

dealing with XML, 336–341
examples of use of, 345–346
method_missing used with, 344
narrow focus of, 336
overview of, 335
review of, 349
transition from API to DSL, 341–344
when to use as alternative to external DSL, 352
duck typing, 88–89
dynamic typing
    compactness of code and, 85–89
    comparing File and StringIO classes, 94–95
    compensating for lost documentation due to
        required type declarations, 92–93
    extreme decoupling with, 89–92
    overview of, 85
    Set class and, 95–96
    trade offs in use of, 93–94

E

each method
    adding iterator methods to classes, 210–212
    avoiding trouble when iterating arrays, 40
    iteration with, 34
    preferred over for loops, 20–21
    types of iterators and, 217
each_address method, Resolv class, 217
each_cons method, Enumerable module and,
    213–214
each_object method, ObjectSpace class,
    217–218
each_splice method, Enumerable module
    and, 214
eigenclasses. see singleton classes
encryption
    managing with class methods, 309–310
    managing with programming logic in classes,
        308–309
end keyword, in code block syntax, 11
Enumerable module, 213–215
Enumerator class, 214
eql? method
    Hash class using, 152–153
    overview of, 150–152
    restrictive view of equality in, 153

equal? method, for testing object identity, 143
equality
    avoiding trouble when using, 153–154
    broadening the scope of double-equals
        operator, 145–146
    double-equals (==) operator, 143–144
    eql? method, 150–153
    equal? method, 143
    Float and Fixnum classes and <=> operator,
        154–156
    identifiers and, 142
    methods for, 142–143
    overview of, 141
    review of, 154–156
    symbols and, 67–68
    symmetry principal and, 146–147
    transitive property and, 147–149
    triple equals operator (===), 149–150
ERB, 362–363
eval method, Object class, 78
exception handling. see also method_missing,
        error handling with
    with execute around, 228
    handling document errors, 266–267
    internal DSLs and, 347
    logging and, 222, 224
exclusive or (^) operator, 131
executable class definitions. see classes, self
        modifying
execute around
    avoiding trouble when using, 228–229
    for functions that must happen before or after
        operations, 224
    initializing objects with, 225, 229–230
    passing arguments and, 226–227
    returning something from code blocks,
        227–228
external DSLs. see DSLs (Domain Specific
        Languages), external

F

false
    in boolean logic, 23–24
    false as an object, 76
File class, comparing with StringIO class, 94–95

filenames, avoiding name collisions, 378
find method, ActiveRecord, 66–67
find_index, map method compared with, 35
Fixnum class, 154–156
Float class, 154–156
floating point numbers, 296
for loops, 20–21
formatting operator (%), for strings, 137–138
forward slashes (/), in regular expression syntax, 58–59
forwardable.rb, 328–329
Fowler, Martin, 336

G

gem files, 370
gem install command, 374
gem list command, 368–369
Gemcutter, adding gems to Gemcutter repository, 375–376
gems
    automating creation of, 375–376
    avoiding trouble when using, 377–380
    building, 370–374
    creating, 378–379
    examples of use of, 376–377
    installing and consuming, 367–368
    nuts and bolts of, 369–370
    packaging programs as, 367
    review of, 380
    shoulda gem, 108
    uploading to repository, 374–375
    versioning support, 368–369
gemspec file, 373–374
GEM::Specification instances, 229–230
gets method, Object class, 78
global variables, class variables compared with, 174
gsub
    inflection rules based on, 50–51
    passing regular expressions into, 60

H

HAML, 361
hash rocket (=>), 30

hashes
    APIs for, 35
    caution when iterating over, 40–41
    each method, 34, 217
    Hash class, 69
    hash tables and eql? method, 150–153
    hash values, 152
    improper use of, 41–42
    method-passing with, 33
    order of, 38
    overview of, 29
    public methods, 36
    shortcut for accessing, 30
    symbols as hash keys, 68–71
HashWithIndifferenceAccess class, 71
helper methods, Rails, 203–204
hoe, for automating creation of gems, 376–377
hooks
    avoiding trouble when using, 257–259
    examples of use of, 259–260
    informing when a class gains a subclass, 250–253
    informing when a module gets included in a class, 253–255
    informing when time is up, 255–256
    method_missing. see method_missing
    overview of, 249
    review of, 261
    set_trace_func, 256–257
    value of, 332
HTML
    HAML for HTML templating, 361
    Rails helper methods for creating, 203–204

I

identifiers
    creating document identifier, 142
    testing object identity, 143
if statements
    case statement compared with, 23
    code capturing values of, 25
    example of use of, 17–18
    modifier forms of, 20
included method, informing when a module gets included in a class, 253–255

indentation, Ruby conventions, 5–6
indexing strings, 52
inflection rules, for strings, 50–51
inheritance
 ancestors method, 199
 class variables searching for associated classes, 171, 173
 mixin modules and, 201–202
 superclasses in inheritance tree, 193
inherited method
 avoiding trouble when using, 257–259
 hook for informing when a class gains a subclass, 250–253
initialization
 defining classes, 294
 of objects using execute around, 225
 saved code blocks used for lazy initialization, 237–239
 of variables, 26
initialize method, for defining classes, 294
inject method, collection methods, 35–36
instance _of?, 145
instance methods
 class methods that build, 321–323
 instance_methods method, 307
 instance.method_name, 74
instance variables
 attaching to class objects, 174
 instance variables method, 79
 naming conventions, 8
instances
 classes as factory for creating, 74–75
 class/instance approximation in defining methods, 157
 inheriting methods of Object class, 78
 singleton methods defined for single object instance, 158–159
integers, 154–156
interfaces, 285. see also APIs
internal DSLs. see DSLs (Domain Specific Languages), internal
intersection operations, mapping boolean operators to, 135
IronRuby implementation, 382
iteration
 adding an iterator, 209–210

adding multiple iterators, 210–211
avoiding trouble when using, 215–216
caution when iterating over arrays and hashes, 40–41
code blocks used as iterators, 207
Enumerable module and, 213–215
spectrum of iterator types, 217–218
through collections, 33–36
writing iterators for collections that do not yet exist, 211–213

J

JAR file Hell, 370
Java
 examples of general purpose languages, 336
 JRuby and, 387
Java Virtual Machine (JVM), 387
JRuby
 overview of, 382, 387–388
 support and documentation, 389
JVM (Java Virtual Machine), 387

K

kind_of? method
 double-equals (==) operator and, 146
 locating modules in classes with, 199

L

lambda method, creating default Proc object using, 239–241
lazy initialization, 237–239
"leave it to the last minute" technique, 88
left shift operator (<<), 131, 135
lib directory
 organizing for gems packaging, 372
 sow command generating, 377
lines, strings as collections of, 50
listeners, for call backs, 234–236
literals, shortcuts for accessing collections, 29–30
load methods, managing logging with, 221–222
logging
 adding to database interactions, 220
 capturing return values, 228

logging (*continued*)
  for debugging, 219
  load and save methods for managing, 221–222
  passing arguments and, 227
  silence method for turning off, 231
  using code blocks for, 222–223
  using explicit log messages, 220–221
long running tests, 110
lstrip method, for strings, 47

M

magic methods. *see also* method_missing,
      building APIs with
  example in ActiveRecord, 291–292
  example in OpenStruct class, 290–291
  overview of, 288
map method, for collections, 35
Matsumoto, Yukihiro, 382
Matz's Ruby Interpreter. *see* MRI (Matz's Ruby
      Interpreter)
metaclasses. *see* singleton classes
metadata, gems and, 370, 373
metaprogramming
  hooks. *see* hooks
  monkey patching. *see* monkey patching
  need for testing in, 315–316
  overview of, 249
  self modifying classes. *see* classes, self modifying
  superclasses as basis for class modifying code.
        see classes, that modify subclasses
  when to use, 331–332
method_added, 256
method_missing
  types of hooks, 256
  used in conjunction with internal DSL, 344
  value of, 332
method_missing, building APIs with
  avoiding trouble when using, 289–290
  building form letters one word at a time,
        286–288
  examples of use of, 290–292
  overview of, 285
  review of, 292
  user focus in creating easy-to-use APIs, 289

method_missing, delegation with
  avoiding trouble when using, 279–281
  example of use by ActiveRecord, 282–283
  overview of, 273
  problems with traditional style of delegation,
        275
  process of applying delegation, 277–278
  pros/cons of delegation, 274–275
  review of, 283
  selective approach to delegation, 278–279
  SimpleDelegator class, 281–282
method_missing, error handling with, 263–264
  avoiding trouble when using, 270–271
  handling document errors, 266–267
  overriding, 265
  review of, 271
  what occurs when Ruby fails to find a method,
        264–265
  whiny nil facility in Rails as example of use of,
        268–269
methods
  array method-passing feature, 30–32
  calling on object instances, 74–75
  class methods that build instance methods,
        321–323
  classes as container for, 74
  class/instance approximation in defining, 157
  creating code blocks by tacking on to end of
        method calls, 207–208
  define_method for creating, 324
  defining module-level, 189
  defining operators vs. using methods, 135
  determining when methods are defined, 307
  dynamic typing and, 85
  for equality, 142–143
  fundamental nature of method calls in Ruby,
        81–82
  handling missing. *see* method_missing
  hash method-passing feature, 33
  "if the method is there, it is the right object," 94
  inheriting default set from Object class,
        77–78
  looking for in superclasses, 75–76
  mixing instance methods with class methods,
        254–255

modifying classes and, 295
modifying subclasses from superclass methods, 324–326
modules as container for, 182, 184–185
naming conventions, 8
operator-to-method translation, 130
parentheses in calling/defining, 9–10
public, private, and protected, 79–81
public methods for arrays and hashes, 36
redefining on broken classes, 295–296
reflection-oriented, 79
renaming using alias_method, 297–299
singleton methods overriding class-defined methods, 159–160
that take code blocks, 223–224
methods, writing
  ActiveRecord::Base class example, 127–128
  composed method way of building classes, 122–123
  compressing specifications, 117–121
  overview of, 117
  qualities of good methods, 121–122
  review of, 128
  single-exit approach, 123–126
  troubles arising from decomposing methods, 126–127
MiniSpec, 110
MiniTest, 110
mixin modules
  as alternative to superclasses, 193–195
  avoiding trouble when using, 198–202
  constants stored in, 204–205
  DataMapper example of use of, 202–203
  for extending modules, 197–198
  inheritance relationships and, 201–202
  overview of, 193
  Rails helper methods using, 203–204
  review of, 205
  as solution for sharing code between unrelated classes, 195–197
mocha
  singleton methods and, 165
  utilities for Test::Unit, 109

mocks
  RSpec, 107–108
  singleton methods and, 165
models, object oriented programming as support system for, 157
modifier forms, of control structures, 19–20
modifiers, strings, 48
module variables, 178–179
module_eval, for creating methods, 329
modules
  accessing classes in, 182–183
  accessing constants in, 183
  adding module variables to, 178–179
  avoiding name collisions, 377–378
  avoiding trouble when using, 189–190
  benefits of dynamic typing, 85
  building incrementally, 185
  class hierarchy and, 201
  as containers, 181–182
  economical use of, 190–191
  extending, 197–198
  grouping related classes in, 182
  grouping utility methods in, 184–185
  hook for informing when a module gets included in a class, 253–255
  including in classes, 195–196
  mixing into class. see mixin modules
  nesting, 183–184
  review of, 191
  treating as objects, 186–189
modulo (%) operator, 131, 152
monkey patching. see also open classes
  do anything to any class, anytime, 297–299
  examples of use of, 299–302
  how it works, 307–308
  modifying existing classes, 296–297
  renaming methods using alias_method, 297–299
MRI (Matz's Ruby Interpreter)
  overview of, 382–385
  support and documentation, 389
  YARV as next generation implementation of, 385
multiline strings, 46, 61–62

multiplication (*) operator, 131
mutability, of strings, 51–52

N

names
 accessing classes in modules by, 182–183
 alias_method for renaming methods, 297–299
 avoiding collisions, 377–378
 example in set.rb class, 14
 execute around and, 228–229
 gems and, 371
 method, 122
 objects and name collisions, 82–83
 Ruby conventions, 8–9
 variable, 8
namespaces, creating name-space modules, 189
NaN (Not a Number), 296
nesting modules, 183–184
nil
 boolean logic and, 23–25
 initializing variables and, 26
 as an object, 77, 84
 whiny nil facility in Rails, 268–269
Not a Number (NaN), 296
not operator, 132
numeric classes
 accepting Float as equals, 154–156
 not supporting singleton methods, 159

O

object oriented programming
 Ruby as OO programming language, 73
 as support system, for models, 157
object relational mappers
 ActiveRecord. see ActiveRecord
 DataMapper. see DataMapper
objects
 avoiding trouble when using, 82–84
 BasicObject, 280–281
 classes, instances, and methods, 74–76
 consistency of Ruby object system, 76–77
 dynamic typing. see dynamic typing
 equality. see equality

fundamental nature of method calls in Ruby, 81–82
 "if the method is there, it is the right object," 94
 initializing using execute around, 225, 229–230
 methods, 77–79
 modules as, 186–189
 name collisions and, 82–83
 Object class, 77
 overview of, 73–74
 public, private, and protected methods, 79–81
 referencing with variables, 77
 review of, 84
 singleton methods, 158–159
ObjectSpace class, 217–218
open classes. see also monkey patching
 avoiding trouble when using, 303
 creating self-modifying classes, 305
 defining classes, 294
 examples of use of, 299–302
 fixing broken classes, 295–296
 improving existing classes, 296–297
 modifying classes, 295
 overview of, 293–294
 renaming methods using alias_method, 297–299
 review of, 303–304
 value of, 332
OpenStruct class, 290–291
operators
 cases/situations calling for, 135–137
 commutative, 137
 defining, 129–131
 overview of, 129
 review of, 139
 string formatting, 137–138
 types in Ruby, 131–133
 using across classes, 134–135
or (|) operator, 131
order, of arrays and hashes, 38
overloading operators, 129
overriding methods
 errors and, 83
 method_missing, 265
 methods in superclass unable to override
  methods in subclasses, 200

P

packaging programs, as gems. *see* gems
parentheses (())
  readability and, 12
  Ruby conventions for calling
       defining/methods, 9–10
`parse_statement` method, 357
parsers
  based on regular expressions, 356–358
  building for XML processing language,
       353–356
  examples of external DSLs, 364
  HAML and, 361–362
  Treetop for building, 358–360
`Pathname` class, 299–300
pattern matching, 150
period (.)
  for matching any single character, 54
  in module syntax, 185
  using asterisk (*) in conjunction with, 58
polymorphism, 88
`pop` method, for arrays, 37
`print` method, `Object` class, 78
private methods, 79–81
`Proc` class, 239–241
`Proc.new`, 240–241
programming
  metaprogramming. *see* metaprogramming
  object oriented, 73, 157
  trade offs in programming languages, 336
programming logic, adding to classes, 308–309,
      314
programs, packaging as gems, 367
protected methods, 81
public methods
  overview of, 79
  returning all public methods of an object, 69
`public_methods`, `Object` class, 79
`push` method, for arrays, 37
`puts` method, `Object` class, 78

Q

question mark (?), using with regular
      expressions, 62–63

R

RACC, for building parsers, 359
Rails
  example of `const_missing` hook, 270
  example of on-the-fly class modification,
      312–313
  example of saved code blocks, 243
  helper methods using mixins, 203–204
  whiny nil facility, 268–269
Rake
  as build tool, 335
  example of `const_missing` hook,
      269–270
  example of saved code blocks, 243–244
  examples of internal DSLs, 345–346
  specifying executable scripts in gems, 374
`rake` command, 374
`rake push` command, 376
`Rakefiles`
  automating creation of gems, 375–376
  `sow` command generating, 377
ranges
  of characters in regular expressions, 56
  indexing strings and, 52
readability, of code, 12–13
reflection-oriented methods, 79
`Regexp` data type, 58
regular expressions
  asterisk (*) symbol in, 57–58
  `case` statement detecting match, 23
  HAML and, 361
  matching beginnings and endings of strings,
      60–62
  matching one character at a time, 54–55
  mistakes to avoid, 63
  as objects, 76
  overview of, 53
  parser based on, 356–358
  pattern matching against strings, 150
  resources for use of, 394
  review of, 64
  sets, ranges, and alternatives, 55–57
  `time.rb` example, 62 63
repository, uploading gems to, 374–375
`require` method, `Object` class, 82

required type declarations, compensating for lost documentation due to, 92–93

`Resolv` class, 217

resources, for Ruby, 393–395

`respond_to` method, 146–147

return, in code blocks, 216

reverse method, for arrays, 36–37

REXML XML parsing library, 338–339

Ripper DSL, 352–353

RSpec
  double-equals (==) operator, 138
  examples, 104
  independence of test, 111
  internal DSLs and, 345–346
  MiniSpec, 110
  mocks, 107–109
  overview of, 102–104
  parameters, 105
  saved code blocks and, 243
  shoulda gem providing RSpec-like example, 108
  singleton methods and, 165
  specifying executable scripts in gems, 374
  stubs, 106–107
  as testing utility, 335
  tidy and readable specs, 104–105

`rstrip` method, for strings, 47

Rubinius, 382, 388–389

Ruby implementations
  avoiding trouble when using, 389
  extending, 389
  JRuby, 387–388
  MRI, 382–385
  overview of, 381
  review of, 390
  Rubinius, 388–389
  versions and, 381–382
  YARV, 385–387

Ruby versions
  comparing Ruby versions, 381–382
  managing transition between, 311–312
  MRI supporting Ruby 1.8, 383
  YARV supporting Ruby 1.9, 381–382

RubyForge, 375

RubyGems. *see* gems

ruby-mp3info, 368

RubySpec project, 109–110

run-time decisions, putting programming logic in classes and, 308

S

`save` methods, 221–222

scope (closure)
  avoiding trouble when using, 241–242
  code blocks drag scope along to wherever they are applied, 225–227

scope, of class methods, 165–166

scripts, specifying executable scripts in gems, 374

`self`
  class methods and, 309
  as default object in method calls, 75
  knowing value of during class definition, 330–331

semicolon (;), for separating statements in Ruby code, 10–11

set
  regular expression for matching any one of a bunch of characters, 55–56
  using asterisk (*) in conjunction with, 58

`Set` class
  dynamic typing and, 95–96
  mapping boolean operators to union and intersection operations, 135

`set_trace_func` hook, 256–257

`setup` method, Test::Unit, 100

`shift` method, for arrays, 37

shoulda gem, utilities for Test::Unit, 108

`silence` method, for turning logging off, 231

`SimpleDelegator` class, 281–282

simplicity, as solution to code complexity, 92

single quotes ('), use with string literals, 44–45

single-exit approach, to writing methods, 123–126

singleton classes
  adding convenience to class instance variables, 176–177
  class methods, 162–165
  visibility of, 160–161

singleton methods
  alternative syntax for, 160
  avoiding trouble when using, 165–167
  class methods, 162–165

defining, 158, 163–164
extending modules and, 198
invisibility of singleton class, 160–161
overriding class-defined methods, 159–160
overview of, 157–158
review of, 167
software
  resources for building software with Ruby, 394
  trade offs in software engineering, 335
sort method
  <=> operator and, 214
  for arrays, 37
source code, for Ruby projects, 394
sow command, generating directory structure of
    gems, 377
spec command
  running specifications with, 103–104
  specifying executable scripts in gems, 374
specs. *see also* tests
  MiniSpec, 110
  mocks and, 107–108
  overview of, 103
  RubySpec project, 109–110
  running with spec command, 103–104
  stubs and, 105–107
  tidy and readable, 104–105
  when to write, 113
splat, for star jargon, 32
split method, working with strings, 48
square brackets. *see* [ ] (square brackets)
squish! method, adding to String class, 301–302
static typing
  adding type-checking code to methods and, 91
  bulkier code with, 89
  dangers of dynamic typing and, 93
  overview of, 85
StringIO class, comparing with File class,
    94–95
strings. *see also* regular expressions
  adding methods to String class, 300–302
  APIs supported, 47–49
  converting symbols to/from, 69
  formatting operator (%) for, 137–138
  indexing, 52
  inflection rules based on gsub, 50–51
  mutability of, 51–52

as objects, 76
optimizing String class for data processing, 67
options for writing, 44–46
overview of, 43
pattern matching regular expressions against
    strings, 150
review of, 52
String class, 43
symbols as, 65–66
types of thing collected in, 49–50
uses of, 66–67
when to use symbols vs. when to use strings,
    70–71
strip method, 47
stubs
  RSpec, 105–107
  singleton methods and, 165
sub method, working with strings, 47–48
subclasses
  calling private methods from, 80
  class instance variables and, 175–176
  difficulty of subclassing, 319–321
  example of paragraph subclass, 317–319
  examples of subclass-changing methods, 327
  hook for informing when a class gains a
      subclass, 250–253, 257–259
  methods in superclass unable to override
      methods in subclasses, 200
  no limit to modifying from superclass method,
      324–326
  practical basis of, 95
subtraction (-) operator
  as binary or unary operator, 132
  overloading, 131
sudo, for running gems, 368
superclasses
  in inheritance tree, 193
  methods in superclass that can add methods to
      subclasses, 324
  methods in superclass unable to override
      methods in subclasses, 200
  mixins as alternative to, 193–195
  modules and, 198
  no limit to modifying subclasses from
      superclass method, 324–326
  overview of, 75–76

swapcase method, working with strings, 47
switch statement, case statement compared
        with, 21
symbols
    compared with strings, 65–66
    confusing nature of, 69–70
    converting strings to/from, 69
    as hash keys, 68–69
    immutability of, 68
    not supporting singleton methods, 159
    as objects, 76
    overview of, 65
    review of, 71
    single instance of, 67–68
    using strings as symbolic markers, 66–67
    when to use symbols vs. when to use strings,
        70–71
symmetry principal, double-equals (==) operator
        and, 146–147

T

tabs, Ruby indentation conventions and, 5–6
TAR files, 370
teardown method, Test::Unit, 100
ternary operator (?:), in expression-based
        decision making, 26
test directory, sow command generating, 377
test-first development, 113
tests
    applying to gems, 380
    assertions in Test::Unit, 101
    automated testing for resolving bugs, 94
    limitations of Test::Unit, 101–102
    MiniTest, 110
    mocha utilities for Test::Unit, 109
    mocks and, 107–108
    overview of, 97
    qualities of good tests, 110–113
    review of, 113
    RSpec testing framework, 102–104
    RubySpec project, 109–110
    shoulda gem utilities for Test::Unit, 108
    stubs and, 105–107

tidy and readable specs, 104–105
    when to write, 113
Test::Unit
    at_exit hook used in, 259–260
    assertions in, 101
    limitations of, 101–102
    mocha utilities for, 109
    overview of, 98–100
    shoulda gem utilities for, 108
text processing, strings and, 43
TextCompressor class, 119
time zones, regular expression for offsetting,
        62–63
time.rb, regular expressions and, 62–63
times method, iterators, 211–212
to_s method
    of Object class, 77–78
    turning symbols into strings, 69
to_sym method, turning strings into symbols, 69
transitive property, of double-equals (==)
        operator, 147–149
Treetop
    for building parsers, 358–360
    examples of external DSLs, 364
triple equals operator (===), for case
        statements, 23, 149–150
true, as an object, 76
two space rule, Ruby indentation convention,
        5–6
type declaration
    documentation and, 92
    dynamic typing. see dynamic typing
    static typing. see static typing
type-checking code, disadvantages of adding, 91

U

unary operators, 131–132, 134
union operations, mapping boolean operators
        to, 135
unique_index_of method, 120
unit tests. see also Test::Unit
    minimum tests, 112–113
    speed as factor in, 110

Unix, 370

`unless` statements
example of use of, 18–19
modifier forms of, 20

`until` statements
comments, 6
example of use of, 19
modifier forms of, 20

`upcase` method, working with strings, 47

URIs
using class variables with, 177–178
using modules with, 191

user interfaces, 285. *see also* APIs

V

values
`case` statement returning, 22
code blocks returning, 208–209

variables
adding module variables to modules, 178–179
attaching instance variable to class objects (class instance variables), 174–175
class variables. *see* class variables
documenting declaration of, 92
initializing, 26
modules and, 186
naming, 8
open classes and, 294
referencing objects with, 77

VCIS (Version Conflict Induced Insanity), 370

versions
Ruby implementations and, 381–382
versioning support in gems, 368–369

vertical bar (|), in syntax of alternatives in regular expressions, 56–57

visibility, of methods, 79–81

W

`while` statements
code capturing values of, 25
example of use of, 19
modifier forms of, 20

whiny nil facility, Rails, 268–269

white space, managing in strings, 47

`with_logging` methods
capturing return values, 228
managing logging with, 222
passing arguments and, 227

X

XML
accessing/manipulating data in, 336–337
building parser for, 353–356
creating reader for, 251–252
processing in Ruby with REXML, 337–339
`XmlRipper` class for writing XML processing scripts, 340–341

`XmlRipper` class
building parser for XML processing language, 354
transition from API to DSL and, 341–344
for writing XML processing scripts, 340

XPath, 338–339, 344

XSLT, 337

XUnit testing frameworks, 98

Y

YAML
compared with XML, 250
example of use of modules in, 191

YARV
overview of, 385–387
support and documentation, 389

`yield`, firing code blocks, 233